The Strategy of Economic Development

BOOKS BY ALBERT O. HIRSCHMAN IN NORTON PAPERBACK

*Journeys Toward Progress: Studies of Economic Policy-Making
in Latin America*
The Strategy of Economic Development

THE STRATEGY OF

ECONOMIC DEVELOPMENT

ALBERT O. HIRSCHMAN

W·W· NORTON & COMPANY

NEW YORK · LONDON

FOR S, K, AND L

Copyright © 1958 by Yale University Press, Inc.
Published simultaneously in Canada by George J. McLeod Limited,
Toronto. Printed in the United States of America.

All Rights Reserved

First published in the Norton Library 1978 by arrangement with
Yale University Press.

Books That Live
The Norton imprint on a book means that in the publisher's
estimation it is a book not for a single season but for the years.
W. W. Norton & Company, Inc.

Library of Congress Cataloging in Publication Data

Hirschman, Albert O.
The strategy of economic development.

Original ed. published by Yale University
Press, New Haven.
Includes bibliographical references and index.
1. Economic development.   I. Title.
HD82.H49   1978   338.9   78–11720
ISBN 0-393-00900-9

1 2 3 4 5 6 7 8 9 0

Preface

"THE ELUCIDATION of immediate experience is the sole justification of any thought; and the starting point for thought is the analytic observation of components of this experience."

At an early stage of planning this book, I found much encouragement in this statement by Whitehead.* For I knew that I was engaged primarily in an attempt to elucidate my own immediate experience in one of the so-called underdeveloped countries. In the course of this attempt, the various observations and reflections I had gathered began to look more and more like variations upon a common theme. So I undertook to discover this theme and then used it in reinterpreting a variety of development problems.

Disagreement with prevailing doctrines is a natural concomitant of such an effort. Sometimes I became aware of it only in the course of working out my own ideas. But in some areas I had long felt dissatisfaction with the present state of our knowledge: for instance, existing theories had seemed to me to be particularly unhelpful to the decision-maker in underdeveloped countries when he has to determine basic strategic issues in development planning, such as the assigning of sector or area priorities or the kind of industrialization effort to be pursued. An attempt is here made to evolve some new ways of thinking about these problems.

I have clearly left myself open to the twin charges of overgeneralization and underdocumentation. To the former I would reply that any theory is built on a limited number of observations; and that intimate acquaintance with an individual country has in fact produced many of our most useful generalizations about the social process. On the other hand, I am very conscious that many of my statements must be considered hypotheses which remain to be tested. Nevertheless, I have confined myself to a predominantly theoretical outline, largely because this was all I managed to accomplish in the time at my disposal. I also feel that at this stage the paucity of testable hypotheses has become an even more serious bottleneck in studying economic development than

* *Process and Reality* (New York, Macmillan, 1930), p. 6.

the shortage of data. Hypotheses beget data, and I certainly hope that some of my propositions—on efficient sequences, on linkage effects, on productivity differentials, etc.—will lend themselves and be subjected to critical empirical research.

My appointment as Irving Fisher Research Professor at Yale University during the academic year 1956–57 provided me with a unique opportunity to reflect on my Colombian experience. A grant from the Rockefeller Foundation made it possible to complete the manuscript during the following year.

Finding it difficult to do much reading after sitting down to write, I have ordinarily not been able to take full account of books and articles that appeared after mid-1957.

I am very grateful to Thomas Schelling on whom I first tried out my ideas and rough drafts; to Charles Wolf, Jr., and Paul G. Clark of the RAND Corporation who criticized the entire manuscript; to James Tobin who commented on Chapter 9; and to Lloyd G. Reynolds who was unfailingly helpful at all stages. In deciphering and typing my manuscript, Mrs. Caroline H. Logan displayed remarkable patience, judgment, and skill.

Portions of this book were originally published in the *American Economic Review* of June and September 1957 and in *Investment Criteria and Economic Growth* (ed. M. F. Millikan), Center for International Studies, Massachusetts Institute of Technology, 1955. Thanks are also due to the International Economic Association for letting me use parts of a paper presented at the Roundtable at Rio de Janeiro in August 1957. The discussions during this Roundtable proved very stimulating to me. In particular, I was heartened by the discovery that students of Brazilian and Latin American economic problems, such as Roberto Campos and Alexandre Kafka, had come independently to conclusions similar to mine on some essential aspects of the development process.

The help and helpfulness of my wife covered an astonishingly wide area. The efficient guidance she provided to the anthropological literature permitted some forays into a territory whose rich resources are too often left unutilized by the economist.

A final word of gratitude is due to Colombia, whose guest I was from 1952 to 1956, first as official economic advisor and then as private consultant. The disruptive political situation which the country experienced during this period made its continuing economic progress stand out by contrast. Fortunately, the country is now turning its energies to the task of political reconstruction. That it may be successful in this endeavor is my wish as I express deep-felt thanks to the many Colombians who have helped me in my attempts to understand the "ambiente."

New Haven, Connecticut
May 1958

Preface to the Paperbound Edition

A WASHINGTON FRIEND of mine, worried about the dangerous thoughts he had detected in my manuscript, told me some three years ago that he would like to see its distribution limited to a few sophisticated officials and experts directly concerned with economic development. I confessed to a preference for the printed over the mimeographed word, but did my best to reassure my friend by pointing out that a severely limited distribution of my book was guaranteed in any event because of occasional use of technical language and numerous footnote references. Here I happily turned out to be wrong as is shown by the present paperbound edition; the question arises, therefore, whether I should now caution the unwary reader on some particularly insidious points.

On the whole, the reception of my book has made it clear that my Washington friend, like all defenders of new orthodoxies, was far too apprehensive of dissenting opinions and of the support they might lend to older orthodoxies. My book has not turned into grist for the mill of those who are hostile to development planning. It was, of course, never meant to be that; rather, my hope was and is that it will contribute to making planning and programming activities more effective.

In any event, self-imposed censorship would have been to no avail. With the ever more widespread interest in economic development, it was inevitable that certain of my findings should have occurred independently to others. For example, Edward C. Banfield, in *The Moral Basis of a Backward Society* (Glencoe, Ill., 1958), reaches conclusions very similar to mine on the obstacles to cooperative decision-making in certain underdeveloped areas. Similarly, the view I take of inflation and balance-of-payments difficulties has much in common with that of a group of Latin American economists, largely of the Economic Commission for Latin America, now frequently designated as "structuralists," in opposition to the "monetarists." Finally, Paul Streeten's article "Unbalanced Growth" in the June 1959 issue of *Oxford Economic Papers* is a particularly striking case of convergence.

It is my continuing regret that I was not able to discuss the completed book with the late Ragnar Nurkse whose writings on balanced growth had played the crucial role of adversary-helper in giving shape to my thinking. In a recent lecture I reformulated my own position in the following way which may be helpful in resolving what should certainly not be made into an irreconcilable conflict:

> Those who stress the importance of balanced growth have made an important contribution by recognizing that various investments and economic activities depend on each other, but from this insight they have drawn the too facile conclusion that all these interrelated activities have to be put into place together. True, automotive vehicles are not much good without highways and modern highways are rather useless without vehicles. But this does not mean that the only or even the best way in which we can develop our transportation system is by expanding simultaneously and evenly both the automotive industry and the highway network. Why not take advantage of the stimulus that is set up by expansion of the one toward that of the other? In other words, I do not deny by any means the interrelatedness of various economic activities of which the balanced growth theory has made so much. On the contrary, I propose that we take advantage of it, that we probe into the structure that is holding together these interrelated activities. As in the atom, there is much energy here that can be and is in fact being utilized in building up economic development nuclei. *Later on* these nuclei look as though they could never have been separated even for a single instant when in actual fact they might never have been assembled had not a sequential solution, i.e., an unbalanced growth sequence been found, by accident,

instinct, or reasoned design. To look at unbalanced growth means, in other words, to look at the dynamics of the development process *in the small*. But perhaps it is high time that we did just that.

I hope this statement will serve to calm down the debate. It is remarkable how the question of balanced versus unbalanced growth together with the analysis of linkages (chapters 3 to 7) seems to have caught the exclusive attention of many readers. I should like to plead for a correction of this bias; in my opinion, the topics discussed in the chapters on motivations (1), technology (8), and regional transmission of growth (10) are no less central to development strategy and require much further investigation.

New York
January 1961

CONTENTS

	Page
Preface	v

1. Preliminary Explorations — 1
   The Search for the Primum Mobile — 1
   The Importance of Being a Latecomer — 7
   The Idea of Change as an Obstacle to Change — 11
   The group-focused image of change. The ego-focused image of change. Exaggerated expectations and personalized liquidity preference.
   The Need for Inducement Mechanisms — 24

2. Growth Models and Development Processes — 29
   The Economics of Growth—Help or Hindrance? — 29
   Explaining Investment Activity — 33
   The Ability to Invest — 35
   The Complementarity Effect of Investment — 40
   The Forces Corroding Development — 44

3. Balanced Growth: A Critique — 50
   Is Balance in Demand Required? — 50
   The Paradox of the Internalization Doctrine — 55
   Different Types of Internalization and Their Effect on Growth — 57

4. Unbalanced Growth: An Espousal — 62
   Is Balance in Supply Required? — 62
   Development as a Chain of Disequilibria — 65
   A Definition of Induced Investment — 70
   Some Related Points of View — 73

5. Investment Choices and Strategies — 76
   Efficient Sequences versus Investment Criteria — 76
   Social Overhead Capital (SOC) versus Directly Productive Activities (DPA) — 83
   Definitions and biases. Development via shortage and via excess capacity of SOC. Suitability of the various sequences. Limits to development via SOC shortage.

xi

6. Interdependence and Industrialization   98
    Backward and Forward Linkage Defined   98
    A Mental Experiment   104
    Backward Linkage at Work   109
    A Model of Capital Formation Based on Backward Linkage   113
    Combining Backward and Forward Linkage   116

7. Industrialization: Further Characteristic Aspects   120
    The Role of Imports in Inducing Industrial Development   120
    The Reason for Dualistic Development   125

8. Efficiency and Growth of the Individual Firm   133
    The Need for Built-In Spurs   133
    The Maintenance Problem and a Suggested Solution   139
    Generalizing the Solution   143
    Capital-Intensive Technology?   150
    Production versus Administration Tasks   153

9. The Role of Disturbances   156
    Inflation   156
      Types of upward pressure on prices. The price-price spiral. Balanced growth and inflation.
    Balance-of-Payments Pressures   166
      Supply imbalances and the demand for imports. The foreign exchange illusion. "Exportability" of fast-growing outputs as a condition of external balance. Growth-inducing effects of fluctuations in foreign exchange earnings.
    Population Pressures   176

CONTENTS

10. Interregional and International Transmission of Economic Growth 183
    "Growing Points" and Lagging Regions 183
    Trickling-Down and Polarization Effects 187
    The Regional Distribution of Public Investment 190
    Interregional and International Transmission Compared 195
      The case for separatism. The case for surrender of sovereignty.
    Optimal Institutional Arrangements 199

11. Conclusion: Functions of Government and Foreign Aid 202
    The Two Functions of Government 202
    The Role of Foreign Capital and Aid 205
    The Argument in Perspective 208

Author Index 211

Subject Index 214

CHAPTER 1

Preliminary Explorations

The Search for the Primum Mobile

THE INTENSIVE STUDY of the problem of economic development has had one discouraging result: it has produced an ever lengthening list of factors and conditions, of obstacles and prerequisites. The direction of the inquiry has proceeded from thoroughly objective, tangible, and quantitative phenomena to more and more subjective, intangible, and unmeasurable ones. For a long time, certainly until 1914 and perhaps until 1929, natural resources held the center of the stage when the chances of a country's development were considered. Later on capital, a man-made and quantifiable entity, came to be considered the principal agent of development. The view is still widespread that if only the underdeveloped countries could obtain, through their own efforts or through outside assistance, sufficient amounts of capital, they would be able to "finish the job." But this belief in the strategic importance of capital has itself been increasingly challenged. Among the proximate causes of economic development, the supply of entrepreneurial and managerial abilities now occupies in official documents a position of pre-eminence at least equal to that of capital.[1] The contribution to be derived from "nonconventional inputs" such as investment in people as productive agents and the introduction of improved techniques not embodied in physical capital goods has also been stressed.[2]

If one turns to the conditions that indirectly determine development by their influence on the supply of capital, entrepreneurship,

1. See, e.g., United Nations, *Processes and Problems of Industrialization in Underdeveloped Countries* (New York, 1955), pp. 30–8.
2. Theodore W. Schultz, *The Economic Test in Latin America*, New York State School of Industrial and Labor Relations, Cornell University, Bulletin 35 (Aug. 1956).

and skills, the spectacle becomes far more bewildering. It is usual at this point to list the need for minimum standards in public order, law enforcement, and public administration. In attempts to dig more deeply, economic historians and sociologists, starting with Max Weber, have identified a number of beliefs, attitudes, value systems, climates of opinion, and propensities which they have found to exert a favorable influence on the generation of enterprise and of developmental initiative. They have also stressed the role of minorities and of deviant behavior in the formation of entrepreneurial groups. Joining in the search for the *primum mobile*, psychologists have recently undertaken to establish the dependence of development and of entrepreneurial activity on the presence of achievement motivation, as measured by experimental tests.[3]

In spite of the many valuable insights gained from these theories, their cumulative impact on the unwary reader could well raise serious doubts about the possibility of any economic development at all. For how can any stagnating country ever hope to fulfill simultaneously so many necessary conditions?

Fortunately, the very multiplicity of attempts at explanation can be made to yield another and radically different conclusion. As one explanation is proposed, a previous one is disputed. This is usually done by demonstrating that if only factor B can be generated, and development thereby got under way, then factor A, hitherto regarded as so important, will be forthcoming without much trouble. This process began when experience demonstrated conclusively that, under appropriate conditions, industrial skills can be learned by any people, race, or human group, and that countries poorly endowed with natural resources can achieve high levels of per capita output and income.

With respect to savings and capital, anthropologists have long known that primitive people who, by Western standards, live "on the margin of subsistence" insist nevertheless on devoting a considerable portion of their time, energies, and resources to ceremonial purposes, gift-making, and other activities not directly related to consumption. In recent years, increasing numbers of economists have also come to doubt that insufficiency of savings is the most important factor hold-

3. I am referring to the work of David C. McClelland and his associates; cf. also Everett E. Hagen, "The Process of Economic Development," *Economic Development and Cultural Change,* 5 (April 1957), 202–4.

ing back development. For one thing, they have noticed, in addition to the above phenomena, the luxury consumption of the rich, the widespread hoarding, and the ubiquitous instances of misdirected and unproductive investment. For another, they have realized that savings and productive investment are as much a result as a cause of development.[4] For once the latter is under way windfall profits are realized at many points in a developing economy; more important, when economic opportunity is perceived, consumption-savings and work-leisure patterns are drastically readjusted. That the supply of capital is remarkably elastic to improved profit expectations has been brought out particularly with respect to capital formation in agriculture in underdeveloped areas. The expansion in the cultivation of slow-yielding tropical tree crops such as coffee, cocoa, and rubber by independent peasant producers is a case in point.[5] But in manufacturing also, shortage of capital is seldom found to hold back the fruition of projects that have been carefully planned and give promise of being competently managed.[6]

The initiatory role of capital is usually belittled by those who stress the importance of entrepreneurship and of technical and managerial knowledge. But again it has been convincingly shown that entrepreneurial ability as such is not usually lacking in underdeveloped countries, but that, because of a foreshortened time-horizon and insufficient knowledge and experience, it is often deflected from the promotion of industry to other more familiar pursuits in trade and real estate.[7] It has even been asserted that enterprise, just as capital, is a "by-product of the process of economic development, and has seldom been found wanting in a society favorable to its exercise."[8] The sud-

4. A. K. Cairncross, "The Place of Capital in Economic Progress," in *Economic Progress*, ed. L. H. Dupriez, Louvain, 1955; see also his review of W. A. Lewis' *The Theory of Economic Growth* in *The Economic Journal*, 66 (Dec. 1956), 694–7.

5. P. T. Bauer and B. S. Yamey, *The Economics of Underdeveloped Countries* (Chicago, 1957), pp. 29–31.

6. C. Wolf, Jr. and S. C. Sufrin, *Capital Formation and Foreign Investment in Underdeveloped Areas* (Syracuse, 1955), pp. 11–29; and William Diamond, *Development Banks* (Baltimore, 1957), pp. 7–13.

7. Henry G. Aubrey, "Industrial Investment Decisions: A Comparative Analysis," *Journal of Economic History*, 15 (Dec. 1955), 333–51.

8. James Baster in the discussion on Aubrey's article, ibid., p. 355.

3

den outbreak of industrial entrepreneurship in Pakistan after the partition, in the Middle East during World War II, and again in Latin America since the thirties confirms the view that underdeveloped countries may harbor a "reserve army" of entrepreneurs that are as achievement-motivated as any Puritan ever was. Similarly, it is hard to argue that there are some countries whose citizens are basically corrupt or unable to keep law and order.

The discovery that the ability to tend a machine and the propensity to invest or to act as entrepreneur are widely spread over the globe and only need suitable occasions to manifest themselves is in line with recent trends in anthropology. Thus Kluckhohn writes: "The anthropologist for two generations has been obsessed with the differences between peoples, neglecting the equally real similarities upon which the 'universal culture pattern' as well as the psychological uniformities are clearly built." [9]

When it was increasingly realized that economic backwardness cannot be explained in terms of any outright *absence* or *scarcity* of this or that human type or factor of production, attention turned to the attitudes and value systems that may favor or inhibit the emergence of the required activities and personalities. To some extent we shall ourselves be concerned with this line of inquiry. But whenever any theory was propounded that considered a given value system a *prerequisite* of development, it could usually be effectively contradicted on empirical grounds: development had actually taken place somewhere without the benefit of the "prerequisite." Moreover, here again different theories neutralize one another. For instance, it seems difficult to argue at one and the same time that the general climate of opinion must be favorable to industrial progress *and* that a strategic factor of particular importance is the presence of minority groups or of individuals with deviant, i.e., socially disapproved, behavior. One rather suspects that when economic opportunity arises it will be perceived and exploited primarily by native entrepreneurs or by deviant minorities, depending on whether or not the traditional values of the society are favorable to change.

9. Clyde Kluckhohn, "Universal Categories of Culture" in *Anthropology Today*, ed. A. L. Kroeber (Chicago, Univ. of Chicago Press, 1953), p. 515. See also G. P. Murdock, "The Common Denominator of Cultures" in *The Science of Man in the World Crisis*, ed. Ralph Linton (New York, 1946), pp. 123–40.

Thus, while we were at first discouraged by the long list of resources and circumstances whose presence has been shown to be needed for economic development, we now find that these resources and circumstances are not so scarce or so difficult to realize, *provided, however, that economic development itself first raises its head.* This is of course only a positive way of stating the well-known proposition that economic development is held back by a series of "interlocking vicious circles."[10] Before it starts, economic development is hard to visualize, not only because so many different conditions must be fulfilled simultaneously but above all because of the vicious circles: generally the realization of these conditions depends in turn on economic development. But this means also that once development has started, the circle is likely to become an upward spiral as all the prerequisites and conditions for development are brought into being.

This approach permits us to focus on a characteristic of the process of economic development that is fundamental for both analysis and strategy: development depends not so much on finding optimal combinations for given resources and factors of production as on calling forth and enlisting for development purposes resources and abilities that are hidden, scattered, or badly utilized.[11] Economists have long realized this situation with respect to labor and have coined the term "disguised unemployment" to describe it. But just as an underdeveloped economy can mobilize vast hidden reserves of unskilled labor from its redundant peasantry, so it is able to make capital, entrepreneurship, and all the other "prerequisites" climb unexpectedly on the bandwagon of economic development once it has started to roll.

If this is correct, then too much has perhaps been made of the difference between a situation of cyclical unemployment in a developed economy and the problem of development in an underdeveloped coun-

10. H. W. Singer, "Economic Progress in Underdeveloped Countries," *Social Research*, 16 (March 1949), 5.

11. A recent contribution makes the same point: "There are always and everywhere potential surpluses available. What counts is the institutional means for bringing them to life. . . . for calling forth the special effort, setting aside the extra amount, devising the surplus." Harry W. Pearson, "The Economy Has No Surplus: Critique of a Theory of Development," in *Trade and Markets in the Early Empires*, ed. K. Polanyi, C. M. Arensberg, and H. W. Pearson (Glencoe, Ill., Free Press, 1957), p. 339.

try. It has often been said that the two situations have nothing in common and demand therefore totally different cures: during the typical depression in a developed country unemployed labor exists side by side with unutilized plant and equipment and all that needs to be done is to "reunite what should never have been parted"; whereas, so it is pointed out, in an underdeveloped economy we have at best disguised unemployment but no other unutilized factors of production, so that the problem is "structural" rather than "cyclical." True, in an underdeveloped economy we have no idle capital or trained labor resources that cry out to be utilized; but we do have not only under-utilized labor in agriculture but unutilized ability to save, latent or misdirected entrepreneurship, and a wide variety of usable skills, not to mention the modern industrial techniques that are waiting to be transferred from the advanced countries. The task here is to *combine* all these ingredients, a task far more difficult than, but not entirely different from, the *recombining* of idle factors of production that must be accomplished to end a depression.

In both situations the need is for a binding agent. The difference is that in a situation of underdevelopment a far stronger agent is required than deficit spending or similar Keynesian remedies for unemployment. But, as we shall see, the way in which these remedies are expected to perform is not entirely devoid of lessons for the problem of development.

What is gained by considering resources and production factors latent and conditionally available rather than outright absent or scarce? The advantage appears to be that in this way attention is properly focused on the essential dynamic and strategic aspects of the development process. Instead of concentrating exclusively on the husbanding of scarce resources such as capital and entrepreneurship, our approach leads us to look for "pressures" and "inducement mechanisms" that will elicit and mobilize the largest possible amounts of these resources. To consider them as irremediably scarce and to plan the allocation of resources on that basis may mean bottling up development, just as a child's mental growth will be badly stunted if an attempt is made to obtain the maximum yield from its manifest abilities at a given point of time rather than to call forth its potential endowments. In this view, then, planning for development consists primarily in the systematic setting up of a series of *pacing devices*.

6

The formulation of the development problem which is here proposed calls particular attention to the fact that the use of different economic resources has very different repercussions or "feedback" effects on the available stocks of these resources. In the case of some natural resources such as mineral deposits there is no feedback at all: the resources become depleted. In the case of capital, on the other hand, a well-known feedback operates: by generating income and then savings, the capital that is used up in the production process is ordinarily more than replenished.[12] More directly, the use of capital in one venture may lead to complementary capital formation in another. Finally, in the exercise of entrepreneurial and managerial ability the feedback is so immediate that it is hard to recognize it as such: these are resources that increase directly with and through use (much as the ability to play the piano or to speak a foreign language improves with exercise) while more indirect effects similar to those characteristic of capital are also at work. Thus, the latter resources which are probably the scarcest at the beginning of the development process are those that may show the fastest increase because of the directness and strength of the feedback effect and because their expansion is limited only by learning ability.

The Importance of Being a Latecomer

To view development as a process of drawing together a variety of conditionally available resources and latent abilities may seem to make light of the task. This is by no means the intention. On the contrary, the approach is motivated by the conviction that development is much more difficult than is often realized. As long as one thinks in terms of a missing component, be it capital, entrepreneurship, or technical knowledge, he is likely to believe that the problem can be solved by injecting that component from the outside or by looking for ways and means of producing it within the country. If one concentrates instead on the need for a "binding agent" which is to bring together various scattered or hidden elements, the task becomes vaguer, to say the least, and may well turn out to be more complex. We may even be considered to be guilty of a fairly meaningless, almost

12. See the formulation of the Harrod-Domar model as a feedback in R. G. D. Allen, *Mathematical Economics* (London, 1956), p. 282.

tautological diagnosis. Are we not simply saying that development depends on the ability and determination of a nation and its citizens to organize themselves for development?

Perhaps this is not as tautological and vague as it sounds. By focusing on determination, for instance, we are taking hold of one of the specific characteristics of the development process in today's underdeveloped countries, namely, the fact that they are latecomers. This condition is bound to make their development into a less spontaneous and more deliberate process than was the case in the countries where the process first occurred.

Some theories of development fail to include in their structures this fundamental fact of *contact* between the advanced and backward countries. The question they ask: why have some countries developed while others have failed to do so? [13] seems to us relevant primarily to the inquiry why the Industrial Revolution took place in England rather than elsewhere. Once economic progress in the pioneer countries is a visible reality, the strength of the desire to imitate, to follow suit, to catch up obviously becomes an important determinant of what will happen among the nonpioneers.

A comprehensive account of the development process as a deliberate attempt at catching up on the part of various groups of economic operators is given by Gerschenkron. In his view, the intensity and other specific characteristics of the developmental efforts of the principal Continental European countries in the nineteenth century were conditioned by the *relative degree of backwardness* vis-à-vis the industrial leaders that was exhibited by each of these countries when it started its industrialization in earnest. The delay in starting the process and its sudden inception are explained by the consideration that "a point will be reached at which the advantages implied in rapid economic development will more than offset those obstacles to economic progress which are inherent in the state of economic backwardness." [14] This theory clearly implies that the development of the

13. This question is, for example, the starting point of the inquiries of T. Haavelmo, *A Study in the Theory of Economic Evolution*, Amsterdam, 1954.

14. Alexander Gerschenkron, "The Problem of Economic Development in Russian Intellectual History" in *Continuity and Change in Russian and Soviet Thought*, ed. E. J. Simmons (Cambridge, Mass., Harvard Univ. Press, 1955), p. 13. For a more detailed statement of his point of view, see in particular his article "Economic Backwardness in Historical Perspective" in *The Progress of Underdeveloped Areas*, ed. B. F. Hoselitz, Chicago, 1952.

latecomers is not generally held back by objective scarcities or by the absence of specific "prerequisites," [15] a view which we have ourselves expressed in the preceding pages.

We find it more difficult to follow Gerschenkron in his explanation of the launching of the development effort. According to his analysis, the economic operators do not at first deem the putative rewards worth the tedious effort of overcoming the backwardness of their society, of introducing all kinds of reforms and institutional changes, of reconstructing their own value systems, etc. But, as relative backwardness increases owing to further advances of the industrial leaders, the advantages to be reaped from economic progress loom larger and larger until finally the effort is undertaken. In a way, the underdeveloped country is thus pictured in the role of an Oblomov who can bring himself to leave his beloved bed and room only if the outside weather is irresistibly splendid.

The implication here is that the operators really know all the time what needs to be done to shed backwardness and to achieve development and are therefore able to weigh the costs against the expected benefits of development. But this point must be questioned. Just as there is no given set of "prerequisites" for economic development, so it is impossible to define a fixed number of backwardness features. What is a hindrance to progress in one setting and at one stage may be helpful under different circumstances. To give just one example, the institution of the extended family has often been considered as an obstacle to development because it dilutes individual incentives; [16] but it can also play a constructive role as it permits a primitive society to adapt itself to new technical activities: maximum use can be made of available spare time and new tasks can be undertaken without prior mastery of such complications as hiring labor and keeping accounts.[17]

In any event, the underdeveloped countries see only the fruits of economic progress and have little advance knowledge of the road they

15. Gerschenkron, "Reflections on the Concept of Prerequisites of Modern Industrialization," *L'Industria* (April–June 1957), pp. 357–72.

16. See, e.g., B. Higgins, "The Dualistic Theory of Underdeveloped Areas," *Economic Development and Cultural Change*, 4 (Jan. 1956), 111; a good general treatment is in Bauer and Yamey, pp. 64–7.

17. C. S. Belshaw, *In Search of Wealth. A Study of the Emergence of Commercial Operations in the Melanesian Society of South-Eastern Papua* (Vancouver, 1955), chs. 5 and 7.

need to travel to obtain them. If they desire these fruits, they will somehow set out after them. Thus they will find out about the changes required in their own society in the course of the development process as they make false starts and as they meet with, and overcome, successive obstacles. It is in this fashion rather than a priori that they will determine which of their institutions and character traits are backward and must be reformed or given up. The tension of development is therefore not so much between known benefits and costs as between the goal and the ignorance and misconceptions about the road to that goal.

Thus determination is not enough after all. It needs to be combined with a perception of what needs to be done, and this perception is acquired only gradually, in the course of the development process. For one thing, few areas of human affairs exhibit such a lack of correspondence between ends and means: to achieve higher per capita incomes, current consumption must be reduced; to make available more leisure time, work must be more rigorously scheduled; to obtain a more equitable distribution of income, new inequalities may first have to be created, etc., etc. No wonder, then, that economic development has so often been a by-product of the quest for political and military power. The choices and decisions that need to be made to achieve development are far more germane to the pursuit of power and prestige than to that of increased welfare.[18]

The nature of the "binding agent" which somewhat mysteriously is supposed to organize and achieve cooperation among the many factors, resources, and abilities needed for successful development is now becoming clearer. It seems to consist in a "growth perspective" which comprises not only the desire for economic growth but also the perception of the essential nature of the road leading toward it.

The question is once again whether we are much advanced by looking at matters in this way. If a "growth perspective" is needed for

18. For this reason, it is interesting to note that a country's standing in the international community is increasingly affected by the extent to which it is achieving economic development. This new international competition is already becoming a force hastening economic advance in many countries. It is facilitated by the increase in the speed and volume of communications and has become formally possible as a result of the invention of a—still very imperfect—scoring method, namely the compilation of national income and income per capita estimates.

growth, we have also just pointed out that this perspective can only gradually be acquired in the course of growth. So it would seem that all we have achieved is to saddle ourselves with yet another vicious circle. But, to paraphrase Orwell, while all development circles are vicious, some are more vicious than others. All circles result from the two-way dependence between development and some other factor, be it capital or entrepreneurship, education, public administration, etc. But the circle to which our analysis has led us may perhaps lay claim to a privileged place in the hierarchy of these circles inasmuch as it alone places the difficulties of development back where all difficulties of human action begin and belong: in the mind. An aspect of this difficulty which seems to us of particular interest will now be explored in greater detail.

The Idea of Change as an Obstacle to Change

It has become fashionable to declare that the desire and drive for economic development has caught the imagination of people everywhere. Admittedly there are still many millions who have failed to let themselves be caught. Nevertheless, the awareness that economic progress does not need to remain the monopoly of a few nations has been widening rapidly and certainly has penetrated some social groups in practically all countries.

The feeling that change and progress is possible and desirable is bound to represent a highly dynamic force in a hitherto stationary society. But if this feeling is due primarily to outside demonstration rather than to one's own experience, it may lead to a variety of misconceptions about the process of change that inhibit the achievement of the new goal until a modicum of learning has been achieved.

The group-focused image of change. To understand why this may be so, we shall first look at the well-known—and frequently romanticized—communal, cooperative, cohesive type of society. The individual members of such a society usually have a definite place and role assigned to them, and the possibility of change and improvement in their economic fortunes hardly enters their horizon. The total product having long been stationary, individual improvement could only take place at the expense of other members and of the cohesiveness of the group. Exceptional performance is therefore discouraged and penalized by a variety of social mechanisms of which the accusation of practicing witchcraft is the best known. An isolated advance is not even desired by the "well-adjusted" member of the group since social controls will so fashion character that "people want to act as they have to act and at the same time find gratification in acting according to the requirements of the culture." [19]

When the idea of the possibility of economic progress is forcibly impressed upon the consciousness of such a society, it will be interpreted to apply only to society as a whole. In other words, individuals will think of economic change as something that must affect equally all members of the group with which they identify themselves. The idea of change then transforms the "image" [20] of a stationary society where everybody plays his assigned role into one of a progressive or dynamic society with the individuals remaining at their previous places in relation to the group. We shall refer to this "image" of change or progress as *group-focused*.

The question must now be asked whether it is possible for the reality of economic change to correspond to this image of it; in other words, is an exclusively group-focused conception of progress favorable to its realization? Within certain limits the question can be answered in the affirmative. Most community development projects, and many technical assistance activities from malaria control to seed improvement, are perfectly compatible with, and indeed are based on, the idea that the benefits from them must accrue equally to all. Where this idea prevails, such "grass roots" projects and activities have therefore a good chance of success.

Considerable care must be taken, however, not to violate the "image" of change that alone is acceptable. The belief or suspicion, however mistaken, that a project will lead to individual enrichment rather than to collective benefits may easily spell its failure,[21] and,

19. Erich Fromm, "Psychoanalytic Characterology and Its Applications to the Understanding of Culture" in *Culture and Personality*, ed. S. S. Sargent and M. W. Smith (New York, The Viking Fund, 1949), p. 10.

20. On this concept see Kenneth E. Boulding, *The Image*, Ann Arbor, 1956.

21. For a good example, see A. R. Holmberg, "The Wells that Failed: An Attempt to Establish a Stable Water Supply in the Viru Valley, Peru," in *Human Problems and Technological Change*, ed. E. H. Spicer (New York, 1952), pp. 113–23. Cf. also P. S. Taylor, "Can We Export the 'New Rural Society'?," *Rural Sociology, 19* (March 1954), 13–20.

in this fashion, any developmental project becomes a rather delicate operation. But what is much more serious is that the group-focused image of change is incompatible with any large-scale development aiming at a fundamental transformation and modernization of an economy. It is the very nature of such development that priorities are established and that certain activities and communities receive temporarily preferred treatment; that economic opportunities are created through public investment in transportation, power, irrigation, etc. which may be seized by some individuals but will be left unexploited by others; and that in general social mobility will be vastly increased as whole social classes and groups are created *ex novo* through industrialization and urbanization.

How difficult it can be to accept this kind of transformation has been shown by Gerschenkron in a revealing analysis of the attitudes toward economic development of the Russian intelligentsia in the nineteenth century. Typically most Russian writers on economic and social issues desired economic development in the expectation and on the condition that it would result in a strengthening of the *obshchina* —the communal use of land; they had remarkably little use for industrialization and railroadization. Therefore, according to Gerschenkron, "the prophets of the Russian intelligentsia . . . were unable to grasp the nature of the forces that were pushing the country's economy in a direction *which was so repulsive to them*," [22] and he also shows how such attitudes, through their influence on university students and others, had a retarding effect on economic development.

In today's underdeveloped countries the resistance to certain typical features of the development process does not often find a similarly full-blown intellectual expression. But the group-focused image of change is strongly at work in many of these countries. The appeal of communism to traditional societies may derive in part from the fact that it pretends to reconcile the requirements of economic change with the group-focused image of change. Economic development under communism naturally involves the setting up of priorities, the acceptance of uneven advances for individuals, economic sectors, and regions within a country, and in general brings with it vast social transformations, but the process formally takes place in the name of

22. "Economic Development in Russian Intellectual History," p. 34 (my italics).

the community and the—admittedly faraway—target is a return to a static society.

A typical manifestation of the group-focused image of change is the reluctance of many governments in underdeveloped countries to pick priorities and to maintain them in a consistent manner. For instance, when countries first undertake ambitious highway and electrification programs, they frequently tend to disperse the available funds among the greatest number of towns and roads. This tendency has no doubt political causes and can also be explained by the fact that the smaller projects are easier to engineer than the larger ones.[23] But most fundamentally the unwillingness to make choices that is often maintained with remarkable stubbornness can perhaps be explained by a basic feeling that progress ought to be equally shared by all sections of the community.

The ego-focused image of change. In contrast to the group-focused image of economic progress, change may be conceived as possible (and beckoning) for the individual while it is not visualized at all for the group. This ego-focused image is likely to arise in hitherto stagnant but not closely integrated societies. The individual member of such societies who is brought face to face with the evidence of economic progress will reinterpret it to mean that he can improve his own lot. On the other hand, he will dismiss such a possibility for society as a whole simply because, not identifying himself with society, he will relate new experiences to himself alone. Therefore, the experience of the possibility of change will change his image of his own chances in life but will not affect the image he has of society as an essentially static conglomerate.

Vivid accounts of societies with such an ego-focused image of change are available in anthropological studies of Ladino and mestizo society in Latin America.[24] The "passive self-restraint and submissive

23. See p. 191.

24. John Gillin, *The Culture of Security in San Carlos: A Study of a Guatemalan Community of Indians and Ladinos,* New Orleans, 1951; and "Ethos and Cultural Aspects of Personality" in Sol Tax and others, *Heritage of Conquest,* Glencoe, Ill., Free Press, 1952. Also William C. Sayres, "Disorientation and Status Change," *Southwestern Journal of Anthropology,* 12 (Spring 1956), 79–86; and "Personality Problems and the Value System in a Rural Colombian Community," *Anthropological Quarterly,* 29 (Jan. 1956), 11–23.

self-resignation" of the Indian way of life is contrasted with the "active concern with self-promotion and ambitious self-determination and manipulation" characteristic of the Ladino and mestizo societies. The latter are strongly competitive, individuals show domineering attitudes toward persons of lower status and frequently feud with members of the same class.

> The individual strives for prominence, a feat in which he is often assisted by his family. Competition or conflict is typically encountered along the road to power, and the average male must learn techniques of open or covert aggression. High status means the right to plan and order subordinates, but also demands a certain deference to their desires if one's subordinates are not to desert to a rival. The caudillo pattern, whether in military affairs, or otherwise, is well established in Ladino culture. But a given caudillo seldom stays in power very long because of the variant drives of his followers. Political advancement is regarded as a legitimate means of advancing one's own interests, if necessary at the expense of other members or factions of the community, including other Ladinos.[25]

In distinguishing "corporate" and "open" peasant communities on the basis of economic and cultural rather than purely ethnographic factors, another anthropologist characterizes the difference between these two types in the following terms:

> The corporate community frowns on individual accumulation and display of wealth and strives to reduce the effects of such accumulation on the communal structure. It resists reshaping of relationships; it defends the traditional equilibrium. The open-ended community permits and expects individual accumulation and display of wealth . . . and allows this new wealth much influence in the reshaping of social ties. . . .
>
> Open communities are marked by the repeated 'circulation of the elite.' Blocs of wealth and power form, only to break up and be replaced by similar blocs coming to the fore.[26]

25. Gillin, "Ethos and Cultural Aspects of Personality," p. 201.
26. Eric Wolf, "Types of Latin American Peasantry: A Preliminary Discussion," *American Anthropologist*, 57 (June 1955), 462 and 465.

Although the anthropological research on which these observations are based was conducted within the last decade, the observed competitive pattern appears to antedate any "demonstration" from the outside of the possibility of dynamic economic development. But it is clear that such demonstration could only serve to reinforce the pattern and to make the struggle for wealth and power even more intense as the stakes increase.

At first blush it might appear that this kind of society is favorable to economic growth. Everybody is ambitious, dissatisfied with his present lot, and believes in the possibility of change. Appetites are unlimited—just the opposite of the usual picture of primitive societies where people's wants are supposed to be limited and fixed, and supply curves consequently slope backward. But, upon closer scrutiny, it will be granted that we have here far too much of a good thing.

The reasons why the ego-focused image of change is inimical to economic development are several. In the first place, success is conceived not as a result of the systematic application of effort and creative energy, combined perhaps with a "little bit of luck," but as due either to sheer luck or to the outwitting of others through careful scheming. The immense popularity of lotteries in the Latin American countries and the desperate intensity of the political struggle testify to the strength of the belief in, and desire for, change through sheer luck or through scheming, respectively.

These attempts to reach success through various short-cuts obviously diminish the flow of energies into activities that will stimulate economic development. But an exclusively ego-focused conception of progress will act as a drag on economic growth in several other serious ways. Most fundamentally it tends to obstruct a series of processes that are part of the entrepreneurial function.

Following Schumpeter's lead, economists and historians alike have hitherto considered the innovating entrepreneur primarily as a strong individualist. His leadership, his willingness to assume risk, his breaking through old patterns of finance, production, and distribution were emphasized and almost made him look like a rebel against society. To stake success on a process or product that has not been tried out before no doubt takes courage, imagination, and a certain willingness to defy the old order, and did so particularly in the tradition-minded European societies during the first stages of the Industrial Revolution.

16

In any event, these qualities were then the most spectacular aspect of entrepreneurship—so much so that the other necessary component was practically overlooked.

This other component involves the ability to engineer agreement among all interested parties, such as the inventor of the process, the partners, the capitalists, the suppliers of parts and services, the distributors, etc., etc.; the ability—so important in underdeveloped countries today—to enlist cooperation of official agencies in such matters as customs duties, permits, exchange control regulations, etc.; the ability to bring and hold together an able staff, to delegate authority, to inspire loyalty, to handle successfully relations with labor and the public, and a host of other managerial talents.

In the United States, of course, the need for this "cooperative" component of entrepreneurship has long been recognized and indeed cultivated, and "human engineering" has come to occupy an increasingly prominent place in the training and thinking of corporation executives. Coordination has been identified as the principal function of business leadership and the prevalence of group, rather than individual, action in all major decisions has been firmly established.[27] In fact, much concern has lately been voiced lest the "creative" component of entrepreneurship and management be smothered by too much cooperation, conformism, "other-directedness," smoothness in human relationships, and consequent insufficient "willingness to disagree."[28]

To keep a proper balance between the equally vital "cooperative" and "creative" components of entrepreneurship is obviously a difficult task. This is not the place to judge whether the cooperative com-

27. See, e.g., R. A. Gordon, *Business Leadership in the Large Corporation* (Washington, 1945), pp. 52 ff. and 99 ff.

28. "The current trend toward emphasizing smooth human relationships as the principal qualification for administrative responsibility tends to militate against the rise of innovators to top positions. Executive committees of enterprises are often afraid to choose a 'strong man' for fear of his disruptive force." R. W. MacLaurin, "The Sequence from Invention to Innovation and its Relation to Economic Growth," *Quarterly Journal of Economics*, 67 (Feb. 1953), 105; cf. also William Whyte, *The Organization Man*, New York, 1956. For an interesting dissent affirming that "the enterprise performs better with the emphasis on cooperation and teamwork than when the charismatic leader asserted himself roughshod over his colleagues," see Theodore Levitt, "The Lonely Crowd and the Economic Man," *Quarterly Journal of Economics*, 70 (Feb. 1956), 112–13.

ponent has actually been overdeveloped in the United States; but in part at least, the present concern can be explained by the contrast between the typical entrepreneurial personality of today and the traditional picture of the entrepreneur as a bold, rugged, and ruthless individual.

This one-sided picture and the traditional emphasis on the creative aspect of entrepreneurship, combined perhaps with an apologetic feeling about the cooperative component, have prevented us from fully noticing the importance of the latter and its lack in many underdeveloped countries. This lack can now be understood as a direct consequence of a strongly ego-focused conception of progress and the consequent diffusion of tension and hostility between people. When the total social product is believed to be rigidly fixed, the idea that both parties can profit from an agreement is not likely to arise; on the contrary, the more closely one approaches agreement, the more suspicious one becomes about the other fellow's having "put something over." Therefore negotiations even over simple matters are likely to bog down or to be protracted, and cooperative action in general becomes singularly difficult, at least outside the inner family circle. Thus the agreements and decisions needed to establish new business organizations or to undertake expansion are often delayed, and efficient staff work within the organization is also frequently threatened.

The argument applies to both the private and the public sector. In fact, the necessarily and overtly limited size of public funds available for spending serves to confirm in the minds of ministers and public officials the generally prevailing idea that A's gain is necessarily B's loss. As a result, feuding and lack of cooperation among and within government agencies is intense and even dictatorships are often incapable of organizing themselves for decisive and quick action. One of the principal functions of the five-, six-, or ten-year plans is precisely to create a growth perspective through the simultaneous presentation of data for several successive years, in place of the concept of a fixed total that is necessarily conveyed by the elaboration, one at a time, of annual budget figures.

Much of the sometimes amused, but often exasperated, feeling of foreign observers and advisers that everything is so unnecessarily complicated and slow in underdeveloped countries derives from these difficulties. But it will now be understood how deep-seated they are and why the usual techniques of group relations and conflict resolution are less readily transferable than industrial knowledge and techniques. The "human relations" component of entrepreneurship, the art of agreement-reaching and of cooperation-enlisting, will remain a critical bottleneck of constructive action for economic development until experience modifies the exclusively ego-focused image of change into one which takes cognizance of the possibility of mutual benefits and all-round growth. Such a modification will be effected through practical, direct experience with development as it proceeds, but it is bound to take time, like any correction of a deeply implanted idea about the nature of the world in which we live.

The shortage of the cooperative component of entrepreneurship in many underdeveloped countries is the more unfortunate as, under present conditions, the need for this component is particularly pronounced. In the first place, the more active role everywhere assumed by governments and official agencies makes it necessary for prospective investors to negotiate many aspects of their proposed operations with official agencies, if only to remove obstacles (e.g., customs duties on raw materials which are to be processed) or to obtain the full benefit of tax incentive schemes or of special financing arrangements. More importantly, the effort involved in persuading prospective partners and associates to participate in a new venture is probably more arduous in today's underdeveloped countries than it ever was in the leading industrial nations. Whereas, during the latters' development, new opportunities arose successively as a result of invention and innovation so that *at any one time* investors were powerfully attracted by the few new products or processes that had just been perfected, the range of possibilities open to investors in underdeveloped countries is seemingly infinite. Unexploited opportunities beckon from every stage of industrial development, from railroads to helicopters, from textiles to electronics. Under these conditions, it is far more difficult to reach agreement and to convince prospective partners and associates of the decisive advantages of any one proposed venture. It matters little that in reality only very few ventures are likely to be feasible and profitable. Even though it may be largely based on illusion, the feeling that there exists a wide range of conceivable ventures is likely to slow down materially the pace of investment decisions.

Exaggerated expectations and personalized liquidity preference. The difficulty of reaching agreement and of deciding on a venture is also rooted in the psychological situation of a society which is having the first, heady taste of economic development. Here again we have too much of a good thing. While an awareness of economic opportunity is essential to call forth initiatives leading to economic development, an unrealistic overestimate may constitute a drawback for several reasons. In the first place, it may lead to wholesale and hasty abandonment of useful ongoing ventures and forms of production in favor of some new "get rich quick" activity. Examples are provided by some of the many "rushes" (into rubber, coffee, cotton, and a variety of other products) which mark the economic history of Brazil. That overresponding to monetary incentives through rapid shifts in production may lead to serious economic waste and losses has long been familiar to economists as a result of the analysis of the cobweb model.[29]

Another frequently observed manifestation of the same excessive alertness to new opportunities consists in the rejection or the postponement of perfectly good projects on the ground that far more profitable schemes are bound to exist or to come along. As a result of just these oversanguine expectations one frequently notices among investor-entrepreneurs in newly developing countries a phenomenon that has much in common with *liquidity preference*. Investors keep their funds in liquid form or engage in a holding operation by investing in foreign exchange, inventories, or real estate, because the prospective profit rate on currently proposed projects does not come up to their (exaggerated) expectations. In other words, they hold money or easily realized assets because they expect the profit rate on tomorrow's ventures to be higher than that on today's ventures, just as according to liquidity-preference theory some investors are holding money because they anticipate higher interest rates.

29. The losses to producers resulting from cobweb-type reactions of supply and demand are examined in Norman S. Buchanan, "A Reconsideration of the Cobweb Theorem," *Journal of Political Economy, 47* (Feb. 1939), 100–10.

We are not concerned here with general bullishness, i.e., with the feeling that the profit rate will rise in the future on *all* ventures whenever undertaken. A bullishness of this kind would not hold back equity investment today, provided only that the profit rate expected for the immediate future is higher than the rate of interest. Our assumption is rather (1) a peculiar kind of optimism which expects tomorrow's ventures to be more profitable as a class during their lifetime than today's ventures are anticipated to be during theirs; and (2) a situation in which the investor-entrepreneurs cannot shift out of their investment once it has been selected. The latter is a fairly realistic assumption in underdeveloped countries where capital markets are either nonexistent or extremely imperfect. Under such conditions it is easily visualized how investor-entrepreneurs may hold their funds *and themselves* in "liquid" or quasi-liquid readiness for a long time before taking the momentous decision to sink their monies and energies into a new venture.

The extension and personalization of the liquidity-preference concept helps to account for the somewhat puzzling spectacle of so many able and wealthy persons in underdeveloped countries ("where there are so many opportunities") keeping themselves and their funds uncommitted or "liquid" so as to take advantage of the unusual opportunity whenever it comes. From the monetary point of view, a strong liquidity preference of this kind will not necessarily act as a brake on inflation because of the likelihood that funds will be invested in the easily realized asset categories already mentioned.

The working of the extended and personalized liquidity preference in underdeveloped countries is illustrated in Figure 1. We measure capital [30] available for investment per unit of time along the horizontal axis and the anticipated profit rate for today's investments along the vertical axis. We may assume that at a certain level of the profit rate—OM—all the capital available during the specified time period—OA—will be forthcoming. At lower rates progressively smaller amounts will be invested as shown for instance by the curve B_1P. This curve is here assumed to stand for the supply curve of capital that would obtain if the level of profit expectations from tomorrow's opportunities either were not taken into account at all or were to coincide with today's level. In the latter case, there would obviously be no point in waiting

30. Capital must here be understood to be combined with entrepreneurship.

for tomorrow's opportunities. Curves B_2P, B_3P and B_4P, on the contrary, correspond to more and more sanguine expectations about tomorrow's opportunities. They are all drawn through P because it is assumed that at some fully satisfactory expected profit rate for today's opportunities, capital would not be held back no matter how hopeful

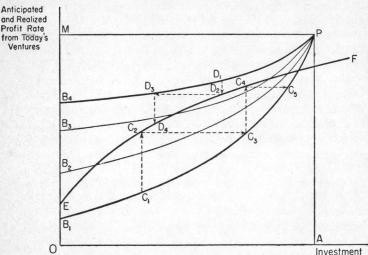

Fig. 1. Tomorrow's ventures and today's investment

one might feel about profits from tomorrow's opportunities. While actual convergence of the whole family of supply curves on one such point is not necessary, it does seem likely that the curves will get closer and closer together the higher the expected profits from today's ventures. When, however, these profits fall below a certain level, then tomorrow's imaginary brighter prospects will make a real difference and actual capital formation will then fall significantly below what it might be.

A further effect of these different degrees of optimism about tomorrow's profit on economic development can be seen if we draw into the figure a curve of realized profits. It may be expected that in an underdeveloped country the actual profit rate increases with the volume of capital that has been invested, but that this "increasing returns" effect is itself subject to diminishing returns. These assumptions are incorporated into the shape of the "realized profit rate" curve EF. Now, if B_1P is the capital supply curve, i.e., if expectations about tomorrow's profits are not unduly optimistic, then realized profits are likely to be higher than expected profits and therefore next time a larger supply of capital is likely to be forthcoming. The dynamic path is shown by the broken line $C_1C_2C_3C_4C_5$.[31] This is obviously a healthy situation. If, on the other hand, excessive optimism prevails about tomorrow's profits, then the supply curve is going to be very elastic and even a high expected rate of profit for today's ventures may elicit only a comparatively small amount of capital formation, with the result that realized profits may well fall below the expectations. In this case capital formation in the next period will be adversely affected as is shown by the dynamic path $D_1D_2D_3D_4$.

To summarize the argument of this section: two different kinds of images of change that are likely to arise in previously static societies have been distinguished: the group-focused image where change is conceived as affecting primarily the group while the individual's relative position remains untouched; and the ego-focused image where the individual conceives change as something that is open to him, essentially at the expense of the rest of society. Both images have been shown to be inimical to genuine economic development, the group-focused image because it impedes the more dynamic patterns of change, the ego-focused image because it is harmful to what was termed the cooperative component of entrepreneurship. On the other hand, this cooperative component, which consists essentially of the agreement-reaching and decision-making processes, was found to be a particularly strong need of the underdeveloped countries today. Finally we discussed other possibly harmful consequences of the sudden appearance of the idea of change and economic advance: excessive mobility and exaggerated expectations of profit from "tomorrow's" ventures holding back action on today's projects.

To acquaint a hitherto static country, society, or group with the idea that change is possible will therefore almost invariably lead to strange, unintended, and unexpected results. The *group-and-ego*-focused idea of change which seems so natural to us, namely, that the individual can advance at his own speed within an expanding economy,

31. It eventually leads to the intersection of the EF and B_1P curves.

is likely to be adopted only after a considerable span of experience has convincingly shown the possibility of such a development. Rather than accept this idea, the leaders of underdeveloped countries will sometimes be found to oscillate between the group-focused and the ego-focused image of change. Such oscillation explains perhaps why many of the "strong-man" regimes in underdeveloped countries come to power with a genuine desire to distribute more equally the fruits of economic progress among all the people, but often end up pitifully in a frantic and unabashed drive for self-enrichment on the part of the dictator and his clique.

The group-and-ego-focused image of change is likely to penetrate first among those who have experienced modern processes of economic development through having been actively involved in them; in the meantime, others will hold firmly to the exclusively ego-focused image. The coexistence of these two images accounts for another character-istic feature of underdeveloped but developing countries, namely, the gulf that separates their two typical leader-personalities: on the one hand, those that get things done, the "réalisateurs" [32] who build busi-ness organizations and hydroelectric stations, who run factories or fly airplanes, and who are always ready to lose themselves in yet another back-breaking job usually involving the transformation of nature, the use of machines, or the production of commodities; on the other hand, those who use their often remarkable intellectual gifts exclusively for the purpose of manipulating *people*. The polarization and lack of communication between these two types symbolizes, and at the same time renders more arduous, the transition from stagnation to dynamic development.

The Need for Inducement Mechanisms

Thus far our investigation is just as discouraging as all other theories of economic development: it has led us to uncover a new difficulty. On the other hand, it is also encouraging since it holds, like the other theories, that if only we can remove or neutralize our difficulty, then

32. As with "entrepreneur," there seems to exist no full equivalent for this French term in the English or American language in spite of the great value that our culture attaches to the personality type.

24

the other bottlenecks, serious as they may be, can also be removed in due course. Nevertheless, our diagnosis has one special characteristic: it is not concerned with the lack of one or even of several needed factors or elements (capital, education, etc.) that must be combined with other elements to produce economic development, but with the deficiency in the combining process itself. Our diagnosis is simply that countries fail to take advantage of their development potential because, for reasons largely related to their image of change, they find it difficult to take the decisions needed for development in the required number and at the required speed. As such, this diagnosis is less meaningful than others: it does not focus immediately on the factor which, once imported or generated within the economy in sufficient quantities, will solve the problem. Rather, the shortages in specific factors or "prerequisites" of production are interpreted as a manifestation of the basic deficiency in organization. For instance, capital or technical education are scarce or the banking system is inadequate because the country has found it difficult to take the steps necessary to create, direct, or procure capital, to spread education, and to introduce the proper financial institutions. Our diagnosis of backwardness therefore reduces all "scarce" factors to one basic scarcity.

If backwardness is due to insufficient number and speed of development decisions and to inadequate performance of developmental tasks, then the fundamental problem of development consists in generating and energizing human action in a certain direction. This finding is at variance with much of the existing literature on development, which has largely concentrated on identifying various *obstacles* to economic progress, be they land tenure systems, the extended family, administrative instability, lack of technical education, or lack of savings. It is usually an implication of such analyses that, through the removal of one or several obstacles, the forces making for development would be released, much like race horses after the lifting of the starting gate. Our approach leads us to doubt the existence of a pent-up energy that is held back by villainous obstacles. It rather views the obstacles as reflections of contradictory drives and of the resulting confusion of the will. Everyday language expresses this interdependence between will and obstacles when a person who does not act is said to be "*inventing* all kinds of difficulties and obstacles."

In such a situation obstacles hardly have a life of their own, and the removal of specific obstacles would be an unreliable method of inducing action.

Economists have long been aware of this type of situation in connection with the problem of getting an economy to move out of the depression doldrums. The weakness of monetary policy in this situation resides precisely in the fact that even a policy of extreme monetary ease is purely obstacle-removing; it is no more than permissive of the needed recovery decisions. Fiscal policy, on the other hand, is considered a more reliable means of curing a deficiency of demand because it can increase the economy's spending stream directly and makes or forces re-employment decisions in the process; it does so in the absence of any *prior* improvement in the "business climate."

In a situation of underdevelopment we are in even greater need of a mechanism of this type. The "lack of confidence" that rules in a depression is easily dispelled compared to the hindrances we have discussed, namely, the reluctance to agree to priorities and to uneven change in the case of the group-focused image of change, and the difficulties of agreement-reaching and cooperation-enlisting in the case of the ego-focused image. These reluctances and difficulties can be overcome only slowly. In the meantime, then, the taking of development decisions [33] is held back not by physical obstacles and scarcities, but by imperfections in the decision-making process. Development theory and policy therefore face the task of examining under what conditions development decisions can be called forth in spite of these imperfections, through pacing devices or inducement mechanisms.

Economics is familiar with the idea of induced decision-making. A first example is the distinction between autonomous and induced investment decisions. Certain investment decisions are considered to be induced and therefore the more reliable component of the investment total because they are related to, *and virtually compelled by*, past increases in income. They are undertaken by firms that experience the pressure of rising demand. These firms produce or expect soon to be producing in conditions of steeply rising marginal costs, and feel they have to expand if they are to keep their share of the total market.

33. We are using this term in the broad sense to cover required institutional changes and reforms as well as investment decisions proper.

Autonomous investment, on the other hand, depends on much more uncertain factors such as new inventions and innovations. Similarly, in a situation of cyclical unemployment, an initial expansion of employment is believed to be rather reliably connected with further expansions through the portion of the newly created income that is spent on domestic consumption. The portion that is saved or spent on foreign goods may or may not lead to additional re-employment, depending on what happens to domestic investment and foreign import demands. Finally, in the analysis of individuals' savings, the distinction between institutionalized and other savings has long been found useful and has more recently been reformulated as a distinction between genuine and habitual or routinized savings decisions.[34] Again, the latter component of the total is more easily predicted because it is forthcoming almost automatically as a result of the near-compulsory features of the various schemes in virtue of which payments are made.

In every one of these cases, an economic magnitude has been broken down into two separate components because one of the two could be considered more predictable and reliable than the other. In each case one of the components refers to decisions we feel confident will be taken *because there is some extra pressure behind them* as a result of pacing, routine responses, threatened penalties, certain and high profitability, or other forces.

This is exactly what we are looking for in the case of development decisions. We have identified the ability to make such decisions as the scarce resource which conditions all the other scarcities and difficulties in underdeveloped countries. However, the nature of this resource is such that it cannot be economized in the usual sense of this term. A scarce factor of production is economized by reducing its proportion relative to other factors, by spreading it thinly over the other factors that are available in greater abundance. But this method is not available in the case of decision-making, since each development move requires "its" decision. Being unable to dilute it, we must call forth as

34. George Katona, "Variability of Consumer Behavior and the Survey Method" in *Contributions of Survey Methods to Economics* (New York, 1954), pp. 48–88. Katona shows that spending decisions can be similarly broken down and that the classification of income-disposing decisions into genuine and routinized decisions may from certain points of view be more meaningful than the traditional distinction between consumption and savings.

much decision-making ability as possible by maximizing induced or routinized decision-making. Much of this book will therefore be concerned with the search for some reasonably effective inducement mechanisms.

CHAPTER 2

Growth Models and Development Processes

The Economics of Growth—Help or Hindrance?

ONE OF THE astounding feats of modern economics is the way in which the analysis of the growth process of advanced industrial countries has yielded an apparatus of seemingly ready applicability to the most primitive economies. This is the kind of "external economies" which accrue frequently in the course of scientific progress: one branch profits from the discoveries and insights of another. In principle, therefore, there is nothing reprehensible in the attempt to make our underdeveloped "economics of development" benefit from the recent vigorous advances of the "economics of growth." [1]

But in the social sciences we must be more than ordinarily suspicious of such short-cuts. The reason is that theories which, because of their high level of abstraction, look perfectly "neutral" as between one kind of economic system and another, often are primarily relevant to the conditions under which they were conceived. They usually originate in attempts to illuminate possible solutions to specific problems encountered at a given time, and are sometimes directly designed to do so. If they are useful theories, they will have focused on variables that in a particular setting are both strategic and subject to change by policy-makers. Therefore, the more useful they are in one setting, the less they are likely to be so in a completely different one. An attempt to "apply" them nevertheless may turn out to be a lengthy detour rather than a short cut. For, as we have become used to looking at reality through certain theoretical glasses, we may for a long time be unable to see it as it really is.

The attempt to apply the economics of growth to the economics of development may be a case in point. The economics of growth, whose

1. We are applying the first term to underdeveloped and the second to economically advanced countries.

principal originators are Harrod and Domar, grew directly out of the stagnation and postwar slump fears of the late thirties and World War II. From the point of view of the history of ideas, they are of course filial descendants of the Keynesian system, even though they have achieved considerable advances over that system in several respects.[2]

Domar's system has many appeals not the least of which is its basic simplicity. A society has a certain income, Y. A portion sY of this income is saved and, in equilibrium, invested: $I = sY$ where s is the propensity to save. This investment results in new capacity. If this capacity is fully utilized, the resulting increase in production and, hence, income per unit of time is $\dot{Y} = \dfrac{I}{k}$ where k is the capital-output ratio. Therefore $\dot{Y} = Y \cdot \dfrac{s}{k}$ and $\dfrac{\dot{Y}}{Y} = \dfrac{s}{k}$, which means that income will have to grow at a rate equal to the quotient of the propensity to save by the capital-output ratio if capacity is to be fully utilized and if savings-investment equilibrium is to prevail. Of course, this summary does not do justice to many aspects of Domar's incisive thought, but in its bare outline this is the theory. The best measure of its success is that today we must pinch ourselves to remember that it is theory rather than a faithful photographic copy of reality.

Harrod has focused attention on an additional relationship which has proven more elusive. While Domar is satisfied to relate investment *forward* to the increase in income that will have to be achieved if the additional capacity resulting from investment is to be utilized, Harrod stresses the way in which investment can be traced *back* to the rate of increase in output (and hence income) that is being experienced by the entrepreneurs. While recognizing the *technological* relationship between capital formation and subsequent full-capacity output growth, he also posits a *behavioral* relationship between growth in demand and, hence, in curent output on the one hand and capital formation on the other.

This functional relationship yields "induced" investment; in addition, Harrod makes allowance for "autonomous" investment which is

2 The standard references are R. F. Harrod, "An Essay in Dynamic Theory," *Economic Journal, 49* (March 1939), 14–33; *Towards a Dynamic Economics,* London, 1948; and E. D. Domar, *Essays on the Theory of Economic Growth,* New York, 1957, in particular Essays 1, 3, 4 and 5; the latter three were first published in 1946–48.

not closely related to current fluctuations in demand and which he thinks can be made partially to depend, like consumption, on the *level* of income rather than on its rate of increase. By adding this explanation of investment behavior to the previously noted relationships, Harrod is able to explore the question which type of behavior is compatible with full employment and full-capacity growth of the economy.

There is no need to go further into these theories here. Our only interest was in recalling as briefly as possible the basic functional relationships on which they are based. For the discussion about growth in advanced economies has remained anchored to the principal concepts just mentioned: the savings function, induced vs. autonomous investment, the productivity of capital.[3] The validity of the reasoning in terms of *a* capital-output ratio has appeared to be vindicated by empirical research. In the United States and the United Kingdom, the ratios have shown remarkable stability over long periods although there is of course considerable variation from one industry to another, and, from the point of view of economic policy, the concepts appear meaningful in analyzing alternative courses of action to maintain or accelerate growth.[4]

Strangely enough, however, the theory has found its principal field of application in the planning of development for underdeveloped countries. The reason is perhaps that the growth models were primarily designed to illuminate a condition which had been thought to be threatening the advanced industrial countries—secular stagnation—but which during the postwar period has been one of the few worries from which we have been entirely free. Being thus relatively underutilized the newly perfected models were employed in a setting quite different from the one for which they were designed. The Domar model, in particular, has proven to be remarkably versatile: it permits us to show not only the rate at which the economy must grow if it is

3. There have of course been major new contributions since the original articles of Harrod and Domar. My point is that the refinement, disaggregation, and qualification of their categories still sets the tone of the discussion.

4. The stability of the ratios is shown in William Fellner, "Long-Term Tendencies in Private Capital Formulation" in *Long-Range Economic Projections*, National Bureau of Economic Research, Princeton, 1954; and E. H. Phelps-Brown and M. Weber, "Accumulation, Productivity and Distribution in the British Economy, 1870–1938," *Economic Journal, 63* (June 1953), 263–88.

to make full use of the capacity created by new investment but, inversely, the required savings and capital-output ratios if income is to attain a certain target growth rate. In such exercises, the capital-output ratio is usually assumed at some value between 2.5 and 5; sometimes several alternative projections are undertaken; with given growth rates, over-all or per capita, and with given population projections in the latter case, total capital requirements for five- or ten-year plans are then easily derived.

Now, there is no harm in making these computations if all they are expected to yield is an approximate idea of the amount of capital that is likely to be used in the course of the growth process. But if one thinks that the functional relationships assumed in the model are a meaningful description of the development process, a point may be reached at which the model becomes a hindrance rather than a help in the understanding of the reality of underdeveloped countries.

In advanced economies, savings and investment decisions are independent of one another to a substantial extent and income per capita is one important determinant of the supply of savings. Therefore the equality between savings and investment is an equilibrium condition, and to write sY for S is a meaningful start in the analysis of typical savings behavior. In an underdeveloped economy, on the other hand, investment and savings decisions are largely interdependent. At the same time, additions to savings depend far more on the opening up of investment opportunities and on the removal of various obstacles to investment activity than on increased income.

Similarly, the capital-output ratio may on the whole be considered a technological coefficient in advanced countries where during any one period a variety of projects with some kind of balanced distribution of capital coefficients will come into existence. This is far less certain in underdeveloped countries where, moreover, "normal" productivity is often held back by shortages and bottlenecks and where their elimination may suddenly produce a considerable increase in the productivity of already invested capital.

For these reasons, a model based on the propensity to save and on the capital-output ratio is bound to be far less useful in underdeveloped than in advanced economies. Its predictive and operational value is low. It does not really tell us much about the key mechanisms through which economic progress gets under way and is carried forward in a backward environment.

The reason for this state of affairs has already been mentioned: while the model appears to be quite general, its principal parameters have been chosen so as to give it maximum relevance within the environment with which it was intended to deal. But the very success of this enterprise makes it virtually certain that the model will have minimum relevance in any radically different environment. The economics of development dare not therefore borrow too extensively from the economics of growth; like the underdeveloped countries themselves, it must learn to walk on its own feet, which means that it must work out its own abstractions.

Explaining Investment Activity

The theory of investment has remained the most unsatisfactory aspect of the growth models of advanced economies. In spite of empirical studies and periodic surveys of investment programs of business firms, investment decisions have not been adequately explained by other observable economic variables. True, the relation between consumption and income has also turned out to be far more complex than was once thought, and that between investment and incremental output potential is certainly not a technological constant unaffected by such matters as relative factor prices, technological progress, etc. Nevertheless, investment is still comparatively the most volatile and least predictable among the more important variables that are involved in the growth process. Harrod, Hicks, and others have used the device of dividing *ex ante* investment into two parts: first, the "induced" portion, resulting from recent increases in demand or, somewhat more realistically, from past profits, and secondly "autonomous investment" which is described as principally influenced by new inventions, expectations, public overhead investments, etc. This is of course a helpful first step in sorting out the known from the unknown factors in the determination of investment. But as long as there remains an "autonomous" investment, i.e., a portion that cannot be convincingly explained by economic variables, we are still without a comprehensive theory of investment. This is probably what Domar

33

sensed when he limited himself essentially to defining the rate of capital formation *required* for steady growth, regardless of the question whether it is in fact likely to be achieved.

The lack of such a theory is not really much lamented. Any attempt at making investment a completely endogenous variable would not be received with great joy at the discovery of a missing link, but on the contrary would meet with much resistance and incredulity. For the notion that investment is subject to many unpredictable outside shocks is firmly rooted in our concept of the investment process in advanced industrial countries.

Exaggerating a little, we may describe this concept in the following terms: at any time, capitalist economies dispose of an ample supply of entrepreneurs who are especially trained in the art of perceiving and ferreting out economic opportunity: who know how to rank all available opportunities according to their profitability: and who can perform or procure everything that is needed to transform the projects into reality, provided only that "finance" is available to them at appropriate terms and conditions. Investors are thus pictured as a hungry lot that throw themselves on and devour any new investment opportunity that comes along. No wonder that the system is unstable and is alternatively suffering from deflation, because of a temporary exhaustion of investment opportunities, or from inflation, because of a temporary excess.

Naturally everything depends on the supply of investment opportunities. If these were to be forthcoming in a steady stream, the chance for investment to flow smoothly would be much increased. But since new inventions must be included among the determinants, and since various accelerators and decelerators are at work, the flow of investment will be far from even.

In the real world, the instability of investment is of course reduced by the fact that reactions to the appearance of investment opportunities are not instantaneous: in fact there is a considerable lag between invention and innovation and this lag is helpfully distributed over several years. Nevertheless, the resulting smoothing of the investment flow does not modify the process in its essentials. In the advanced industrial economies we cannot help feeling that investment is constantly living from hand to mouth. How much more confident we would be about the chances of these economies to maintain a steady growth pace if investments did not always follow so hard on the heels of technical progress!

This brings us of course straight back to our subject, the under-developed countries. They are in the "fortunate" position of facing a huge accumulated reservoir of technical progress on which they may draw steadily for many years to come. But *their* difficulty, on the other hand, lies with the processes that are largely taken for granted in advanced countries, namely, with the perception of investment opportunities and their transformation into actual investments.

With investment not depending on the uncertain appearance of a fresh supply of attractive investment opportunities, it may actually be easier to construct a theory of investment for them than for the advanced countries. This is fortunate, for any theory of development must start with a consideration of the forces that determine investment in underdeveloped countries, especially when it is realized that savings are by no means the only limiting factor and may be low because investments are low rather than vice versa. Hemmed in between the simplifications of the growth models with their smooth exponential paths and the unnerving choppiness characteristic of the growth process in underdeveloped countries, current writings on development are almost devoid of attempts at building up a theoretical framework in answer to this question. One finds in them many valuable hints on how investment should proceed, on investment criteria useful for policy makers, but little systematic discussion of the forces that govern the process of capital accumulation. Perhaps all the knowledge we need and can hope to attain may indeed be summarized by the statement that investment depends on savings and a number of other factors, such as technical education, organizational know-how, presence of enterprising minorities, etc. Nevertheless, at the risk of attacking a trivial problem, we shall now attempt to go beyond this type of statement.

The Ability to Invest

In the theory of growth relating to advanced countries, attention is properly centered on two points: the generation of savings on the one hand, and the availability of investment opportunities and their productivity on the other. Since it is taken for granted that investment will automatically take place provided savings and investment opportunities are both available, it is only natural to focus on what are in effect the two *terminal points* of the savings-investment process.

In underdeveloped countries, such telescoping of the process would be highly unrealistic: the factors limiting growth are here most generally connected, not with the two terminal points themselves, but with the difficulties of connecting them. In other words, development is held back primarily by the difficulties of channeling *existing* or potentially existing savings into available productive investment opportunities, i.e., by a shortage of the ability to make and carry out development decisions. Some of the reasons for this shortage of what we shall call briefly the "ability to invest" were set out in the first chapter.

The ability to invest is acquired and increased primarily by practice; and the amount of practice depends in fact on the size of the modern sector of the economy. In other words, an economy secretes abilities, skills, and attitudes needed for further development roughly in proportion to the size of the sector where these abilities are already required and where these attitudes are being inculcated. For instance, in an economy with 1000 plants, about ten times as many managers and engineers can be expected to be available for the manning of new managerial and engineering jobs than in an economy with 100 plants. More intangible factors, such as the ability to promote new enterprises and to enlist cooperation for this purpose, the ability to perceive new opportunities and to act on them, may, in a first approximation, be supposed to be similarly related to their actual breeding ground.

We may therefore think of the ability to invest as a coefficient v that, applied to the total income Y_m of the economy's modern sector, yields the investment $v \cdot Y_m$ that *can* and will be undertaken provided the finance is available. The propensity to save, s, on the other hand, is the ratio of all savings to the total income of the economy, Y. Let us examine briefly the relationship between these quantities.

At an early stage of the developing country's growth, the investment volume permitted by the ability to invest is likely to be low, not necessarily because v is low, but simply because Y_m is small in relation to Y. We are up against one of the famous vicious circles: a modern sector is needed to generate investing ability and vice versa. Whether or not the distribution of income is very uneven, it is likely that total mobilizable savings in such an economy exceed total investing capacity. The excess may actually show up in unadulterated forms such as hoarded gold or foreign exchange; more likely, an excess of potential over actual savings may be indicated by luxury consumption of the rich, by occasional large-scale spending and gifts even among the poor, and by considerable amounts of time devoted to leisure and similar phenomena ubiquitous in underdeveloped countries.

We have here the opposite of the "forced savings" concept which describes the involuntary cut in consumption that is inflicted upon the public at large when inflationary finance is made available to investors. In underdeveloped countries, on the contrary, we may perhaps say that a readiness to save and invest exists, but is being *frustrated*—or at least this is how the situation might be characterized by someone who would look back upon it after development has made important forward strides. Of course, it is not easy to define this concept of potential or frustrated savings; generally it just stands for what an outside observer thinks should or might be saved. But as in the case of disguised unemployment, a precise definition is not necessary; we may say that frustrated savings exist whenever the total supply of savings is highly responsive to the appearance of new investment opportunities, again a condition characteristic of many underdeveloped countries.

As the modern sector expands, $v \cdot Y_m$ expands also and, provided v is larger than s, will eventually catch up with sY. From that point on, we are back at the traditional model, with the further expansion of the economy essentially limited by the supply of savings and with the latter responding more to increase in income than to the appearance of new investment opportunities. Such opportunities then result primarily in a reshuffling of the order in which investments will actually be undertaken.

Clearly our "ability to invest" is closely related to what has sometimes been termed "absorptive capacity."[5] It has of course been realized that a country's capacity to absorb capital may be lower than the investment funds available to it because of shortages of skills and

5. M. F. Millikan and W. W. Rostow, *A Proposal: Key to an Effective Foreign Policy* (New York, 1957), pp. 60–3; G. M. Meier and R. E. Baldwin, *Economic Development: Theory, History, Policy* (New York, 1957), pp. 351–5.

other obstacles. But this situation has always been considered a deviation from the norm, i.e., the full absorption of all available finance. In this fashion, attention has been centered on the removal of the various hindrances to absorption, an activity which is then detached from the purview of economic analysis and relegated to prehistory under the heading "laying down the prerequisites for economic development." In our opinion, it is more fruitful to investigate directly how investment activity is determined and grows in underdeveloped countries than to start with some preconceived idea of what it should be. For this reason, we prefer the term "ability to invest" which suggests a phenomenon that has an expansion path of its own. The path which we have traced thus far is a very schematic one. Nevertheless some implications are evident even at this stage of the argument.

"Only the capitalists save." Arthur Lewis has clearly seen that the growth of underdeveloped countries is held back by the smallness of the modern (capitalist) sector rather than by any absolute inability to save resulting from low income levels. However, he maintains savings in their traditional role as principal agent of growth; and since he wishes to relate growth to the size of the modern sector rather than to that of the whole economy he is naturally led to the "classical" proposition that only the capitalists save (or that only their savings count).[6] But why not take one more step and rely for growth on the composite abilities produced by the modern sector which include, inter alia, the ability to mobilize the savings of the rest of the community? This course not only has the advantage of realism and simplicity; it also gives us a model of development that is applicable regardless of the economic system under which a country chooses to live.

The role of foreign capital. It is clear from our analysis that foreign capital plays two different roles in the course of the development process: in the first phase, when domestic savings are not the factor limiting development, foreign capital is needed not so much qua

6. W. A. Lewis, "Economic Development With Unlimited Supplies of Labour," *Manchester School of Economic and Social Studies, 23* (May 1955), 153–60; and *The Theory of Economic Growth* (Homewood, Ill., 1955), pp. 225 ff.

capital as because it brings with it certain abilities and skills that are in particularly short supply. This does not mean that the capital contribution should be necessarily and entirely divorced from the provision of skills and know-how, through licensing arrangements, management contracts, and the like. Certain abilities and attitudes are extremely hard to divorce from capital and yet are among those that it is most important to acquire for a developing country. An example is what has become known as growth mentality, which, among other things, stands for the plowing back of profits in substantial quantities rather than for the "milking" so often practised by local capitalists.

During the subsequent phase, foreign capital is needed qua capital. The entrepreneurial and managerial abilities are there, but the community now does not produce a sufficient amount of savings to employ these abilities fully. Foreign capital now does not need all the trappings of the first phase: it may best take the form of general development loans. Attempts to direct and supervise closely are not only likely to produce resentment but are almost certain to be futile: for when a country has reached the stage where its entrepreneurial skills outrun its supply of domestic capital, it will usually know how to rearrange its planned investments so as to present foreign lenders with the projects it knows to be acceptable while reserving its domestic capital resources for those projects which it knows to be less popular abroad.[7]

The supply of savings as a ceiling for the growth path. The transition from the first to the second stage of growth, i.e., from the point where the growth-limiting factor turns from the ability to invest into the supply of savings, should not be considered as a turning point neatly defined in time. Since intersectoral mobility is far from perfect, both for savings and for developmental skills, the transition is likely to occur at different times for the different sectors of the economy. Nevertheless, the coming of this transition may mean that the country will from then on have to follow a slower expansion path than hitherto unless it takes special measures that range from the procurement of large-scale foreign capital imports to fiscal and monetary reforms as well as to the forcible compression of mass consumption.

7. The foregoing paragraphs are a preliminary formulation; see Chs. 9 and 11 for further consideration of the role of foreign capital.

It is likely that a country that hits the savings ceiling is going to make such an attempt to break through it in some manner; if it does not succeed, it may well fall below it in true Hicksian fashion, for some kind of accelerator is likely to have been at work during the growth process up to the ceiling; therefore, as the rate of advance slows down, economic progress may in fact drop below the ceiling. In any event, this period of transition is likely to be a particularly crucial and turbulent one for a developing country and one during which public opinion may well become ready for extreme solutions.

The Complementarity Effect of Investment

Thus far our theory is still quite anemic. That development is being bred in some fashion in the developed sector of an economy is not only a rather unexciting statement, but it does not permit one to account adequately for the sudden spurts or the unexpected relapses into stagnation that developing countries have often exhibited. We have made development proceed along a path which, although somewhat different from the one traditionally trodden, still has much in common with other, equally unrealistic, models of growth. Development seems impossible of achievement at the early stage (because of the various vicious circles) and well-nigh irresistible later on. We shall now attempt to remedy these defects of our construction.

The role of the ability to invest in the growth process is very similar to that traditionally occupied by the propensity to save. Inasmuch as savings set an effective ceiling to the amount of investment that an economy can actually undertake, they have been considered a necessary condition for investment activity to take place.[8] But because of the independence of savings and investment decisions, savings do not by themselves call forth investment activity and this fact has led precisely to the various attempts to account independently for the latter, through the innovating entrepreneur, past changes in output (induced investment), profits, etc.

The ability to invest is of course more directly related to investment activity. It comprises the ability to perceive investment op-

8. Inversely, investment may be considered a necessary condition for savings plans to be realizable—a relationship that was stressed by Keynes.

portunities, and since, in an underdeveloped country, a large supply of such opportunities presumably exists, the expanding ability to invest may be considered to supply the necessary *and* sufficient condition for investment to come about. Do we then need any additional apparatus to account for growth? I think we do. Perhaps we can conceive of the investment generated by the ability to invest *not as a ceiling but as a floor*.[9] After all, we related it exclusively to the modern sector, ruling out any contribution from the rest of the economy. The investment undertaken as a result of the growth of the ability to invest is that which is undertaken by people who have been effectively transformed into modern decision-makers by the working of the advanced sector of the economy. They do not exhibit any more the difficulties in acting, in cooperating, in establishing priorities on which we dwelt in the first chapter. But if the economy is to rely only on this process, its growth is going to be painfully slow. Is there not some way in which the energies of the rest of the economy can be utilized so as to produce growth in addition to the trickle that, in the first stages of development, results from the ability to invest?

To be able to give a positive answer to this question, we must locate a mechanism that will make for investments with a force capable of compensating for the characteristic difficulties of underdeveloped countries. I believe that such a mechanism can be encountered in a certain characteristic of investment itself, namely in its contagious effect on more investment. For want of a better expression and for reasons that will become clear, I shall call it the complementarity effect of investment.

Investment is a many-sided actor on the economic scene. Its simultaneous performance as income-generator and capacity-creator is the foundation of modern growth theory. Now we will stress a third role which it plays occasionally on top of the other two: that of pace-setter for additional investment.

Ordinarily, the road from investment to more investment is considered to be rather indirect: investment increases capacity and if the economy expands in such a way as to accommodate this capacity, the

9. At least as long as we take only positive, development-promoting forces into account. The next section will deal with negative forces which may make the "floor" cave in.

additional income based on the increased capacity will result in more savings, which, in turn, allow additional investments. Also, according to the doctrine of "induced investment," if there is an increase in investment activity from one period to another, "induced" investment in capital goods industries will result. But there is no room in these constructions for any direct effect of the investment of one period on that of the next period.

The fact that such direct effects exist, i.e., that the investments of one period are often the principal motivating forces behind some additional investments of subsequent periods, is of course well known, but for some reason this knowledge has not been fully transferred from the theory of production to the theory of growth. The former has long taught that an increase in production of commodity A may require more production of commodity B or that, because of technical complementarity, it may lower the marginal cost of producing commodity C.[10] Thus investment in the production of A sets up strong pressures for an increase in the production of B and strong incentives for the start of production of C. The reason for which the theory of growth for advanced economies has not made much of these sequences is that they are expected to take place automatically and almost instantaneously; also, with a complete universe of commodities already in production, the needs aroused or opportunities opened up by additional investment result only in marginal adjustment in outputs from *existing capacity*. In underdeveloped countries, on the contrary, these processes are absolutely basic in determining the expansive path of the economy; and in the next chapters we will try to examine the principal types of such sequences in some detail. The complementarity effect thus reinforces and supplements the slowly growing ability to invest of underdeveloped countries. The investments of one period call forth complementary investments in the next period with a will and logic of their own; they block out a part of the road that lies ahead and virtually compel certain additional investment decisions. These decisions are therefore comparatively "easy to take" and are likely to attract newcomers who will join the rolling development bandwagon while the operators who have had the benefit of the education afforded by the modern sector of the economy may be spared for the

10. See, e.g., Tibor Scitovsky, *Welfare and Competition* (Chicago, 1951), pp. 139–40.

many difficult investment decisions that still remain to be taken.[11] In the language of the Swedish economist Dahmén, their job is to start new development "blocks," whereas less well-trained operators may be left to finish them.[12]

The complementarity effect of investment is therefore the essential mechanism by which new energies are channeled toward the development process and through which the vicious circle that seems to confine it can be broken. To give maximum play to this effect must therefore be a primary objective of development policy.

What can we say in general about the likely quantitative importance of the effect? Very little. Formally, it would be possible to construe the effect as a multiplier-type relationship so that each investment would lead to investments in the next period in an amount smaller than the original investment; if the relationship were of the opposite type, the complementarity effect would soon swamp all investment. Now it may be expected that the structural repercussions will slowly become exhausted and will be finite in the aggregate; but there is no reason for thinking that this finite sum is likely to be the result of a smooth geometric progression.

On the other hand, for reasons already noted, it is likely that the complementarity effect will lose importance as the economy reaches higher levels of development. New investments no longer lead necessarily to a chain of related new investments once the economy is well rounded out, with all activities nicely dovetailed with one another. It is probably for this reason that the analysis of complementarity has been relegated by economic theory to microprocesses of partial equi-

11. As already mentioned (Ch. 1, n. 34), Katona has distinguished between genuine and routinized economic decisions. Routinized is not a good term for a decision the taking of which has been considerably facilitated by previous decisions, but which nevertheless may be taken only once in a lifetime. Our "easy" decisions include, but are by no means limited to, those taken by Schumpeter's "imitators."

12. Erik Dahmén, *Entrepreneurial Activity in Swedish Industry in the Period 1919–1939*, Stockholm, 1950 (in Swedish). In a review article about what seems to be a very interesting work, Gerschenkron explains that a "development block" is for Dahmén "spread over several industrial branches . . . for reasons of technological and economic complementarities." At its early stages, it is "shot through . . . with structural tensions." *Review of Economics and Statistics, 39* (Nov. 1957), 471.

librium; but for underdeveloped countries it deserves a place of honor in any macroeconomic analysis of the growth process.

The point of view which we have acquired thus far can best be made clear by illustrating it through a concrete issue in economic development policy. In a valuable article on the role of small industry in economic development, Aubrey has argued in favor of small industry in a rural or small-town setting on the ground that in this way it is possible to economize on the overhead capital expenditures (water, power, housing, etc.) required by urbanized industry and its labor force.[13] This position is of course entirely valid on the assumption that the supply of capital is fixed. But if we drop this assumption and let ourselves be guided by the rule that during a prolonged phase the essence of development strategy consists in maximizing induced decision-making, then we would favor rather than oppose the establishment of industries in cities precisely because it compels additional or complementary capital formation that otherwise might never have taken place.

Obviously, what we are opposing here is not the principle of husbanding capital in general but a policy which in the name of this principle would reduce the stimuli and pressures toward additional capital formation that might emanate from the investments of a given period. Such a policy would indeed economize on capital requirements in the next period, but it would equally inhibit the supply of capital; in effect, therefore, it would "economize" on capital *formation* rather than on capital!

The Forces Corroding Development

It is not my intention in this section to add to the vast literature on "obstacles to economic development." Whatever small contribution I had to make to this subject has been presented in Chapter 1. My purpose here is rather to remind the reader that these obstacles do not only block or hold back development, but remain very much at work once the development process has started. They then turn into forces making for abortive development and for the stagnation and decay of ventures that looked hopeful at first.

13. Aubrey, "Small Industry in Economic Development," *Social Research, 18* (Sept. 1951), 296–7.

Because of the simplified growth models that are so deeply embedded in our thinking, there is a tendency to concentrate on the *initial* obstacles which have to be removed if development is to be launched at all. While the possibility of decay and stagnation has long been recognized, it has been seriously studied only for the mature economies of Western Europe and the United States. The reason lies no doubt in strong mental habits: we are fond of interpreting events in terms of biological growth patterns (birth-youth-maturity-old age-death), historical cycles (rise and decline), and perhaps logistic growth curves (acceleration followed by deceleration), but we seem to be unwilling to admit that growth can be halted or stunted even in its early stages.

These habits are reinforced by observation of the behavior of individual industries in economically advanced countries which indeed have frequently exhibited the cycle: accelerating progress—decelerating growth—stagnation—decline.[14] Over-all growth of the economy has been assured as a result of growth leadership passing from one industry to another.

However, the idea that development, once started, will proceed smoothly for some considerable time until the problems of "maturity" and "old age" appear, gives a misleading image of the growth problems of underdeveloped countries. A more apt analogy has been proposed by Rostow: that of the take-off of an airplane.[15] Here at least attention is duly focused on the early phase of a country's economic development which may or may not result in a cumulative growth movement depending on the momentum that is gathered. It certainly is true that, during this phase, considerable uncertainty prevails about the chances of success of the country in its bid to join the developed countries. Forward steps are halting and scattered, difficulties abound, achievements are fragile and continued growth seems extraordinarily dependent on careful nursing, creative individuals, and good luck.

Then, at a later point, we suddenly feel that we no longer need to worry so much, that a solid foundation exists, that economic progress has become institutionalized and routinized to a certain extent. As

14. Simon Kuznets, *Economic Change* (New York, 1953), Essay No. 9, "Retardation of Industrial Growth."

15. Rostow, "The Take-Off into Self-Sustained Growth," *Economic Journal, 66* (March 1956), 25–48.

the principal criterion for determining whether "take-off" is being achieved, Rostow uses a sharp increase in the ratio of investment to national income. But this is at best a diagnostic device. Behind the rise in the investment ratio lie crucial changes in certain characteristic features of the development process.

That development leads a precarious existence during its first stages and can easily become abortive can hardly be doubted. In almost all underdeveloped countries we can find examples of industrial ventures that have gone to seed, and of other hopeful beginnings that have turned into disappointments. I am not now referring to ventures that were badly planned from the start, but to those that, after having worked well for a while, have deteriorated or decayed for one reason or another. It is a common observation in underdeveloped countries that it is far easier to start an industry than to keep it operating efficiently over a period of several years. The difficulty of ensuring regular maintenance and repairs of irrigation canals, highways, buildings, and machinery is one of the most striking common denominators of the underdeveloped world.

How can we build these widespread phenomena into our theory? Are there forces hostile to development that the development process itself brings into being?

Economists have paid attention to this type of sequence mainly in the analysis of the effect of development on population increases. Here a number of neo-Malthusian models have been developed [16] that show how an initial increase in income may result in a population increase that swallows up the increase in income; the models show under what conditions a country will be caught in, or will be able to break out of, such a "low-level equilibrium trap." No doubt the sequence: growth in per capita income→increase in population→decline in per capita income is a particularly fascinating aspect of the possibilities of abortive development, both because of its possible practical relevance in many important underdeveloped countries, and because it is susceptible of easy and fairly meaningful mathematical manipulations.

16. H. Leibenstein, *A Theory of Economic-Demographic Development*, Princeton, 1954; and *Economic Backwardness and Economic Growth*, New York, Wiley, 1957; R. R. Nelson, "A Theory of the Low-Level Equilibrium Trap," *American Economic Review*, 46 (Dec. 1956), 894–908. A different approach to the population problem is suggested in Ch. 9.

But the increase in population is obviously only one of many forces that are set in motion by development and may react adversely on it. If growth starts at a few points rather than everywhere at the same time, then tensions arise naturally between the modern and the traditional sectors, and just as the modern sector breeds the "ability to invest," so will the traditional sector now secrete attitudes and actions that will in effect corrode and undermine the country's economic progress.

Such negative effects must be recognized as a third independent factor determining the growth pattern of underdeveloped countries jointly with the two positive factors that have already been discussed. Consequently, the direction of economic development policy ought to be shaped by some knowledge of these forces of stagnation and decay, of the areas where they attack with particular virulence and effectiveness, and of the manner in which they can be checked. We shall return to these problems in greater detail in Chapter 8.

A learning model applicable to economic development. A few years ago, H. A. Simon suggested that certain types of self-regulated behavior, such as voluntary learning of a foreign language, might be described by what he called the "Berlitz Model." [17] Since I believe the model to be very suggestive for the aspects of the development process I have been discussing, I shall describe it briefly in nonmathematical terms: Simon supposes that an individual who desires to learn French starts out with a given level of difficulty or ignorance. The more he practises, the more he will reduce the difficulty, but for each level of difficulty there is one rate of practice (hours per day) beyond which practising is unpleasant so that if this level is reached or exceeded, practice will be reduced the next day. If the student starts out with a rate of practice that is felt as unpleasant, we are going to witness a race between the rate at which he learns French and the rate at which he reduces his studying. He may give up before he has learned, or alternatively he may advance sufficiently so that one day he reaches a point at which the amount of studying he still engages in is felt as pleasant rather than unpleasant; from then on, he

17. "Some Strategic Considerations in the Construction of Social Science Models" in *Mathematical Thinking in the Social Sciences,* ed. P. F. Lazarsfeld (Glencoe, Ill., Free Press, 1954), pp. 402–5.

will lengthen his daily periods of study and he will surely learn. A third possibility is that, being aware that long periods of study are unpleasant in the beginning, he will start out by studying for short periods so that studying is pleasant all along and will be slowly increased until the subject is mastered.

I find it tempting to look at development with the help of this learning model. Somewhat like a person who decides in a fit of enthusiasm to learn a foreign language, a country that sets out on the road to development often does not realize the difficulties of the task ahead. As these difficulties appear, as it becomes clear that the price of development is a high one in terms of human suffering, social tensions, forced abandonment of traditional behavior and values, etc., "practice" may be reduced, contradictory and harmful economic policies are being adopted, and development will be slowed down and perhaps halted. On the other hand, if income growth reaches a point where the benefits of development are felt to outweigh the dislocations it brings with it, "practice" becomes pleasant and is gradually increased, and the country will reach its developmental goals. This model argues in favor of some forcing of the pace in the early stages of development, to overcome the resistances that then are strongest.[18]

Naturally, a far smoother road toward development would be via the third alternative of Simon's model, i.e., by undertaking development in very small doses at first so that all unpleasantness is avoided from the start. This process may be applicable, and is an excellent model to keep in mind, with respect to situations encountered in small-scale and community development projects as well as in many technical assistance activities of an educational nature. But, as we saw in our discussion of the group-focused image of change, the decisions that have to be made when an underdeveloped country attempts to

18. The model is in a sense a qualified version of the "Gerschenkron model." According to the latter, a backward country compares the expected benefits of development with the expected cost implicit in the effort to shed backwardness. In the Berlitz model, the initial decision may be construed to follow from an *ex ante* weighing of this sort, but the follow-through operations are then influenced by actual experience, i.e., by successive *ex post* weighings of realized benefits against realized costs. In this way, the Berlitz model takes care of the points which in Ch. 1 were raised in criticism of Gerschenkron's view on the development of latecomers.

modernize its economic and social structure are almost certain to imply a certain amount of "painful practice."

It is clear by now that we do not propose a rigid model of economic development. In this chapter we have identified one force that by itself would make for steady growth: the ability to invest. But economic development can in effect be far more rapid or far less successful than would be indicated by this basic factor because of the presence of other dynamic positive and negative forces which we have described. To understand how these forces can be activated or checked, respectively, is then our most important task. Our foray into the theory of development has thus left us with a heightened consciousness of the importance of a theory of development *strategy*.

CHAPTER 3

Balanced Growth: A Critique

Is Balance in Demand Required?

THE GENERAL VIEW of development which we have gained must now prove its usefulness in dealing with important issues of development policy. This process can best be started by reviewing some current views and theories.

It is often said that in spite of all our efforts economics has not produced a real theory of development. What is meant by this phrase? Probably that economists have not been able to construct, much less agree on, a single and unbroken chain of causes and effects that would neatly explain the transition from "underdevelopment" to development. While this "failure" is of course only to the credit of economists, it cannot be denied that in comparison with the elaborate constructs of static partial and general equilibrium theory, our dynamics, particularly those dealing with underdeveloped countries, have themselves an "underdeveloped" look. Challenging generalizations and theoretical insights are conspicuously rare in the writings on economic development. Nevertheless, theoretical reasoning has by now been applied to a few closely interrelated problems such as balanced growth and the determination of investment priorities. Both deal essentially with the path to or the design of development, the principal subject matter of the present essay.

Before setting out I think it only fair to warn the reader that I heartily disagree with the "balanced growth" doctrine. In fact, if I may indulge for a moment in some introspective analysis, it was the experience of finding myself instinctively so much at variance with this theory that made me aware of having acquired a distinct outlook on development problems, which it might perhaps be worth while to explore systematically.

The theory of balanced growth has several authors and aspects. The principal authors are Rosenstein-Rodan, Nurkse, Lewis, and

Scitovsky.[1] In one of its aspects, the theory stresses the need for the different parts of a developing economy to remain in step to avoid supply difficulties. Industry must not get too far ahead of agriculture. Basic facilities in transportation, power, water supply, etc.—the so-called social overhead capital—must be supplied in adequate volume to support and stimulate the growth of industry. We shall have to say something later on about these prescriptions of balance between sectors in the course of growth. But first we shall address ourselves to a version of the theory which is of greater analytical interest.

In this version the requirement of balanced growth is derived from the demand side. It is argued that a new venture—say, a shoe factory —which gets underway by itself in an underdeveloped country is likely to turn into a failure: the workers, employees, and owners of the shoe factory will obviously not buy all of its output, while the other citizens of the country are caught in an "underdevelopment equilibrium" where they are just able jointly to afford their own meager output. Therefore, it is argued, to make development possible it is necessary to start, *at one and the same time*, a large number of new industries which will be each others' clients through the purchases of their workers, employes, and owners. For this reason, the theory has now also been annexed to the "theory of the big push." [2] A big push could, of course, result from one or a few big projects, or from a large number of projects of varying size that dovetail with one another. It is clearly the latter alternative of the "big push" theory that is implied by the theory of balanced growth.

As will be explained below, the theory exists also in a more sophisticated variant, but let us stop here for some basic critical comments.

My principal point is that the theory fails as a theory of *development*. Development presumably means the process of *change* of one

1. P. N. Rosenstein-Rodan, "Problems of Industrialization of Eastern and South-Eastern Europe," *Economic Journal, 53* (June–Sept. 1943), 205; Ragnar Nurkse, *Problems of Capital Formation in Underdeveloped Countries* (Oxford, 1953), ch. 1; Tibor Scitovsky, "Two Concepts of External Economies," *Journal of Political Economy, 62* (April 1954), 143–52; W. A. Lewis, *Theory of Economic Growth,* pp. 274–83. The first two authors stress balance in demand, the latter two balance in supply.

2. Rosenstein-Rodan, "Notes on the Theory of the Big Push," paper submitted to the Rio Roundtable of the International Economic Association, 1957, mimeographed.

type of economy *into* some other more advanced type. But such a process is given up as hopeless by the balanced growth theory which finds it difficult to visualize how the "underdevelopment equilibrium" can be broken into at any one point. The argument is reminiscent of the paradox about the string that is equally strong everywhere and that therefore when pulled cannot break anywhere first: it either will not break at all or must give way everywhere at once. However, as Montaigne pointed out in considering this paradox, its premise "is contrary to nature" for "nothing is ever encountered by us that does not hold some difference however small it may be." [3]

Oblivious of this "difference," the balanced growth theory reaches the conclusion that an entirely new, self-contained modern industrial economy must be superimposed on the stagnant and equally self-contained traditional sector. Say's Law is here made to reign *independently* in both economies. This is not growth, it is not even the grafting of something new *onto* something old; it is a perfectly dualistic pattern of development, akin to what is known to child psychologists as "parallel play." There are indeed instances of this kind of development, but they are usually considered conspicuous failures from both the social and economic points of view: the contrast between the Indian communities of the Peruvian altiplano and the Spanish mestizo economy along the coast comes to mind and so do the much decried enclave-type plantations and mining operations that have been set up in several underdeveloped countries by foreign concerns as perfectly self-contained units, far away from the danger of contamination by the local economy.

Naturally, this is not the picture that was in the minds of the authors of the theory. How can we then explain that they set up so unsatisfactory a model? I suspect the reason is that the very difficulty of the task of development has led them to an escapist solution. How many a Western traveler to an underdeveloped country has been bewildered and dismayed by the ubiquitous poverty and inefficiency, by the immensity of the task, and by the interlocking vicious circles! The temptation is strong then to leave all this backwardness alone and to dream of an entirely new type of economy where, in the words of the poet, "tout est ordre et beauté!"

One of the most curious aspects of the theory is the way in which

3. *Essays,* Bk. 2, ch. 14.

it combines a defeatist attitude toward the capabilities of under-developed economies with completely unrealistic expectations about their creative abilities. On the one hand, the conception of the traditional economy as a closed circle dismisses the abundant historical evidence about the piecemeal penetration by industry that competes successfully with local handicraft and by new products which are first imported and then manufactured locally.[4] It also disregards the evidence that, for better or for worse, some products of modern industrial civilization—flashlights, radios, bicycles, or beer—are always found sufficiently attractive to make people stop hoarding, restrict traditional consumption, work harder, or produce more for the market in order to acquire them. But, on the other hand, a people that is assumed to be unable to do any of these things and that is therefore entirely uninterested in change and satisfied with its lot is then expected to marshal sufficient entrepreneurial and managerial ability to set up at the same time a whole flock of industries that are going to take in each others' output! For this is of course the major bone that I have to pick with the balanced growth theory: its application requires huge amounts of precisely those abilities which we have identified as likely to be in very limited supply in underdeveloped countries. It is altogether inconceivable that a one-floor economy could set up such a "second floor" with its own forces or even with limited help from abroad; without thorough foreign colonization the task would seem to be hopeless. As Singer writes: "The advantages of multiple development may make interesting reading for economists, but they are gloomy news indeed for the underdeveloped countries. The initial resources for simultaneous developments on many fronts are generally lacking." [5] In other words, if a country were ready to apply the doctrine

4. Viner, in a paper prepared for the Rome Congress of the International Economic Association in 1956 ("Stability and Progress: The Problems of the Poor Countries," to be published), has pointed out that from the demand point of view balanced growth is not required whenever a new activity is either cost-reducing rather than output-increasing, or import-replacing or export-oriented. His first category is actually too restrictive, for output-increasing activities can also be introduced in isolation if the outputs are new and highly desired products so that their availability leads to an increase in the demand for income. See, on this point, J. J. Spengler, "Product-Adding vs. Product-Replacing Innovations," *Kyklos, 3* (1957), 249–80. Cf. also Ch. 7.

5. Singer, "Economic Progress in Underdeveloped Countries," pp. 7–8.

of balanced growth, then it would not be underdeveloped in the first place.

It is possible that the theory of balanced growth has been inspired by a variant of the Keynesian analysis of the slump.[6] In a situation of underemployment equilibrium, the rationale for government intervention may be put as follows: an isolated act of increasing production by a single firm is not likely to be "validated" by the market since the demand that is generated by the increase in production and its multiplier effects is not going to converge on the output of the firm; what is needed to fulfill optimistic expectations and therefore to bring such expectations about is a simultaneous stepping up of production by many firms. This simultaneity in turn can be achieved only if a substantial increase in consumer spending induced by fiscal policy provides guideposts to manufacturers and leads to a generalized recovery of output.

The balanced growth doctrine is now seen to be essentially the application of underdevelopment of a therapy originally devised for an underemployment situation. During the cyclical upswing, a balanced recovery of economic activity is indeed possible—for the industries, machines, managers, and workers, as well as the consumption habits, are all there, only waiting to resume their temporarily suspended functions and roles. In a state of underdevelopment this is obviously not so, and a simultaneous solution is therefore out of reach whether or not the government lends a helping hand.

The last clause is important. For the balanced growth doctrine is usually invoked to provide a justification for centralized governmental direction and coordination of the development process. But this justification is hardly convincing. A task that private enterprise or market forces are unable to handle does not ipso facto become ideally suited to performance by public authorities. We must recognize that there are tasks that simply exceed the capabilities of a society, no matter to whom they are being entrusted. Balanced growth in the sense of simultaneous multiple development would seem to be one of them.[7]

6. Domar, "Investment and Monopolies" in *Income, Employment and Public Policy* (New York, 1948), pp. 49–57, and W. J. Baumol, *Welfare Economics and the Theory of the State* (Cambridge, Mass., 1952), pp. 96–7.

7. See p. 65.

The Paradox of the Internalization Doctrine

According to the theory of balanced growth which we have discussed so far, the role of the state is to assure that simultaneity of investments in a large variety of enterprises which is believed to be needed to ensure the success of the individual ventures. A more sophisticated version of the doctrine and of the role it assigns to state action analyzes the anticipations rather than the possible actions of entrepreneurs. It states that, under a private enterprise system, entrepreneurs in underdeveloped countries will invest far less than is profitable from the point of view of society. The reason is that atomistic private producers cannot appropriate the external economies to which their activity gives rise, or that they cannot foresee the repercussions which will eventually make them into recipients of economies external to other firms but internal to their own.[8] Private profit calculations fatally underestimate actual social benefits. In the opinion of Rosenstein-Rodan, the pessimistic anticipations of the entrepreneurs are correct as long at they remain atomistic producers; in that of Scitovsky, they are incorrect since they are eventually going to be recipients of pecuniary external economies. But the conclusions are similar in both cases. Production must be integrated and centrally planned as though it were taking place in a single "trust," for only in that case are the external economies going to be "internalized" with a consequent upward revision of profit estimates.

In one respect, the theory is no more than a variant of the balanced growth doctrine. It says: if ten projects could be undertaken jointly, lending each other mutual support in demand, any one of them would be more profitable than the same project undertaken in isolation. On the premises stated, this is undoubtedly correct. But it is also true that a country cannot undertake any number of projects just because they would turn out to be profitable *if* it undertook them. At any one time the available developmental skills of a country set some kind of a ceiling on the number of projects that can be undertaken simultaneously.

Nevertheless, if we allow a certain degree of flexibility, it is legiti-

8. The former situation is described by Rosenstein-Rodan, the latter by Scitovsky. For references, see p. 51, n. 1.

mate to inquire whether centralization of investment decisions would tend to be growth-promoting. Is it really true that the wider the area over which internalization takes place the greater the incentive to invest is going to be? This would be the case if *all* the repercussions of a new venture were going to be favorable. However, if the repercussions include losses (pecuniary external diseconomies), they will ordinarily be internalized along with the gains and it is no longer certain where we will come out.[9]

The case for centralized investment planning as growth-promoting per se would of course be entirely convincing if it permitted production to be organized in such a way that *only external economies were internalized* while all the external diseconomies and social costs resulting from new ventures remained strictly external to the central authority or were negligible. In this eventuality we would indeed obtain a highly dynamic system, but the question is: can it be done? Here again, the image that was in the minds of the authors of the "internalization" doctrine must have been that of a backward economic sector which would be left pretty much alone, and a brave new sector to be built from the ground up and in isolation; in this fashion, all those who might possibly suffer losses in the course of the development process are effectively assumed away. We do not exclude the possibility that the picture may be fairly realistic in certain special situations such as the reconstruction of an economy devastated by war, or the development of *undeveloped* regions and open spaces through colonization schemes: here the repercussions on existing productive activities may be a small matter compared to that mutual interdependence of the new activities which makes joint planning essential. But in general economic development means transformation rather than creation *ex novo:* it brings disruption of traditional ways of living, of producing, and of doing things, in the course of which there have always been many losses; old skills become obsolete, old trades are ruined, city slums mushroom, crime and suicide multiply, etc., etc. And to these social costs many others must be added, from air pollution to unemployment, so much so that a whole book has recently been devoted to their detailed analysis.[10]

9. In the paper cited on p. 53, n. 4, Viner also makes the point that external diseconomies must be taken into account.

10. K. William Kapp, *The Social Costs of Private Enterprise,* Cambridge, Mass., 1950.

The paradoxical character of the internalization doctrine is now becoming apparent. Assumption of responsibility by the state in the economic field has most frequently been urged, not to provide more impetus to development through the adding up of all the gains, but to *introduce some of the social costs into the economic calculus* and thus to temper the ruthlessness and destructiveness of capitalist development. Presumably the advocates of this course thought that some sacrifice in the speed of the process of creative destruction would be well worth while if it could be made a bit less destructive of material, cultural, and spiritual values. And, admittedly, a major difficulty for the speedy industrialization of today's underdeveloped countries consists precisely in the fact that they are not prepared to incur those social costs that were so spectacularly associated with the process during the early nineteenth century in Western Europe. They are forcing their young entrepreneurial class (as well as their taxpayers in general) to internalize a good portion of these costs through advanced social security, minimum wage, and collective bargaining legislation, through subsidized low-cost housing and similar "welfare state" measures.

Different Types of Internalization and Their Effect on Growth

It is tempting to embark on a short digression and to speculate about the probable effect on development, particularly on its speed and character, of different institutional arrangements with respect to the "internalization of external economies and diseconomies." Historically, there have been some characteristic changes in the comprehensiveness with which information about the social benefits and costs deriving from economic changes is signaled to the economic decision-makers and enters into their calculations.

Under the guild system, for instance, an innovation in producing a given commodity could only be introduced by someone who was already engaged in its production by the old process. As we know from Schumpeter, this fact would in itself militate against many innovations that might render painfully acquired skills useless and valuable equipment obsolete. Moreover, even if the individual guild member planned an important change in the method of production or a substantial modification of the product, he would ordinarily have to seek the explicit authorization of the guild, which was not likely to encourage innovations that might cause severe damage to the interests of members. Heckscher quotes a telling ordinance from the late seventeenth century in France: "If a cloth-weaver intends to process a piece according to his own invention he must not set it on the loom but should obtain permission from the judges of the town to employ the number and length of the threads that he desires, after the question has been considered by four of the oldest merchants and four of the oldest weavers of the guild." [11] The introduction of new products was more difficult to control than that of improved processes, but attempts at such control were also frequently made. For instance, the manufacture of buttons covered with loom-made cloth which competed with the hand-stitched variety was prohibited around the same time on the ground that such manufacture "would lead to the total destruction of a collectivity consisting of a considerable number of workers whose livelihood depends entirely on their profession." [12] In this way, then, the external diseconomies of innovations were fully taken into account by the guild system, and, to the extent that the regulations worked, technological progress was seriously held back.

The system broke down precisely to give way to another one that did not require this kind of internalization, and that proved, therefore, immensely more dynamic. When anyone can enter a trade or industry, he can take advantage of the latest inventions and innovations, and the damages suffered by traditional producers are no concern of his. Better still, if there are important mutually profitable repercussions and complementarities between two lines of production, the capitalist system ordinarily (i.e., in the absence of the strictest kind of antitrust legislation) interposes no obstacle to the combination of such activities into a single firm. So that from the point of view of investment incentives, the capitalist system, especially as it existed in the nineteenth century, is hard to beat: there was a minimum of internalization of external diseconomies and there was no limitation on the internalization of pecuniary external economies through acquisitions, combinations, or mergers with closely interdependent economic activities. Finally, the state provided important external economies by supplying law and order, basic education, and some public utilities.

11. E. F. Heckscher, *Mercantilism* (London, Allen & Unwin, 1935), *1*, 171.
12. Quoted in E. Levasseur, *Histoire des classes ouvrières en France avant 1789* (Paris, 1859), *2*, 332.

And even though there certainly existed external economies that could not be appropriated by the individual entrepreneur, the balance between the social costs he caused but escaped and the social benefits he failed to turn into profits was likely to be favorable for many entrepreneurs. This was so particularly with respect to the introduction of new products that competed successfully with close substitutes, and of new technology that resulted in the abandonment of traditional processes. In other words, it was the peculiar *lack* of internalization implicit in the private enterprise system—the way in which the institutions of that system "hid" certain costs from the entrepreneurs —that was largely responsible for the dynamic economic changes that took place. Admittedly, such an explanation of economic progress in the nineteenth century has little in common with Adam Smith's Invisible Hand; it is far more reminiscent of Hegel's *List der Vernunft*.

Let us now consider how the pattern of internalization likely to prevail in a centrally planned and directed economy will affect its capacity for economic growth. In such an economy, by definition, internalization is supposed to be complete with respect to what in capitalist economies appears as external economies and diseconomies. Thus, if the kind of growth experienced by capitalist economies can be largely understood as a consequence of the lack of internalization, an economy which has achieved internalization is likely to have quite a different growth story.

In the first place, inasmuch as production decisions in such an economy are likely to be made largely within an industry-wide frame of reference, the interests of existing firms are going to be taken fully into account.[13] The managers of an industry are likely to identify themselves with these firms, with their workers, and with the non-amortized value of their machines, and are unlikely to favor disruptive changes that would interfere with carefully laid plans and would also mean premature obsolescence of skills and equipment. In this respect, then, a planned economy is likely to behave much like the guild system; the process of "creative destruction" is constitutionally alien to it because destruction here means self-destruction rather than destruction of somebody else. Taking into consideration the interests

13. Provided they are not obviously antiquated. For instance, the existence of transportation by horse-drawn carriages will hardly hold back the development of motor vehicle production.

of existing firms will lead to a tendency to avoid frequent changes in the design and quality of consumer goods or frequent introduction of substitutes that might gratify the foolish whims of the consuming public but could disrupt production schedules and endanger the value of a portion of the country's human and material assets.[14]

There are more general reasons for believing that an economy where the making of investment decisions is centralized is not likely to be particularly aggressive in undertaking certain processes of innovation. Let us assume that the adoption of a given innovation would make A better off and B worse off. Then, according to welfare economics, one way of testing the social desirability of introducing the innovation is to ascertain whether A can afford to "bribe" B into accepting the innovation and still remain better off than before. As was rightly stressed in the discussion of this compensation or "bribery" test, it is not enough to establish that the test *could* be satisfied—compensation must actually be paid if we wish to be certain that total welfare has not suffered as a result of the innovation.[15]

But here arises an additional question to which welfare economists, being unconcerned with growth problems, have not paid attention: [16] Supposing that A who stands to profit from the innovation is also the one who must carry it out, would he still be motivated to do so *if he knew in advance that compensation would have to be paid?* In many cases this would seem unlikely. Even though A might still be able to increase his welfare, he may not consider it worth while,

14. Such tendencies are also at work in certain highly oligopolistic industry branches under capitalism. But they are absent from many other branches, and where they exist they are frequently checked or even reversed by other forces operating in the opposite direction as a result of the over-all lack of internalization.

15. The test was introduced by Kaldor in "Welfare Propositions in Economics," *Economic Journal, 49* (Sept. 1939), 549–52, and refined by Scitovsky in "A Note on Welfare Propositions in Economics," *Review of Economic Studies, 9* (Nov. 1941), 77–88; the requirement that the compensation actually be paid was first pointed out by Baumol, "Community Indifference," *Review of Economic Studies, 14* (1946–47), 44–8. The discussion has since moved on to considerably more sophisticated terrain, but for our purposes it is sufficient to recall these early contributions. For a good treatment of the present state of the "new welfare economics" and bibliographical references, see F. M. Bator, "The Simple Analytics of Welfare Maximization," *American Economic Review, 47* (March 1957), 22–59.

16. With the exception of J. E. Meade, who mentions the problem of disincentives arising from compensation in *Trade and Welfare* (London, 1955), p. 78.

e.g., because of uncertainty, to devote his energies to a task whose rewards are drastically scaled down. Similarly, if the decisions about innovations are centralized, many innovating decisions whose pros do not outweigh the cons by a sufficiently wide margin may also be shelved.

It could be held that internalization serves in this case the function of inhibiting innovations that would yield private gains but not social benefits. This was of course the claim of the guilds. In fact, however, internalization is likely to result in an overestimate of the prospective losses: for it is the nature of most innovations that its beneficiaries are anonymous, inarticulate, and unaware of the benefits-to-accrue (they include among others the consumers that are yet unborn), while those who stand to lose from the innovation are highly vocal vested interests.

A society that centralizes investment decisions may therefore be expected to be biased against innovations whose introduction might cause losses to existing operators by, e.g., improving the design and quality of current output and by increasing its variety through the introduction of substitute goods. On the other hand, there would be no similar reluctance to undertake the production of entirely new articles not meant as substitutes for any one existing good, or of capital goods whose eventual impact on existing producers is hard to evaluate. It is interesting to note that these conclusions fit rather well the pattern of successes and failures of the Soviet economy.

Thus internalization is likely to affect the pace of a country's development unfavorably in some areas and favorably in others—the net effect is by no means clear. Even aside from the fact that internalization as such cannot overnight increase a country's ability to act for development, it is unlikely to lead to a *general* upward revision of profitability estimates because external diseconomies are necessarily internalized along with the economies. To obtain such an upward revision and to convince themselves that they should attempt to step up the rate of their development, centrally planned economies have abundant recourse to the old capitalist trick of shutting out of the economic calculus a variety of social costs that are being incurred in the process of growth. As a result, they may well achieve accelerated growth—not by practising internalization but by reneging on it.

61

CHAPTER 4

Unbalanced Growth: An Espousal

Is Balance in Supply Required?

IN THE LAST CHAPTER we criticized the idea that development must take place simultaneously in many activities to provide the element of "mutual support" that alone will make it possible to clear the market of the newly produced goods. Having discarded this "pure" theory of balanced growth we must still consider a far less rigorous version, one that insists that if growth is not to be stunted the various sectors of an economy will have to grow jointly in some (not necessarily identical) proportion; no sector should get too far out of line, not because of demand but because of supply or "structural" considerations. For instance, if secondary industry grows, the food and raw material input needed by the workers and the machines will go up; if some of these requirements are imported, then an increase in exports is necessary, etc., etc.

In this form, the balanced growth theory is essentially an exercise in retrospective comparative statics. If we look at an economy that has experienced growth at two different points in time, we will of course find that a great many parts of it have pushed ahead: industry and agriculture, capital goods and consumer goods industries, cars on the road and highway mileage—each at its own average annual rate of increase. But surely the individual components of the economy will not actually have grown at these rates throughout the period under review. Just as on the demand side the market can absorb "unbalanced" advances in output because of cost-reducing innovations, new products, and import substitution, so we can have isolated forward thrusts on the supply side as inputs are redistributed among users through price changes, and at the cost of some temporary shortages and disequilibria in the balance of payments or elsewhere. In fact, development has of course proceeded in this way, with growth being communicated from the leading sectors of the economy to the followers, from one industry to another, from one firm to another. In other words, the balanced growth that is revealed by the two still photographs taken at two different points in time is the end result of a series of uneven advances of one sector followed by the catching-up of other sectors. If the catching-up overreaches its goal, as it often does, then the stage is set for further advances elsewhere. The advantage of this kind of seesaw advance over "balanced growth," where every activity expands perfectly in step with every other, is that it leaves considerable scope to *induced* investment decisions and therefore economizes our principal scarce resource, namely, genuine decision-making.

Classical economics, while not taking so positive a view of the imbalances of the growth process, at least was never particularly concerned about them because it relied on prices to signal, and on the profit motive to eliminate rapidly and reliably, any structural disequilibria that might arise in the course of growth. The critics of classical economics, on the other hand, have always pointed to cases in which these "market forces" would not act with adequate strength and speed. Having thus convinced themselves that the adjustment mechanism is beset with virtually insuperable obstacles, some of the critics naturally enough took the defeatist view that growth has to be balanced from the start or cannot take place at all.

This counsel of perfection is not only impractical but also uneconomical. We need not sacrifice the valuable development mechanisms brought into play by unbalanced growth, especially if we go beyond the overly narrow view of the adjustment process that has long dominated economic literature.

Tradition seems to require that economists argue forever about the question whether, in any disequilibrium situation, *market forces acting alone* are likely to restore equilibrium. Now this is certainly an interesting question. But as social scientists we surely must address ourselves also to the broader question: is the disequilibrium situation likely to be corrected at all, by market or nonmarket forces, or by both acting jointly? *It is our contention that nonmarket forces are not necessarily less "automatic" than market forces.* Certainly the almost monotonous regularity with which interventionist economists have come forward—and with which authorities have acted—when the market forces did not adequately perform their task testifies to the fact that we do not have to rely exclusively on price signals and profit-maximizers to save us from trouble.[1]

The case of unbalanced growth provides a good illustration. When supply difficulties arise in the course of uneven progress in sectors—such as education and public utilities—where private enterprise is not operating, strong pressures are felt by public authorities to "do something"; and since the desire for political survival is at least as strong a motive force as the desire to realize a profit, we may ordinarily expect some corrective action to be taken.[1a]

There is no implication here that any disequilibrium whatsoever will be resolved by some combination of market and nonmarket forces. But if a community cannot generate the "induced" decisions and actions needed to deal with the supply disequilibria that arise in the course of uneven growth, then I can see little reason for believing that it will be able to take the set of "autonomous" decisions required by balanced growth. In other words, if the adjustment mechanism breaks down altogether, this is a sign that the community rejects economic growth as an overriding objective.

The inclusion of probable reactions of nonmarket forces not only serves to make economic analysis more realistic. It also protects us

1. Some traditional equilibrium mechanisms were unable to dispense entirely with help from agents outside the market. Thus, the restoration of balance-of-payments equilibrium and the damping of the business cycle was, for a long time, made to depend on correct manipulation by the central bank of the rate of interest, in reaction to developing disequilibria. But this role of the central banker has usually been rationalized as an exception to the rule; and in the minds of many economists, the central banker became a sort of honorary member of the market forces.

1a. Sectoral imbalances have of course been a conspicuous feature of Russian economic development. The resulting difficulties have been described in Soviet literature as "nonantagonistic contradictions" which are not only admitted to exist but apparently considered to perform a useful signaling and corrective function: "The characteristic trait of our difficulties and contradictions consists precisely in that they themselves indicate to us the basis and the means for their solution." V. Kozlovskii, *Antagonisticheskie i neantagonisticheskie protivorechiia* (Moscow, Moskovskii Rabochii, 1954), p. 70. These "nonantagonistic" contradictions which are successfully overcome by administrative action of the Communist party and the government are then opposed to the "antagonistic" contradictions which are said to afflict capitalism and which can be resolved only by revolution.

against a fallacious chain of reasoning that is fairly common in development economics and of which the doctrine of balanced growth is itself an excellent illustration. In this reasoning, one first selects some objective of economic policy that seems desirable enough; then one proves that the objective cannot be attained through the operation of market forces; and one concludes that state action surely will bring the objective about. But this conclusion is clearly a non sequitur. The fact that private entrepreneurs will be unable or unwilling to do certain jobs which we would like to see done does not in itself ensure that the government can handle them. We must examine whether these jobs are likely to be performed satisfactorily by public authorities, which function after all in the same society as the entrepreneurs.[2]

Development as a Chain of Disequilibria

As has been shown, the balanced growth theory results from comparing the initial point of underdevelopment equilibrium with another point at which development will practically have been accomplished. A certain impatience with the process that lies between these two points—i.e., with the process of development—is shown by the following quotation from a well-known article by Scitovsky:

> Profits are a sign of disequilibrium; and the magnitude of profits under free competition may be regarded as a rough index of the degree of disequilibrium. Profits in a freely competitive industry lead to investment in that industry; and the investment in turn tends to eliminate the profits that have called it forth. Thus far, then, investment tends to bring equilibrium nearer. The same investment, however, may raise . . . profits in other industries; and to this extent it leads away from equilibrium. . . . The profits of industry B created by the lower price for factor A, call for investment and expansion in industry B one result of which will be an increase in industry B's demand for industry A's product.

2. Much the same point is made forcefully by Bauer and Yamey with respect to governmental promotion of industrial enterprise: "A general lack of enterprise in a country does not in itself set up a presumption of such initiative in the public sector," *Underdeveloped Countries*, p. 161. However, I do not follow the authors in the conclusions which they draw for the role of governments in economic development. See Chs. 8 and 11.

> This in turn will give rise to profits and call for further investment and expansion in A; and equilibrium is reached only when successive doses of investment and expansion in the two industries have led to the simultaneous elimination of investment in both. It is only at this stage that . . . the amount of investment profitable in industry A is also the socially desirable amount. The amount is clearly greater than that which is profitable at the first stage before industry B has made its adjustment. We can conclude, therefore, that when an investment gives rise to pecuniary external economies, its private profitability understates its social desirability.[3]

To my mind, the first part of this passage is a most pertinent portrayal of how development is set and kept in motion, but Scitovsky, considering the proceedings he describes unnecessarily laborious, proposes to short-circuit them and to reach in a single jump a new point of equilibrium where the "elimination of investment" has been accomplished. But, actually, development is a lengthy process during which interaction of the kind described by Scitovsky takes place not only between two industries, but up and down and across the whole of an economy's input-output matrix, and for many decades. What point in such a virtually infinite sequence of repercussions are we supposed to shoot at? Which intermediate expansion stages ought we to skip, and which ordinarily successive stages ought we to combine? Some skipping or combining may be possible, but with no more than the modest objective of speeding up development here and there. In general, development policy must concern itself with the judicious setting up of the kind of sequences and repercussions so well described by Scitovsky, rather than with any attempt to suppress them. In other words, our aim must be to *keep alive* rather than to eliminate the disequilibria of which profits and losses are symptoms in a competitive economy. If the economy is to be kept moving ahead, the task of development policy is to maintain tensions, disproportions, and disequilibria. That nightmare of equilibrium economics, the endlessly spinning cobweb, is the *kind* of mechanism we must assiduously look for as an invaluable help in the development process.

Therefore, the sequence that "leads away from equilibrium" is pre-

3. "Two Concepts of External Economies," pp. 148–9.

cisely an ideal pattern of development from our point of view: for each move in the sequence is induced by a previous disequilibrium and in turn creates a new disequilibrium that requires a further move. This is achieved by the fact that the expansion of industry A leads to economies external to A but appropriable by B, while the consequent expansion of B brings with it economies external to B but subsequently internal to A (or C for that matter), and so on. At each step, an industry takes advantage of external economies created by previous expansion, and at the same time creates new external economies to be exploited by other operators.[4]

In Scitovsky's example, these external economies are essentially caused by production complementarities of one type or another, and we are thus returning to the complementarity effect of investment which was already invoked in Chapter 2 as a mechanism that would make investment decisions particularly easy or compelling. We were then speaking of the investment-promoting character of investment, not indirectly through additional savings out of the incomes created by investment, but through direct contact or "contagion."

Technical complementarity in the strict sense is usually defined as a situation where an increase in the output of commodity A lowers the marginal costs of producing commodity B. This will happen typically as a result of the following situations:

a. because A is an input of B and is produced under conditions of decreasing costs;

b. because B is an input of A and is itself produced under conditions of decreasing costs;

c. because A and B are joint products (or because B is a by-product of A) and are produced under decreasing costs.

Because situations such as these have long been familiar to economists, complementarity is usually associated with economies of scale.[5] But there is no need for so restrictive an interpretation. We can define complementarity as any situation where an increase in

4. Note that the private profitability falls short of the social desirability of any venture only when its "output" of external economies exceeds its "input" derived from other ventures.

5. W. Fellner, *Trends and Cycles in Economic Activity* (New York, 1956), pp. 199–200. N. S. Buchanan and H. S. Ellis, *Approaches to Economic Development* (New York, 1955), pp. 279–80.

the demand for commodity A and the consequent increase in its output call forth an increased demand for commodity B at its existing price. This happens not only when the connection between the two commodities is via the production process. The connection between A and B may also arise because the increased *use* of A leads to greater demand for B. We are not thinking here of situations where A and B *must* be employed jointly in fixed proportions. In this case it would not make much sense to say that demand for A and the subsequent increase in its output provide an incentive for the production of B, as it is rather the demand for the good or service into which A and B enter jointly which explains the demand for both products. This is the familiar case of derived demand. But there are many situations in the course of economic development where the increased availability of one commodity does not *compel* a *simultaneous* increase in supply of another commodity, but *induces slowly*, through a loose kind of complementarity in use, an upward shift in its demand schedule. The phenomenon has been described under the apt heading "entrained want"; [6] Veblen observed it long ago and effectively summed it up when he said that "invention is the mother of necessity" rather than vice versa.

An example of the rigid type of complementarity in use (best treated as derived demand) is cement and reinforcing steel rods in the construction, say, of downtown office buildings. Examples of the looser, "developmental" type of complementarity (entrained want) can be found in the way in which the existence of the new office buildings strengthens demand for a great variety of goods and services: from modern office furniture and equipment (still fairly rigid), to parking and restaurant facilities, stylish secretaries, and eventually perhaps to more office buildings as the demonstration effect goes to work on the tenants of the older buildings. Here again, failure to arrange for all of these complementary items from the start could be denounced

6. The term is used by H. G. Barnett in *Innovation: The Basis of Cultural Change* (New York, McGraw-Hill, 1953), pp. 148–51, with the exact meaning we have in mind here: "The fulfillment of one need establishes conditions out of which others emerge . . . In most instances it is impossible for people to foresee [these emergent wants] even if they try . . . Entrained wants are a consistent feature of motivational stresses for cultural change" (p. 148).

as "poor planning" which ought to be avoided by centralized decision-making. But, just as in the case quoted by Scitovsky, an attempt to telescope the whole process would be futile because of the virtually infinite number of complementarity repercussions, and because of the uncertainty about a good many of them; moreover, such an attempt would miss the point that the profitable opportunities that arise as a result of the initial development move constitute powerful and valuable levers for subsequent development which are to be carefully nursed, maintained at some optimum level, and if necessary created consciously rather than eliminated.[7]

The common feature of the various complementarity situations is that, as a result of the increase in the output of A, the profitability of the production of B is being increased because B's marginal costs drop, or because its demand schedule shifts upward, or because both forces act jointly.

Put even more generally, complementarity means that increased production of A will lead to *pressure* for increasing the available supply of B. When B is a privately produced good or service, this pressure will lead to imports or larger domestic production of B because it will be in the *interest* of traders and producers of B to respond to the pressure. When B is not privately produced, the pressure does not transmute itself into pecuniary self-interest, and will take the form of political pressure for the provision of B. This is the case for such public services as law and order, education, satisfactory monetary and banking arrangements, highways, water, electric power, etc. Complementarity then manifests itself in the form of complaints about

7. This does not mean that when new buildings are put up one should refrain from planning for new parking facilities. Development itself constantly extends the range of complementarities that are rigidly compelled and necessarily simultaneous: the optional equipment of one period becomes the standard equipment of the next, as a result of social and cultural pressures and needs rather than because of purely technological factors. The process of turning loose complementarities into rigid ones is often called "integrated planning" which is then opposed to "improvisation." These terms, particularly dear to city planners, are quite misleading in their antagonism. "Integrated planning" takes care of *a few* of the *known* repercussions of a development move rather than letting them take care of themselves as best they can independently of that move. But it certainly can never hope to comprehend them all.

shortages, bottlenecks, and obstacles to development. Action in this case does not take place through the operation of the profit motive, but through group pressures on public authorities and agencies.

A Definition of Induced Investment

The complementarity effect provides us with a new concept of *induced* investment which is more meaningful for underdeveloped economies than the conventional one, i.e., investment that is directly related to past increases in output. For this conventional concept of induced investment has validity mainly for countries with a fully built-up industrial and agricultural structure where increases in demand lead to increases in capacity designed to keep marginal costs from entering the area in which they would begin to rise steeply. The required adjustments may cover many industries, but are ordinarily small in any one year in relation to existing capacity. The big dynamic changes in developed economies are expected to originate in "autonomous" investment.

This is not a realistic picture of the growth process in underdeveloped economies. Here an increase in the demand for beer, for example, may lead not only to the expansion of existing brewing capacity but, at a certain point, to the *start* of domestic production of bottles, of barley cultivation, and to a whole chain of similar repercussions. In other words, the investment that is induced by complementarity effects may help to bring about a real transformation of an underdeveloped economy.

One of the difficulties of the concept of induced investment in its traditional meaning is its precise delimitation. The reason for which investment is undertaken is not that demand has increased in the past, but that the experience of the past is taken as a guide to the future. In other words, investment is undertaken because for one reason or another the ensuing output is expected to find a market. But looked at in this way, all investment is obviously induced and the distinction between induced and autonomous investment becomes untenable or arbitrary.[8]

At first blush, it might seem that the same flaw, in an even more pronounced form, affects the distinction we have drawn. Is not every

8. Fellner, *Trends*, p. 319.

investment "induced" in the sense that it complements some other existing investment? With the generously wide definition of complementarity which we have given, cannot every step in the development of a country be considered as called forth by the preceding steps in a never-ending series of "inducements"? Have we then perhaps explained too much?

At this point we may, however, revert to our earlier discussion of external economies:-it was then shown that new projects often appropriate external economies created by preceding ventures and create external economies that may be utilized by subsequent ones. Some projects create more external economies than they appropriate and therefore their private profitability falls short of their social desirability. It is therefore to be expected that the opposite situation can also be encountered—namely, ventures that have a large "input" of external economies and a much smaller "output." The projects thus favored represent the class of "easy-to-exploit" investment opportunities which always abound in newly developing economies.

We can then define our concept of induced investment by the provision that the projects that fall into this category must be *net beneficiaries* of external economies.

This definition makes induced investment look very much like the multiplier: each investment is conceived as inducing a series of subsequent investments and there is an element of convergence as the "output" of external economies diminishes at each step. This, however, does not necessarily mean that the investments themselves converge; there is no rigid connection between the size of an investment and its net "input" of external economies, although some association between these two magnitudes may be expected to exist.[9]

Theoretically, our definition of induced investment is, I believe, more satisfactory than the conventional one and it is far more relevant in the context of development problems. Nevertheless it is extremely difficult to give empirical content to the concept and we shall therefore not attempt to give our reasoning more rigor than it possesses; we shall continue to speak of investment inducing other investments and shall simply be aware that there are widely varying degrees of "inducements."

An ideal situation obtains when, as was pointed out in the last sec-

9. See Ch. 6, the concept of satellite industries.

tion, one disequilibrium calls forth a development move which in turn leads to a similar disequilibrium and so on ad infinitum. If such a chain of unbalanced growth sequences could be set up, the economic policy-makers could just watch the proceedings from the sidelines. It may be noticed that in this situation private profitability and social desirability are likely to coincide, not because of the absence of external economies, but because "input" and "output" of external economies are the same for each successive venture.

In practice, growth sequences are likely to exhibit tendencies toward convergence or potentialities of divergence, and development policy is largely concerned with the prevention of too rapid convergence and with the promotion of the possibilities of divergence.

One more point. The induced investment defined thus far is a gross quantity. In the previous chapter, we made much of the point that development brings with it external diseconomies as well as economies. The external diseconomies brought into the world by new investments refer primarily to the damage done to existing industrial or handicraft establishments by the introduction of modern methods and products. It must be granted, therefore, that new investments will hold back reinvestment in these establishments while leading to complementary capital formation elsewhere in the economy. The effect is, however, quite asymmetrical, as the greatest damage that new investment will cause to pre-existing equipment consists in failure to maintain and replace that equipment. Thus, inasmuch as the external diseconomies of new investments result in negative investment, this destructive effect is likely to be spread over several years; whereas the positive effect of the external economies leads at once to a demand for the total capital requirements of whatever ventures are going to be "induced." Because of this asymmetry, the investment-reducing effect of new investments resulting from competition and substitution effects seems unlikely to match the investment-creating effects of complementarity except where competitive industries are strong and complementarity effects rather weak. This latter situation may be characteristic of the textile industry and may account for the fact that in several underdeveloped countries the setting up of this industry has failed to provide the necessary spark for further development.

Some Related Points of View

The way in which investment leads to other investment through complementarities and external economies is an invaluable "aid" to development that must be consciously utilized in the course of the development process. It puts special pressure behind a whole group of investment decisions and augments thereby that scarce and non-economizable resource of underdeveloped countries, the ability to make new investment decisions.

The manner in which an investment project affects the availability of this resource is for us the principal measure of its contribution to further development. A development strategy that stems from this approach is outlined in the next chapters. Before closing the present one we shall refer briefly to some development theories that are related to the point of view presented here.

One of the principal characteristics of our approach has been the direct connection we have established between the investment of one period and that of the next. The complementarity effect "calls forth" new investment; to the extent that savings are determined by this process, they play a perfectly passive role. This situation is very similar to the one recently described by Domar in his analysis of a growth model elaborated thirty years ago by the Russian economist Feldman. The essence of this model is the division of total investment into investment designed to expand the output of consumers' goods on the one hand, and of producers' goods, on the other. Domar shows that once this division is made "the propensity to save has no life of its own so to speak and is completely determined by the relative productive capacities of the two categories." [10] The limit to investment in the Feldman model as interpreted by Domar is not the ability or propensity to save, but the productive capacity of the investment goods sector. Although the model is admittedly unrealistic, especially for an open economy, it is interesting as an attempt to build a sequence where investment of one period is directly related to the investment of prior periods without the intermediary of the savings ratio.

The rather tormented discussion around an article on investment criteria by Galenson and Leibenstein has yielded a similar line of

10. *Essays*, p. 236.

thought: namely, that savings and reinvestment may depend not only on the productivity of capital but on various other characteristics of the projects in which capital is invested.[11] Although savings out of income are here an important intermediate link in the causal sequence, it is the specific nature of the investment, rather than merely the resulting income flow, that is seen as determining subsequent capital formation.

These are attempts to build generalizations about the required kind and composition of investment into development theory and to establish a closer-than-usual connection between investments of successive periods. However, these results are reached through the use of assumptions that, to my mind, are unnecessarily restrictive. Three other studies come even closer to our viewpoint. First, there is Perroux's concept of the "growth poles" and his incisive description of the growth process as something that is called forth by these poles.[12] Second, mention must be made of the introductory remarks in Svennilson's work on the *Growth and Stagnation of the European Economy*, which come very close to our point of view. Here Svennilson mentions the importance of complementary developments and describes his work as an attempt to overcome the "unhappy division between the cost and price theory on the one hand and the theory of growth and employment on the other." [13] Unfortunately the subsequent analysis, while often ingenious and always interesting, does not entirely fulfill these promises.

Finally, the importance of interindustry interactions because of external economies, economies of scale, and complementarities has been fully recognized by Fellner. He states that these phenomena can account for a rise in the yield of capital even when the latter is growing

11. See O. Eckstein, "Investment Criteria for Economic Development and the Theory of Intertemporal Welfare Economics," *Quarterly Journal of Economics*, 71 (Feb. 1957), 66. This article sets up a model where the income streams resulting from different investment projects are affected by *project-specific* savings propensities. Cf. W. Galenson and H. Leibenstein, "Investment Criteria, Productivity and Economic Development," ibid., 69 (Aug. 1955), 343–70, and discussions in the November 1956, February and August 1957, and August 1958 issues of the *Journal*. See also p. 149, n. 23a.

12. François Perroux, "Note sur la notion de 'pôle de croissance,'" *Economie appliquée*, 8 (Jan.–June 1953), 307–20.

13. U. N. Economic Commission for Europe (Geneva, 1954), p. 8.

at a faster rate than other factors of production and in the absence of technological improvements.[14] But Fellner relegates the action of these forces to the almost prehistoric phase during which "primitive economies" accumulate the "initial capital stock" required for growth. From then on, the only offsets to diminishing returns to capital that are admitted are organizational and technological improvements. I believe that the concept of initial capital stock, like that of "prerequisites," is not a particularly useful one, and that complementarity effects are extremely important in offsetting diminishing returns from capital during a protracted period. Perhaps an economy is never quite through creating its "indivisibilities," i.e., its complex of complementary economic activities!

14. *Trends,* pp. 200 and 341 ff.

CHAPTER 5

Investment Choices and Strategies

Efficient Sequences versus Investment Criteria

WE CAN now begin to consider one of the most crucial problems in development theory and policy: that of investment choices.

Development requires the undertaking of a series of projects producing favorable effects on the flow of income, in a wide variety of fields: public administration, education, health, transportation, power, agriculture, industry, urban development, etc. The limitation of resources, be they savings available for investment or our "ability to invest," compels a choice among these projects. In traditional economics, the market performs this function by equating the productivities of the various projects at the margin. It is recognized, however, that in any economy a substantial proportion of funds must be devoted to projects (in education, health, some public utilities, etc.) whose output has no readily assigned or fully recoverable market value. Moreover, underdeveloped economies tend to exhibit certain systematic discrepancies between private costs and social costs, and in such cases reliance on the market would lead to misallocation of resources.[1]

These considerations and the practical needs of development planners have led to the elaboration of *investment criteria*. The problem that has been discussed in this connection can be formulated as follows: given a limited amount of investment resources and a series of proposed investment projects whose total cost exceeds the available resources, how do we pick out the projects that will make the greatest contribution relative to their cost? In answering this question, econ-

1. There are at least three important areas in which such systematic discrepancies are apt to occur: the wage rate (because of disguised unemployment), the exchange rate (because of overvaluation of the currency), and the interest rate (because of rationing of loan funds on the part of the banks). See J. Tinbergen, *The Design of Development* (Baltimore, 1958), pp. 39 ff.

omists have ordinarily interpreted "contribution" as *direct contribution to output* once the project has been completed. This is only natural if growth is visualized as depending exclusively on aggregate output and income which, via the propensity to save, secretes the means for further growth. On these premises, the measurement of what has been called the "social marginal productivity" (SMP) of different projects—essentially a more or less sophisticated benefit-cost ratio—becomes the instrument that should in theory permit us to rank different projects in the order of their expected contribution to output and therefore to further growth.[2]

Recently, a far more elaborate concept has been proposed by Leibenstein: In addition to the output stream, investment criteria ought to take account also of the differential effects of the proposed ventures on the supply of entrepreneurship and of savings, on consumption habits, population increases, and a variety of other factors affecting further growth.[3] Leibenstein admits that a criterion embodying all these repercussions (in addition to SMP proper) would be of unusually difficult application.[4] In practice, his criticism seems likely to result in an agnostic "it all depends" attitude since it seriously impairs the usefulness of the SMP criterion without replacing it by a manageable new instrument.

In attempting a different approach, we shall first draw a distinction between substitution choices and postponement choices. Consider any choice between project A and project B: If the decision favors A, this may mean either that B is *discarded permanently* or that it is *postponed*. In the former case, the choice is between technical substitutes such as alternative means of providing a city with power or water supply. Many important choices are of this kind. They relate to the best means of attaining a given end or to the best design of a project whose output itself is needed beyond question. In deciding such choices, the usual investment criteria retain considerable usefulness.

2. A. E. Kahn, "Investment Criteria in Development," *Quarterly Journal of Economics,* 55 (Feb. 1951), 38–61; H. B. Chenery, "The Application of Investment Criteria," *Quarterly Journal of Economics,* 57 (Feb. 1953), 76–96; J. Ahumada, "Preparación y evaluación de proyectos de desarrollo económico," *El trimestre económico,* 22 (July–Sept. 1955), 265–96.

3. Leibenstein, *Economic Backwardness and Economic Growth,* ch. 15.

4. Ibid., p. 268.

Nevertheless, we feel that in underdeveloped countries additional considerations must be introduced and we will do so in Chapter 8.

Let us suppose for the time being that all substitution choices have been made and that we have before us a series of useful projects which are ideally designed to accomplish their respective purposes. In this situation, we are only faced with postponement choices.[5] We no longer choose A instead of B; rather, we choose the sequence AB instead of the sequence BA. What is the possible rationale for such a choice? If we suppose that our goal is to have both A and B, but that "now" we can undertake only either A or B, leaving B or A, respectively, for "later," then it is clear that the only conceivable reason for preferring AB to BA is that B will be possible sooner once A is in place than vice versa. In other words, our choice depends entirely on the pressure that the existence of A exerts toward the coming into existence of B as compared to the corresponding pressure that would emanate from B toward A. Once the problem is formulated in this way it becomes quite clear that the comparative productivity of A and B which will both have to be undertaken is likely to be a rather minor factor in the decision assigning the priority.

Although our reasoning has been drastically simplified, it takes hold of an important aspect of the development problem. Essential tasks always abound in underdeveloped countries since backwardness has so many different interrelated facets. From this interrelatedness we do not draw the balanced growth conclusion that a simultaneous attack is essential. But what might be called a sequential or chain solution is indeed required. In other words, isolated progress in one area is possible, but only for a limited period; if it is not to be choked off, it

5. In an earlier paper, "Economics and Investment Planning: Reflections Based on Experience in Colombia" in *Investment Criteria and Economic Growth*, ed. M. F. Millikan (Cambridge, Mass., M.I.T., 1955, multilithed), I argued essentially that economists ought to confine themselves to the making of substitution choices. I still believe that the most urgent task of development planners usually consists in arriving at correct substitution choices; but I realize now that postponement choices cannot be evaded. They must be made at two different stages of the process of development planning: first before it is decided in which sector or sectors substitution choices are to be studied, for the decision seriously to study alternative means of fulfilling a given need usually already implies a decision to give priority to this need; and secondly, after substitution choices have been completed in several different sectors.

must be followed by progress elsewhere. Therefore to compare the productivity increases that result from two projects in, e.g., education and transportation, is an insoluble problem not only in practice but conceptually. Such comparisons must be made on the *ceteris paribus* assumption that progress is being achieved in only one of the areas; and on this assumption the longer-term productivity of both undertakings is simply *zero* since the improved transportation facilities will serve little purpose and will fast deteriorate if education is not also improved in due course and vice versa. Therefore, the question of priority must be resolved on the basis of a comparative appraisal of the strength with which progress in one of these areas will induce progress in the other.[6] In these basic types of development decisions, it is therefore not sufficient to supplement, qualify, and otherwise refine the usual investment criteria. We must evolve entirely new aids to thought and action in this largely uncharted territory of efficient sequences and optimal development strategies.

There is no doubt that the task that we have set ourselves is extremely complex. Let us suppose that we know which are the n steps that need to be taken to, say, double a country's per capita income. Then there exist in principle $n!$ possible sequential arrangements of these n steps! Of course, there can be no question of neatly deducing, through a series of syllogisms, *the* most efficient sequence. Rather, we will strive to "suboptimize"[7] and to develop a few guideposts, principles, and illustrative models.

To begin with, there was a great deal of exaggeration in our statement that there exist $n!$ sequences in which the n steps may be undertaken. Many sequences are unavoidably "one-way" for purely tech-

6. It may be objected that indivisibility could not be such as to prevent us from investing our resources partly in education and partly in transportation. However, the point we are making does not depend on indivisibility in the sense of "lumpiness." Let us assume that we have identified n essential and interrelated projects, costing 200 million dollars, but that we have only 100 million dollars at hand. Suppose that out of the n projects we can put together various collections of $m < n$ projects costing 100 million dollars. Then again the criterion for picking any particular collection of m projects would be the strength with which their execution would induce the remaining projects. Thus indivisibility is assumed only in the trivial sense that some projects will necessarily be undertaken ahead of others.

7. Charles Hitch, "Sub-optimization in Operations Problems," *Journal of the Operations Research Society of America, 1* (May 1953), 87–99.

nical reasons (a road must be built before it can be paved); one also feels that other one-way sequences are imposed not because they are technically determined but because they are necessary if development is to be properly planned, i.e., is to proceed in an "orderly" fashion. But here there may be some doubt as to how far it is advisable to go. Observation tells us that rapid growth of countries, cities, industries, and individual firms hardly ever proceeds in a completely orderly fashion, but that an excess of disorderliness may exert an inhibiting and demoralizing influence on further growth. Can we then perhaps define an optimum degree of orderliness in development? To illustrate this problem, let A, B, C, and D in Figure 2 represent a group of development steps we wish to take and that ought to be

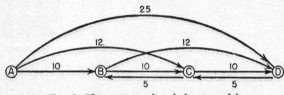

Fig. 2. The optimum disorderliness model

taken in this order if ideal "orderliness" is to be achieved. Let us also suppose that step A *must* be realized before B, C, or D can possibly be undertaken, but that with A accomplished the sequence is no longer imposed. In the absence of limiting factors, the sequence ABCD would be chosen because it provides the smoothest transition from state A to state ABCD. But we now introduce a limited resource, such as decision-making or organizational ability, or simply time, and assume that different amounts of this resource are spent in going from one point to another. We want to minimize the use of this resource. If, say, ten units of this resource are spent in going from A to B, from B to C, and from C to D, then it is natural to think that to go from A directly to C will take a somewhat larger (say 12 units) and from A to D perhaps a much larger amount (say 25 units), because of the absence of the intermediate preparatory stages. On the other hand, less than ten units (say 5) should be needed to "fill in" B or C after C or D, respectively, because once the later steps have been realized the lack of the intermediary ones makes itself felt in so pressing a manner that the decision to undertake them requires far smaller quantities of the scarce ability or time than when they represented genuine forward steps.

If we apply the foregoing illustrative figures, then the expenditure of our scarce resource that is involved in the various possible sequences is as follows:

A to B to C to D	30 (10 + 10 + 10)
A jump to C then fill in B, then D	27 (12 + 5 + 10)
A to B then jump to D, then fill in C	27 (10 + 12 + 5)
A jump to D, then fill in B and C	35 (25 + 5 + 5)

In this example the figures have been selected so as to show that a limited amount of "putting the cart before the horse" may be efficient as compared to both maximum orderliness and maximum disorderliness.

It may be helpful to attempt a translation of this model into more familiar terminology. Let us assume two ventures, m and n, which require equal amounts of capital and have a yield of 10% and 8% respectively. At the beginning of period 1 the interest rate stands at 9%, hence only venture m is undertaken. At the beginning of period 2, with venture m in existence, the expected yield of venture n has risen to 10% and is now also launched. But we are free to suppose that, if n were undertaken first, m would be urgently required and that its expected yield would rise to 14% at the beginning of period 2. In this eventuality, investors would maximize income by selecting in period 1 the investment with the lower yield! Besides they would do everything to rush m to completion. Such strange results are avoided in traditional theory by the implicit assumption which we chose to discard here, that the profitability of different ventures is invariant with respect to the order in which they are undertaken.

The preceding examples are highly artificial as they imply that development proceeds along a single path. Nevertheless, they embody a number of concepts that are recurring throughout this essay: the difference between "permissive" and "compulsive" sequences, the possible rationality of violating "first things first" norms and the fact that the difficulty of taking a development decision is not necessarily proportional to the amount of capital it requires.

A more complex and perhaps more realistic model would be to consider development as the putting together of a jigsaw puzzle. The fitting in of individual pieces would represent the taking of discrete development steps. The problem would again be to minimize the time needed to put the puzzle together. The total time is of course equal to the sum of the time periods spent on fitting in the individual pieces, and the time needed for each piece could be made to depend inversely on the number of contacts with adjacent pieces already in place: with each piece surrounded by several neighbors, the larger the number of neighbors in place, the less time it will take to find and fit into its proper place the common neighbor of these neighbors. Each fitting is more or less "induced," depending on the ease or difficulty with which it may be made.[8] An efficient sequence for putting the puzzle together could be found by trial and error once we have information about the varying amounts of time needed for fitting in individual pieces. For instance, if the time needed fell rapidly toward zero the larger the number of neighbors already in place, then the efficient sequence would turn out to be completely different from the one that would be optimal if the increase in the facility with which pieces may be fitted in were subject to decreasing returns as the number of neighbors increased.

Up to this point, we have considered that the difficulty of taking any development steps (i.e., the fitting in of the individual jigsaw pieces) depends exclusively on the number of neighbors already in place. We can bring our model one step closer to reality by supposing that the taking of the different steps varies in intrinsic difficulty *besides* being affected by the number of neighbors. If this is the case, then the putting together of the puzzle becomes far more determinate than before: for now we would aim at surrounding by "neighbors" those pieces that are intrinsically most difficult to fit in, securing thereby far

---

8. In the usual jigsaw puzzle the task of fitting in a piece also becomes progressively easier as the game progresses and the number of remaining loose pieces declines. Although this feature of a jigsaw puzzle could be related to the "take-off" concept and to Simon's learning model (cf. Ch. 2), it is rather a disturbing element from the point of view of the problem which we wish to illustrate at this juncture. To eliminate it, we may imagine that the jigsaw puzzle goes on forever: only a limited number of loose pieces can be chosen from at any point of time, but as soon as one piece is fitted, a new one is mixed in among the loose pieces on the table. Such a representation of our model is consistent with the view that the growth process is an infinite one, but that at any one point of time only a limited number of steps-to-be-taken is within the horizon of the decision-makers.

greater economies of effort than if we surrounded those pieces that are intrinsically of average or less-than-average difficulty.

These fanciful digressions may illustrate the kind of models in terms of which a general theory of "efficient sequences" might be built. I doubt, however, that it is useful to go very far in this direction. Our short discussion had primarily the purpose:

1. to make the concept of efficient sequence a little more palpable; and

2. to show that efficient sequences will necessarily vary widely from region to region and from country to country depending on the location and stubbornness of the principal development difficulties.

Social Overhead Capital versus Directly Productive Activities

Definitions and biases. The distinction between Social Overhead Capital (SOC) and Directly Productive Activities (DPA) is a recent one. Like all such classifications it must be judged not by its logic, which is far from compelling, but by its theoretical and practical usefulness, which has been considerable. SOC is usually defined as comprising those basic services without which primary, secondary, and tertiary productive activities cannot function. In its wider sense, it includes all public services from law and order through education and public health to transportation, communications, power and water supply, as well as such agricultural overhead capital as irrigation and drainage systems. The hard core of the concept can probably be restricted to transportation and power. Thus limited, SOC can be operationally defined as comprising those activities for the financing of which the International Bank for Reconstruction and Development shows a pronounced preference, just as the behavioral sciences have been said to comprise all those endeavors which manage to obtain financial support from the Ford Foundation. The conditions for including an activity under the category of SOC are probably at least the following three:

1. The services provided by the activity facilitate, or are in some sense basic to, the carrying on of a great variety of economic activities.

2. The services are provided in practically all countries by public agencies or by private agencies subject to some public control: they

are provided free of charge or at rates regulated by public agencies.

3. The services cannot be imported.

The difference between the wide and the narrow meaning of SOC depends on whether one adds a fourth condition, namely:

4. The investment needed to provide the services is characterized by "lumpiness" (technical indivisibilities) as well as by a high capital-output ratio (provided the output is at all measurable).

This last condition clearly focuses attention away from, say, health and education, toward port installations, highways, hydroelectric projects, etc.

Statistical and historical research has shown the importance of SOC in the total investment picture as well as the large share of foreign investment that went into SOC, particularly railroads, during the nineteenth and early twentieth centuries.[9] As a result, economists, and particularly the "developers" among them, have become acutely SOC-conscious. It is widely assumed that enlarged availabilities of electric power and of transportation facilities are essential preconditions for economic development practically everywhere. Here, at least, we have a field where economists have given full recognition to the principle of "efficient sequence." Investment in SOC is advocated not because of its direct effect on final output, but because it permits and, in fact, invites DPA to come in.

The trouble with investment in SOC—or is it its strength?—is that it is impervious to the investment criteria that have been devised to introduce some rationality into development plans. The computation of capital-output ratios often presents almost insuperable statistical difficulties (as in the case of highways) and is moreover considered to be misleading anyway because of the igniting effect SOC investment is expected to have on DPA. As a result, SOC investment is largely a matter of faith in the development potential of a country or region.

The fact that there is so little possibility of evaluating objectively how much investment in SOC is really indicated in any given situation should give us pause. Such a situation implies at least the possibility of wasteful mistakes.

9. Cairncross, "The Place of Capital in Economic Progress"; and Nurkse, "International Investment Today in the Light of Nineteenth Century Experience," *Economic Journal*, 64 (Dec. 1954), 744–58; and *Problems of Capital Formation*, pp. 152–4, and articles by Carter Goodrich there cited.

The absence of ex ante criteria is compounded by the weakness of sanctions when mistakes have actually been made. Underutilized port installations, highways, and even power plants do not present nearly the same administrative and public relations problem as a factory that is idle or suffers losses because of insufficient demand.

Perhaps it is this absence of criteria and of sanctions that has endeared SOC so much to the developers. Development planning is a risky business and there is naturally an attraction in undertaking ventures that cannot be proven wrong before they are started and that are unlikely ever to become obvious failures.

It must be conceded that, to some extent, investment in SOC is "safer" than investment in DPA, not only on this account but also in a real sense: it is diversified investment in the general growth of the economy rather than in the growth of one specific activity. This is the case, for instance, of improvements in a country's *principal* port, of modernization of an *integrated* railroad system, and of additions to the capacity of an *interconnected* electric power production and distribution system. But many SOC investments do not represent similarly diversified risks, and are rather narrowly tied to the anticipated rising fortunes of one city, one valley, or one traffic route; in such cases, it is questionable whether SOC investment is less risky than, for example, investment in an industry whose products might have a nationwide market.

There is another important reason for which the importance of SOC investment may have been overstressed in recent years. In the countries outside the Soviet orbit, directly productive activities in industry, agriculture, and commerce are generally in the hands of individuals or private firms. Therefore, development programs, although often claiming to lay down comprehensive patterns of resource use for the future, are concerned primarily with the allocation of public investment funds among those activities that are considered to be the responsibility of public agencies. The provision of transportation and communications facilities, the production and distribution of electric power, the construction of irrigation and drainage systems are now widely agreed to be appropriate fields of governmental economic activity in addition to the more traditional ones of law and order, defense, education, health, etc. Since economic planners are then spending most of their time on SOC projects, it is only natural that they should claim for them overriding and fundamental importance. This in itself would be innocuous enough were it not for the fact that a combination of taboos, opposing interests, and self-restraint makes it difficult for public investment to enter the DPA sectors. Therefore SOC investment is not only being overadvertised; it also risks being overdone since alternative and possibly more desirable uses of public funds are simply not within the horizon of the planners.

Development via shortage and via excess capacity of SOC. There can be no question whatever that SOC investment is "essential" for economic development. The sizable percentage of total investment occupied by SOC investment in all countries testifies to this fact. But all we know from such statistics is that SOC investment is a most important ingredient of economic development. *They cannot tell us to what extent SOC investment leads or follows DPA investment,* and this is the question we are interested in.

There is no simple answer. Either sequence is conceivable and we must look toward economic analysis and history for indications of the advisability of one or the other under given conditions.

Some SOC investment is required as a prerequisite of DPA investment. Access to an area by sea, road, rail, or air is indispensable before other economic activities can unfold there. But within rather wide limits, the relationship between SOC and DPA is not technologically determined. Within these limits, the cost of producing any given output of DPA will be the higher, the more inadequate the SOC of the economy. This situation is shown in Figure 3. Availability (and cost) of SOC is measured on the horizontal axis. *Total* cost of producing DPA output (including depreciation charges on DPA investment) is shown on the vertical axis. It is assumed that SOC investments do not enter DPA cost calculations. The *a* curve indicates the cost of producing a given full-capacity output of DPA from a given DPA investment as a function of the availability of SOC. The *b*, *c*, and *d* curves show this cost for successively higher amounts of DPA output from successively higher DPA investments.

The slope of the curves is easily explained. Starting at the far right, SOC is plentiful and DPA costs are low; additional SOC hardly makes for any further decline in DPA costs. As we move left, costs for any given DPA output rise slowly at first, then more rapidly; the cost curves eventually become vertical as there is a minimum SOC which is indispensably required for producing any given DPA output.

The cost curves are superficially reminiscent of the familiar iso-quants which show output as a function of two inputs such as labor

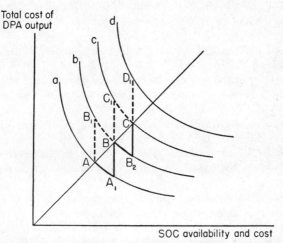

Fig. 3. Balanced and unbalanced growth of DPA and SOC

and capital. Actually the situation is quite different. Our cost curves do not show how a given output can be produced by increasing one input and decreasing another: they are strictly two-dimensional since they reflect the variations in the cost of a given output as only one element, namely the availability of SOC, is being altered. And this element is not even an input in the usual sense, since it does not constitute an "internalized" cost for the DPA producers.

From the point of view of the economy as a whole, the objective is to obtain increasing outputs of DPA at minimum costs in terms of resources devoted to both DPA and SOC. On each curve, the point the *sum* of whose coordinates is smallest is therefore the most desirable one. We have drawn the curves in such a way that the 45° line through the origin connects the optimal points of the different curves. This line expresses the ideal of balanced growth of DPA and SOC: a bit of each at each step no doubt would result in the greatest economy of the country's resources.

87

But it is one of the paradoxes of development that poor countries cannot always afford to be economical. Our principal assumption throughout this essay is that the real scarcity in underdeveloped countries is not the resources themselves but the ability to bring them into play. We shall now apply this notion by stipulating:

1. that SOC and DPA cannot be expanded at one and the same time; and

2. that preference should go to that sequence of expansion steps which maximizes "induced" decision-making.

As a result of the first condition, we can immediately visualize two principal types of sequence: one that starts expansion through increases in the supply of SOC—shown in Figure 3 by the fat line connecting points AA_1BB_2C—and one where the initial expansionary step is always taken by DPA, indicated in the figure by the dotted line AB_1BC_1C. The first sequence may be labeled "*development via excess capacity*" (of SOC) and the latter "*development via shortage*" (of SOC).

According to the second condition, our preference should go to the sequence that shows the greatest promise of being vigorously self-propelling. It is difficult to tell from our figure which one is likely to be superior on this ground. If we start by expanding SOC (sequence AA_1BB_2C), existing DPA production becomes less costly and an increase in DPA investment therefore may well get under way, depending on the response of entrepreneurs to increased profits. If, on the other hand, expansion of DPA is undertaken first, DPA production costs are likely to rise substantially and DPA producers will realize the possibility of making considerable economies through the installation of larger SOC facilities. As a result, pressures for such an increase are likely to come into play and will thus induce the next step in this sequence.

Both sequences therefore set up incentives and pressures, and an evaluation of their respective "efficiency" depends on the strength of entrepreneurial motivations on the one hand and on the response to public pressure of the authorities responsible for SOC on the other.

It may be asked how the sequence could start at all by expanding DPA, in view of the rise in costs that such an expansion, unaccompanied by a concurrent enlargement of SOC, would entail. The answer is that, even at B_1, DPA may still be profitable. Moreover, we have made no institutional assumptions about the way in which either DPA or SOC is organized. In other words, we have not debarred ourselves from undertaking public investment in DPA should we find that the more efficient development sequence is set in motion in this way. Also, if that is our finding, it may represent an important argument for protection and other forms of subsidy to private industry. We have here a new type of infant industry argument: in a situation where SOC is not plentiful it may be more efficient to protect, subsidize, provide special finance for, or to undertake directly investment in DPA than to stimulate DPA indirectly through investment in SOC.

A combination of the two types of sequences is also conceivable. Suppose that investment decisions of both SOC and DPA operators need the special push of SOC shortage or SOC excess capacity, respectively, but that once the push is felt, *both overreact* to it and thereby bring about a pressure situation of the opposite type: then we would obtain a third type of sequence which in the figure would weave around the balanced growth line. For instance, the reaction of the SOC operators to the shortage situation prevailing at B_1 would bring DPA costs down all the way to B_2, whereupon DPA operators would overreact to the excess capacity of SOC by jumping to line d, thereby creating a new SOC shortage at D_1, etc. Such a mixed "staircase" sequence that continually overshoots "balance" and thereby sets up alternate types of investment pressures has interesting points of similarity with the cobweb model. From the point of view of development behavior and strategy, however, the two pure sequences seem more meaningful and will now be considered in greater detail.

Suitability of the various sequences. The principal characteristic of the two varieties of unbalanced growth which we have described is that they yield an extra dividend of "induced," "easy-to-take," or "compelled" decisions resulting in additional investment and output. Excess capacity of SOC, "building ahead of demand," is expected to create this demand by making a country, region, or city attractive to DPA investors. If, on the other hand, DPA is allowed or is made to run ahead of SOC, strong pressures are set up for the provision of SOC in a subsequent period. Development via shortage is an instance of the "disorderly," "compulsive" sequence discussed earlier in this chapter. Development is speeded up because an intermediate stage that is being jumped over can be filled in with comparative ease as pressures and needs arise from the already realized stages. The absence of the intermediate stage is now felt as a shortage and the decisions to remedy it are more readily taken than before the shortage arose. For instance, fiscal measures and utility rate changes which are needed to secure the funds for expansion and whose adoption was out of the question prior to the shortage are suddenly accepted as inescapable.

Thus balanced growth of SOC and DPA is not only unattainable in underdeveloped countries; it may not even be a desirable policy be-

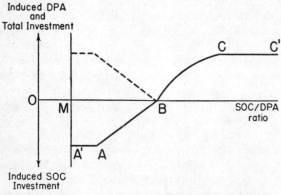

Fig. 4a. Investment induced by SOC shortage or excess

cause it does not set up the incentives and pressures that make for this "dividend" of induced investment decisions.

Let us try to be more explicit. Suppose that, during a first period, a certain number of SOC and DPA investment decisions have been made; they have resulted in some ratio of SOC to DPA output. We are now interested in analyzing the *induced* investment decisions that result from this ratio in a second period. This problem is illustrated in Figures 4a and 4b. Along the horizontal axis we plot the value of the SOC/DPA ratio. We plot induced DPA investment on the vertical axis in the upward direction and induced SOC investment along the same axis but in the downward direction. Total induced investment is shown by a dotted curve or line in the upward direction to the point where it coincides with induced DPA investment.

Point *B* on the horizontal axis is the point of balance corresponding to points *A*, *B*, or *C* in Figure 3, i.e., to the points of optimal allocation of the country's resources from the point of view of static equilibrium.[10] If the SOC/DPA ratio is lower than *OB*, we are in the realm of shortage and of induced SOC investment; if it is higher, we are in that of excess capacity and of induced DPA investment. At first sight, it would appear that the greater the departure of the SOC/DPA ratio from *OB*, the greater will be induced investment in either SOC or DPA; and this situation is indeed portrayed up to points *A* and *C* in Figure 4a. The flattening out of the curve showing induced DPA investment is easily explained; obviously this particular inducement effect is subject

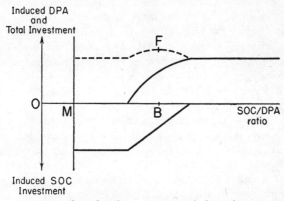

Fig. 4b. Induced investment, with foresight

to decreasing returns as SOC excess capacity rises; within any finite period traffic is not likely to expand in proportion to the number of lanes of a highway. The situation is different for the way in which an SOC shortage induces additional SOC in the next period; here there is no reason for assuming a flattening out. The greater the shortage the greater will be the pressures to remedy it and the greater the amount of capital required to accomplish this end. The limitation is rather a technical one: while the excess capacity of SOC can be as high as we wish to imagine it, there are technological limitations to

10. The value of the ratio does not need to be the same at different levels of output.

a reduction of SOC if a given DPA output is to be maintained. This minimum is shown on our figure as point M.

Another limitation comes into play if we think—as we must—in terms of a finite reaction period: then there is a limit to the amount of investment that can be started during that period, regardless of the strength of the inducement. This consideration applies of course also to the induced DPA investment and it results in the two segments of the inducement curve $A'ABCC'$ in Figure 4a that are parallel to the horizontal axis.

We may now engage in some speculation about the strength of the inducement effects, as reflected in the shape of the inducement curves. First, let us notice that the curve for *total* induced investment as drawn in Figure 4a has its minimum at the point of balance, B. In other words, when the SOC/DPA ratio is such that there is neither excess capacity nor shortage of SOC, and when SOC and DPA are thus in balance, and resources have been optimally allocated between these two categories, then we would actually obtain zero induced investment in the next period. Thus, the contention that balanced growth may be undesirable, besides being unattainable, is illustrated and may well hold true for many underdeveloped countries.

Naturally we can vary our chart to come to quite different conclusions. It is fully conceivable that, once an economy has been progressing over an extended period of time, there will be an overlapping of induced DPA and SOC investments over a significant stretch, a situation shown in Figure 4b. DPA investors who can look back on a long experience of SOC investment being taken care of will be induced to invest prior to the actual point when excess capacity appears; and SOC investment will similarly be undertaken prior to the appearance of an actual shortage. Thus, when the community has acquired the foresight and confidence in further growth characteristic of a progressive economy, the point of balanced growth may also be the point of maximum inducement of further investment, as is shown by point F on the *total* inducement curve in Figure 4b. Under these conditions, balanced growth would therefore be desirable not only from the static but also from the dynamic point of view; moreover, it would no longer be unattainable as our strictures against balanced growth on this count would clearly not apply to the advanced type of economy we are now talking about. Regardless of the existence of a true maximum at *B,* a situation where there is substantial overlapping of the two inducement effects sharply reduces the attractiveness of either variety of unbalanced growth from the point of view of inducing further investment.

We are getting close here to the traditional notions of dynamic equilibrium and induced investment: even though, with SOC and DPA in balance, there exist for the moment neither tensions, pressures, nor special incentives, further balanced growth of these two components of total investment is induced by the anticipation of such pressures and incentives; this anticipation must, in turn, be traced to past experience, which has taught SOC and DPA operators to expect trouble or opportunity, respectively, before either actually arises. In this sense, *it is the experience of unbalanced growth in the past that produces, at an advanced stage of economic development, the possibility of balanced growth.*

But let us return from this El Dorado to our underdeveloped areas, where balanced growth is both unattainable and undesirable. This brings us back to Figure 4a and to speculation about the comparative strength of inducement via SOC shortage or SOC excess capacity.

A basic difference between these two sequences is the type of inducement that is set up. Excess SOC capacity is essentially permissive; while it certainly serves to reinforce motivations that already exist, and may therefore mean the difference between a large flow of DPA investment and a trickle, it invites rather than compels. The opposite holds with respect to the inducement via shortage. A shortage that is experienced as such is bound to lead to attempts to remedy it on the part of those who suffer from it or who stand to gain from its elimination. In situations where motivations are deficient, it therefore seems safer to rely on development via shortage than on development via excess capacity. In other words, if we endow an underdeveloped country with a first-class highway network, with extensive hydroelectric and perhaps irrigation facilities, can we be certain that industrial and agricultural activity will expand in the wake of these improvements? Would it not be less risky and more economical first to make sure of such activity, even though it may have to be subsidized in view of the absence of adequate transportation and power, and then let the ensuing pressures determine the appropriate outlays for SOC and its location? As examples of this type of sequence, one may cite the development of Japan, Turkey and, to a considerable extent, of the U.S.S.R.

As already pointed out, the limits to such a policy are set by technological factors, since a minimum amount of SOC is a prerequisite at any given level of DPA. These limits may sometimes be rather narrow, especially in largely undeveloped regions and areas of new settlement where little or no social overhead capital has as yet been created. Naturally, at this stage, only development via excess capacity is feasible; the points M and B of Figure 4a are merged at the point of origin. The idea that expansion of SOC must under all circumstances precede an expansion of DPA probably originates in the identification of all development situations with such *initial* growth sequences and in the consideration of SOC as a kind of fixed-coefficient "input" that would always have to come into existence prior to "its" DPA-output. But this is surely not a realistic picture for most of today's underdeveloped countries.

The argument in favor of development via SOC shortage applies with particular force to an underdeveloped country's own backward areas. Here we have regions that have, so to speak, hardened in their reluctance to develop and it seems rather unlikely that a purely permissive system—which is moreover a very expensive one—will be effective. In other words, the BC segment of the inducement curve—the one corresponding to excess capacity in SOC—is likely to be pitifully flat.

To place one's faith in purely permissive sequences and to rely on the ability of SOC facilities to call forth other economic activities can, under these circumstances, be just as irrational as the so-called "Cargo Cult" that has been engaged in by some of the New Guinea tribes after the lamented departure of the Allied expeditionary force at the end of World War II: "Those in the coastal villages have built wharves out into the sea, ready for the ships to tie up, and those in land villages have constructed airstrips out of the jungle for the planes to land. And they have waited in expectancy for the Second Coming of the Cargoes." [11] Touching as it is, such a belief in the propitiatory powers of social overhead capital should not be the basis of development policy.

11. Raymond Firth, *Elements of Social Organization* (New York, Philosophical Library, 1951), p. 112.

On the other hand, many underdeveloped but developing countries also have their boom towns and their privileged provinces. Here, of course, a policy of providing for plentiful SOC will lead to beneficial repercussions since in such regions many entrepreneurs are always on the brink of investment decisions and will therefore be pushed over it by an improvement in cost and revenue outlook such as is provided by good SOC facilities. On the other hand, a moderate SOC shortage is not likely to do too much damage to a really dynamic developing area. In such a situation industries will think nothing of bringing in their own diesel generators, of digging for their own water, and of building their own access roads and workers' houses. Thus the *BC* curve is not only likely to surge nicely upward, but may even overlap the *AB* curve as in Figure 4b. In other words, a region that is really booming will be much helped by a policy concentrating on SOC, but will not be decisively harmed by its absence.

Observation certainly bears this out. Rapidly growing centers will usually suffer shortages, sometimes because of lack of proper planning, but often also because it would be illegitimate and wasteful to expand SOC facilities in anticipation of the kind of extremely rapid economic progress that does hit a city or area sometimes, but whose occurrence or continuation can never be predicted with confidence. When these shortages do occur, they do not seem to affect the growth perceptibly, but rather are taken as an additional proof that dynamic development is indeed under way. In an underdeveloped country it is often the city with the worst water, power, and housing shortages that is most favored by private investors.

The foregoing is more valid for domestic than for foreign investment. The latter can choose among dynamic centers of several countries and is likely to give some preference to those where shortages are least harassing. This consideration also applies within a country that has several developing centers competing with one another. In such a situation the positive response to excess SOC may be high for one center because of the competition of the others.[12] In other words, the choice of DPA investors is likely to be made primarily on the basis of

12. The situation is a close analogue to that of price elasticity of demand for the export article of a country when this country is one among many producers. That elasticity, as is well known, is always high even though the elasticity for the commodity as a whole may be low.

the comparative SOC endowments of the different "candidate" areas: [13] the *BC* curve is bulging, and development via excess capacity is definitely the choice in this case.

Limits to development via SOC shortage. Our advocacy of development via SOC shortage in certain situations has been hedged by a number of qualifications. Even so, it will come as a shock to those who feel that the inadequacy of transportation and power has been a principal bottleneck in the growth of many important underdeveloped countries. While some observers attribute this situation to inadequate planning and mistaken priorities in development programs, others account for it more simply and often more convincingly by inflation and its consequences: when a country is in the grip of inflation, economic policy-makers are very prone to attempt to hold prices down wherever the administrative difficulties are not overwhelming. Now the prices of public utility services are among the easiest to hold, and are usually subject to direct control of the authorities. Therefore rates of public utilities such as water, electric power, railroads, streetcars, telephones, etc. usually lag far behind the rise in the general price level, with the double result that wasteful consumption of these services is powerfully encouraged while financing of necessary expansions is rendered difficult if not impossible.

There is no doubt that neglect of public utilities can become a most serious drag on economic progress. We have recognized that there is a minimum SOC/DPA output ratio, i.e., a point where DPA output can only be increased if SOC is expanded. But this does not mean that at this point no further DPA investment can take place at all; rather, total productivity of *aggregate* DPA investment will show no further increases. An individual factory can still be established, and while its output will of course be positive, its *social* marginal productivity will be zero, for the productivity of existing firms is lowered once the new firm claims a share of the already short SOC facilities. This situation may show up in marginal firms going out of business, or in a gen-

13. This is shown by the advertisements of the various state development commissions or boards that usually appear in the *New York Times Annual Economic Review* early in January of each year: these organizations point primarily to power and transportation availabilities, factory space, and more intangible factors such as good labor relations or trained labor force.

erally poorer quantity and quality performance of all firms, or in both. In other words, the disequilibrium between SOC and DPA has become so pronounced that it is automatically kept from increasing through a refusal of DPA to expand or through the destruction of existing DPA investment as new investment is undertaken.

Unfortunately it is not easy to recognize the point where development of DPA ahead of SOC becomes self-defeating in this fashion, precisely because no absolute obstacle ever arises to debar additional DPA investment. It is quite possible that some countries with protracted inflations have come close to this point especially when the reluctance to raise rates has been further strengthened by the desire to "squeeze" foreign-controlled companies.

Nevertheless, we cannot condemn altogether one of our two approaches—development via SOC shortages—solely on the ground that, if overdone, it *may* lead to stagnation rather than to growth. For it will do so only in a community whose behavior has become thoroughly irrational and where creative responses have been choked off. But which development approach can be expected to work in such a community? When the authorities responsible for public utilities and other SOC facilities fail to respond to dangers so clear and present and to needs as obvious as those that are signalled by collapsing bridges, derailed trains, and constant power failures, what hope is there that these same authorities would know how to plan the construction of bridges, railroads, and power stations *ahead of demand*, without the grossest waste of resources?

We are trying to formulate here a set of economic development policies on the assumption that underdeveloped countries have to contend with some special difficulties and scarcities; but our task would be impossible if we had to assume complete lack of response to development stimuli. Such behavior is best explained as a temporary victory of those forces which are opposed to paying the price of development—from their point of view such behavior is of course entirely rational.

CHAPTER 6

Interdependence and Industrialization

Backward and Forward Linkage Defined

OUR SEARCH for efficient sequences and for mechanisms that tend to maximize "induced" investment decisions must now move on to the directly productive activities themselves. Here we meet with such well-known development alternatives as agriculture versus industry, export promotion versus import substitution, heavy versus light industry, etc. Rather than examine in isolation each one of these specific problems we shall attempt to sketch a generalized method of attack.

In our discussion of SOC versus DPA we made two assumptions:

1. that within certain limits the proportions in which investment must be divided between these two categories are variable (this assumption resulted in the possibility of excess or shortage of social overhead capital); and

2. that in case of a shortage, the remedy of imports was not available (this is fairly realistic in the case of transportation and power, not to speak of more basic SOC activities such as education and law enforcement).

Both assumptions will now be reversed; insofar as relations among various directly productive activities are concerned, we shall operate on the assumption, familiar from input-output analysis, that input coefficients are fixed or at least that needed inputs increase monotonically with outputs. In other words, while it was conceivable that an economy is inadequately or overgenerously equipped with technical training facilities, port installations, roads, and electric power stations relative to its endowment of manufacturing capacity, it is plausible to suppose (at least with given techniques) that an increase in the output of cotton yardage requires a larger input of raw cotton. Flexibility is restored, on the other hand, by the assumption that if a required input is not supplied from domestic sources it can be imported.

The pattern of pressures, incentives, and repercussions is therefore likely to be quite different from the one that was characteristic of the SOC-DPA relationship.

In discussing the latter, the concepts of SOC shortage and excess capacity emerged as the principal agents of further development. With our new assumptions, a specific shortage of goods and services required as inputs for a certain newly established economic activity is inconceivable. If the required inputs are not available, the activity will simply not take place. If it does take place, the inputs must already be forthcoming—either as a result of domestic production or through imports. Thus it seems that there is little room here for the kind of direct and strong pressure that leads from one productive activity toward another. But important stimuli result nevertheless from the fact that the setting up of an industry brings with it the *availability of a new, expanding market for its inputs* whether or not these inputs are supplied initially from abroad.

Similarly with what we called excess capacity. At first it would seem that this concept has little place within the DPA sector. An industry must sell its output. It will come into being only if it anticipates being able to do so; if the anticipation turns out to be a miscalculation, the industry will have to close its doors. Thus the coming into existence of an industry must be the result of some pre-existing demand, but can it be held to induce new activities and demand? Such repercussions are less obvious than the road which permanently encourages new traffic flows. Nevertheless, the domestic availability of a product whose output will ordinarily be expanded if necessary does have some features in common with the availability of a basic service.

It may seem that, given our assumption that DPA products can be imported, there is no reason why domestic availability of a new product should prove a better spur to further economic activity involving the product as an input than availability from foreign sources of supply that existed all along. In pure theory, this may indeed be so, but in practice three important considerations make domestic availability a considerably more effective spur to further development:

1. Importing requires special skills and therefore reduces the number of potential entrants.

2. Importing is subject to special balance-of-payments uncertainties, and production largely based on imports is therefore particularly

risky; if inflation is expected to proceed more rapidly at home than abroad and adjustment of the exchange rate is held back, quantitative import restrictions become likely; if, on the other hand, the exchange rate is allowed to depreciate freely, it is likely to do so faster than the domestic purchasing power of the country's currency and there would be a long-run cost advantage in relying as much as possible on domestic inputs.

3. Finally and perhaps most important, the fact that a certain product is produced domestically is likely to result in efforts on the part of the producers to propagate its further uses and in their financial participation in such ventures. The domestic availability of a product thus brings into being active forces that make for its utilization as input in new economic activities catering to newly "entrained wants." In this respect, it is therefore a less purely permissive inducement mechanism than the existence of a road which merely "invites" more traffic.

Thus, in close analogy to the alternative between development via shortage and development via excess capacity which we described for the SOC-DPA situation, two inducement mechanisms may be considered to be at work within the DPA sector:

1. The input-provision, derived demand, or *backward linkage effects,* i.e., every nonprimary economic activity, will induce attempts to supply through domestic production the inputs needed in that activity.

2. The output-utilization or *forward linkage effects,* i.e., every activity that does not by its nature cater exclusively to final demands, will induce attempts to utilize its outputs as inputs in some new activities.

Development policy must attempt to enlist these well-known backward and forward effects; but it can do so only if there is some knowledge as to how different economic activities "score" with respect to these effects. Ordinarily economists have been content with general references to the advantages of external economies, complementarities, cumulative causation, etc. But no systematic effort has been made to describe how the development path ought to be modified so as to maximize these advantages even though the existence of input-output statistics supplies us with a few tools for an analysis of this kind.

First, a further note on the linkage concept itself. What do we imply when we speak of the linkage effects emanating from industry A toward industry B? Language can be quite ambiguous here, for we may have in mind the potential *importance* of the linkage effect in terms of, say, the net output of the new industries that might be called forth; or we may mean the *strength* of the effect, i.e., the probability that these industries will actually come into being. The total effect could be measured by the sum of the products of these two elements; in other words, if the establishment of industry W may lead, through linkage effects, to the establishment of n additional industries with net outputs equal to x_i $(i = 1,2...n)$ and if the probability that each one of these industries will actually be set up as a result of the establishment of industry W is p_i $(i = 1,2...n)$, then the total linkage effect of industry W is equal to $\sum_1^n x_i p_i$.

The probabilities can be interpreted as measuring the strength of the stimulus that is set up. For backward linkage, this strength can be roughly measured as follows: suppose industry W requires annual inputs of y_1, $y_2...y_n$ and suppose that the minimum economic size (in terms of annual productive capacity) of firms that would turn out these inputs is equal to a_1, $a_2...a_n$; then the strength of the stimulus or the probability that the setting up of industry W will lead to the setting up of industries producing the inputs is equal to the ratio of the y's to the a's.[1] Minimum economic size is not a technical concept, but is defined in economic terms relative to normal profits and efficient foreign suppliers. In other words, it is the size at which the domestic firm will be able both to secure normal profits and to compete with existing foreign suppliers, taking into account locational advantages *and* disadvantages as well as, perhaps, some infant industry protection. In this way comparative cost conditions are automatically taken into account.[2]

In the case of forward linkage, an interpretation of the p's is less

1. The ratio is to be defined as having a ceiling of 1, i.e., the value of the ratio is equal to unity, whenever the y's are equal to or *larger than* the a's. Note also that the y's are equivalent to the gross output of the new industries or firms in physical terms whereas the x's are their net outputs in value terms.

2. Data on the economic size of plants in different industries would be the starting point for determining minimum economic size in different countries. Research in this area in relation to economic development is surprisingly scant, except for the pioneering article of K. A. Bohr, "Investment Criteria for Manufacturing Industries in Underdeveloped Countries," *Review of Economics and Statistics, 36* (May 1954), 157–66. Some basic data for small and medium plants are available in a series of Industrial Reports issued by the Office of Industrial Resources of the International Cooperation Administration. For data on optimum plant size in U. S. industry, see J. S. Bain, *Barriers to New Competition* (Cambridge, Mass., 1956), ch. 3.

straightforward. The concept of economic size is not helpful here, since the size of the market for the industries that might be brought into being through forward linkage does not depend on their suppliers. A clue can perhaps be found in the importance of the articles produced by industry W as inputs for the output of the to-be-linked industry. If these inputs are a very small fraction of the industry's eventual output, then their domestic availability is not likely to be an important factor in calling forth that industry. If, on the other hand, these articles are subjected to few further manufacturing operations, then the strength of the forward stimulus is likely to be substantial, provided demand is sufficient to justify domestic production.

In these cases, then, importance and strength—the x's and the p's—of the linkage effect are inversely correlated. Industries where the x's are small and the p's large are sometimes aptly called "satellite" industries. They are almost unfailingly established in the wake of industry W but are of minor importance in comparison to that industry. Thus defined, satellite industries can be established through backward or forward linkage. In the case of cement, for instance, the manufacture of multi-wall bags for packing purposes represents backward linkage while the establishment of a cement block industry represents satellite formation through forward linkage. A satellite industry usually has the following characteristics:

a. it enjoys a strong locational advantage from proximity to the master industry;

b. it uses as principal input an output or by-product of the master industry without subjecting it to elaborate transformation, or its principal output is a—usually minor—input of the master industry; and

c. its minimum economic size is smaller than that of the master industry.

While satellite industries are almost certain to be established once the master industry is in place, the establishment of industry W also results in stimuli toward the setting up of nonsatellite industries. In these cases, the strength of the stimulus is infinitely weaker, but the stake is far bigger. Examples of such a situation are the stimulus that the setting up of a multi-wall bag factory gives toward the creation of a pulp and paper industry or, for the case of forward linkage, the stimulus given by the establishment of an iron and steel industry to

102

all the metal-fabricating industries. Here the establishment of one industry is a contributing factor which by itself is quite unlikely to result in the creation of the others; but when we speak of external economies and complementarities, we think at least as much of these uncertain linkages as of the far more certain, but also far less significant, satellites with which any industry of a certain size surrounds itself. The weakness of the stimulus in the case of nonsatellites can be explained by the absence of the three factors that define satellites. Linkage is reduced to the fact that an input of the newly established industry is an output of the to-be-created industry or vice versa, but the established industry would not be the principal customer or supplier of the to-be-created industry; in fact, particularly in cases of backward linkage, minimum economic size of the to-be-created industry would frequently be larger than that of the industry where the linkage originates.[3]

In spite of the importance of the nonsatellite type of linkage, it seems necessary to provide for some arbitrary cut-off point for small probabilities. It is all very well to say that the establishment of a brewery sends out a stimulus in the direction of a paper industry because of the labels needed for the beer bottles, but by itself this stimulus is not likely ever to lead to the setting up of a paper mill. Thus, if we consider *in isolation* the linkage effects exclusively of the beer industry on further industrial or agricultural development, we should consider only those stimuli whose probability exceeds a certain critical value, say one-half.[4]

If we proceed in this way, the joint linkage effects of two industries, say beer and cement, considered as a unit, are likely to be larger than the sum of their individual linkage effects, since some of the xp products which are omitted in computing the individual effects because

3. To the extent that the minimum economic size of an industry is larger the farther away one moves from the finished consumer or producer goods stage. This is, of course, by no means universally true as is shown, e.g., by the large minimum size of the motor vehicles makers.

4. It is a good rule of thumb that an industry can properly be established in an underdeveloped but developing country as soon as existing demand is equal to one-half of the economic size of the plant as defined above. The additional demand needed to justify the investment can be expected to come from the growth of existing demand and from the development of new demand through forward linkage, once the plant is in existence.

the p's are below the critical value will exceed this value if added together for both industries. Here we have an argument in favor of multiple development that we would consider convincing were it not that our principal argument against it is concerned with its feasibility rather than with its desirability.

The fact that the linkage effects of two industries viewed in combination are larger than the sum of the linkage effects of each industry in isolation helps to account for the cumulative character of development. When industry A is first set up, its satellites will soon follow; but when industry B is subsequently established, this may help to bring into existence not only its own satellites but some firms which neither A nor B in isolation could have called forth. And with C coming into play some firms will follow that require the combined stimuli not only of B and C but of A, B, and C. This mechanism may go far toward explaining the *acceleration* of industrial growth which is so conspicuous during the first stages of a country's development.

A Mental Experiment

Let us attempt to take a closer look at the cumulative effect of industrialization. The problem is now simply formulated: how are linkage effects maximized? Obviously, even if we had the necessary quantitative information about these effects, an answer to this question would yield only *one* investment criterion among several others. Therefore, the usefulness of the criterion lies in the guidance it could provide in specific situations with respect to alternatives that arise in the course of development, rather than in the design of any rigid sequence that might be derived from it.

As a first step, it is instructive to look at the various sectors of an economy with the aim of appraising the amount and kinds of linkage effects which they exert. With linkage most fully developed in advanced industrial countries, it is tempting to turn to them to discover those sectors or subsectors that ought to receive high ratings in any development program, not only on account of the intrinsic usefulness of their output, but because of the further development stimuli which are likely to emanate from them.

What use can be drawn from the statistical results of input-output analysis in this connection? We may, of course, measure the degree of interdependence shown by any one industry by computing

1. the proportion of its total output that does not go to final demand but rather to other industries, and

2. the proportion of its output that represents purchases from other industries.

But these two measures of the extent to which any one industry interlocks with others within a national economy can be taken to represent forward and backward linkage effects only on the basis of a mental experiment: we would have to imagine for every industry in turn that the country's development started with it, so that all its sales to and purchases from other domestic industries are fancied to have developed as a sequel to its foundation. In fact, of course, an industry W which shows the highest degree of interdependence could very well have been set up last, thus proving that maximum interdependence is quite compatible with complete absence of active linkage effects. Nevertheless, *if* W had been set up first, and assuming that the total output and its commodity composition would have come out to the same final result shown in the input-output table, then the industries that are using W's products in their own manufacturing processes, and those that are suppliers of W, would have received important growth stimuli from it. Since we are interested in appraising the comparative importance of such hypothetical stimuli in different industries to help us find, precisely in a nonindustrial country, the most efficient sequence for its industrialization, the results of this mental experiment are pertinent to our inquiry.[5]

In a recent study by Chenery and Watanabe,[6] the degree of interdependence of various industries has been computed and averaged for Italy, Japan, and the United States, and the resulting figures reproduced in the table below can be taken as a general indication of the ranking of these industries from the point of view of backward and forward linkage effects. Because of the proviso contained in note 5, averages for countries with different industrial structures are perhaps better suited to provide such indications than individual country figures.

5. On the condition that we expect the commodity composition of the underdeveloped country's output to bear eventually some resemblance to that of the country on whose input-output statistics we perform the experiment.

6. H. B. Chenery and T. Watanabe, "International Comparisons of the Structure of Production," paper presented at the Cleveland Meeting of the Econometric Society, Dec. 1956 (dittoed), to be published in *Econometrica*.

Average Degree of Interdependence of Economic Sectors in Italy, Japan, and the United States

	Interdependence through Purchases from Other Sectors [a] (Backward Linkage)	Interdependence through Sales to Other Sectors [b] (Forward Linkage)
1. "Intermediate Manufacture" (backward and forward linkage both high)		
Iron and Steel	66	78
Nonferrous Metals	61	81
Paper and Products	57	78
Petroleum Products	65	68
Coal Products	63	67
Chemicals	60	69
Textiles	67	57
Rubber Products	51	48
Printing and Publishing	49	46
2. "Final Manufacture" (backward linkage high, forward linkage low)		
Grain Mill Products	89	42
Leather and Products	66	37
Lumber and Wood Products	61	38
Apparel	69	12
Transport Equipment	60	20
Machinery	51	28
Nonmetallic Mineral Products	47	30
Processed Foods	61	15
Shipbuilding	58	14
Miscellaneous Industries	43	20
3. "Intermediate Primary Production" (forward linkage high, backward linkage low)		
Metal Mining	21	93
Petroleum and Natural Gas	15	97
Coal Mining	23	87
Agriculture and Forestry	31	72
Electric Power	27	59
Nonmetallic Minerals	17	52

	Interdependence through Purchases from Other Sectors [a] (Backward Linkage)	Interdependence through Sales to Other Sectors [b] (Forward Linkage)
4. *"Final Primary Production"* (backward and forward linkage both low)		
Fishing	24	36
Transport	31	26
Services	19	34
Trade	16	17

a. Ratio of interindustry purchases to total production (%).
b. Ratio of interindustry sales to total demand (%).

Source: Chenery and Watanabe, "International Comparisons," p. 11. Reproduced by permission of the authors.

The four categories in the table have been established by Chenery and Watanabe, and they are meaningful within our own conceptual framework. Within each category, the industries have been ranked according to their combined score (backward plus forward linkage). As we attribute more importance to backward than to forward linkage,[7] we place industries with high backward and low forward linkage ahead of those that have the inverse characteristic.

The ranking does an injustice to machinery and also to transport equipment. The low value of forward linkage in their case is probably due to the fact that sales of these industries to other industries are construed in input-output tables as final demand deliveries because they are accounted for under capital formation. Looking at interindustry transactions from the point of view of linkage effects, there is no essential difference between the stimulus toward setting up an insecticide mixing plant and that toward installing a tractor assembly plant which emanates from insecticide or tractor purchases by agricultural establishments.

In some cases, the mental experiment through which we identify interdependence with linkage effects takes on a somewhat eerie flavor. For instance, the largest value for backward linkage is found for grain mill products, but it is highly unrealistic to think of wheat and rice cultivation as being "induced" by wheat and rice mills; rather the mills must be regarded as satellites (through forward linkage)

7. See p. 116.

107

of the foodcrop-growing activities. Nevertheless, even in this instance, backward linkage is sometimes experienced in underdeveloped countries as will be seen below.

In any event it is interesting to note that the industry with the highest combined linkage score is iron and steel. Perhaps the underdeveloped countries are not so foolish and so exclusively prestige-motivated in attributing prime importance to this industry!

The interdependence ratios of the table are very rough indexes of the potential linkage effects that might be introduced into nonindustrial economies by specific industrial sectors. A more refined measure of backward linkage can be obtained by considering the inverse of the input-output matrix. This inverse matrix makes it possible to estimate the *direct and indirect* repercussions of an increase in final demand requirements for any one industry on the other sectors of the economy. Since indirect repercussions are not taken into account when one computes simply the ratio of an industry's purchases from other industries to the total value of its output, the measure derived from the inverse matrix is more comprehensive. A Danish economist has proposed this measure—he calls it "power of dispersion"—as one way of identifying "key industries," and has argued that knowledge of these measures could be of value in a depression because it would permit us to focus recovery policy on those industries whose expansion would "lead to a general increase in economic activity embracing all or at least most industries." [8] In addition, we believe that computation of these indexes may be of interest not only to those who seek to reactivate a developed economy but also to those who attempt to activate an underdeveloped economy.

The knowledge of the approximate ranking of an industry from the point of view of forward and backward linkage effects as derived from existing developed economies through their input-output tables is, I believe, useful to the economist-planner in underdeveloped areas. It· is something to be added to his criteria-box. But excessive reliance should obviously not be placed on these rankings, based as they are on a mental experiment subject to numerous qualifications. Industrial development clearly cannot be started everywhere with an iron and

8. P. N. Rasmussen, *Studies in Inter-Sectoral Relations* (Copenhagen, Einar Harcks, 1956), p. 141. Unfortunately the empirical studies included in the book do not do justice to Rasmussen's very interesting analytical tools because of excessive aggregation. Thus, all manufacturing is brought together in a single sector!

steel industry just because this industry maximizes linkage. It is far more useful to look at the structure of underdeveloped countries and to examine how linkage effects normally make their appearance: such an analysis is likely to yield some hints about the possibility of influencing development in such a way as to strengthen these effects.

Backward Linkage at Work

The lack of interdependence and linkage is of course one of the most typical characteristics of underdeveloped economies. If we had homogeneous input-output statistics for all countries, it would certainly be instructive to rank countries according to the proportion of intersectoral transactions to total output; it is likely that this ranking would exhibit a close correlation with both income per capita and with the percentage of the population occupied in manufacturing.

Agriculture in general, and subsistence agriculture in particular, are of course characterized by the scarcity of linkage effects. By definition, all *primary* production should exclude any substantial degree of backward linkage although the introduction of modern methods does bring with it considerable outside purchases of seeds, fertilizers, insecticides, and other current inputs, not to speak of machines and vehicles. We may say that the more primitive the agricultural and mining activities, the more truly primary they are.

Forward linkage effects are also weak in agriculture and mining. A large proportion of agricultural output is destined directly for consumption or export; another important part is subjected to some processing in industries that can be characterized as satellite inasmuch as the value added by them to the agricultural product (milling of wheat, rice, coffee, etc.) is small relative to the value of the product itself. Only a comparatively small fraction of total agricultural output of underdeveloped countries receives elaborate processing, which usually takes place abroad.

The case for inferiority of agriculture to manufacturing has most frequently been argued on grounds of comparative productivity. While this case has been shown not to be entirely convincing,[9] agriculture certainly stands convicted on the count of its lack of direct stimulus

9. Viner, *International Trade and Economic Development* (Glencoe, Ill., Free Press, 1952), pp. 63–73; and Buchanan and Ellis, *Economic Development,* pp. 259–63.

to the setting up of new activities through linkage effects: the superiority of manufacturing in this respect is crushing. This may yet be the most important reason militating against any complete specialization of underdeveloped countries in primary production.

The grudge against what has become known as the "enclave" type of development is due to this ability of primary products from mines, wells, and plantations to slip out of a country without leaving much of a trace in the rest of the economy. Naturally hostility to the profits earned by foreign companies plays an important role in such attitudes; but the absence of direct linkage effects of primary production for export lends these views a plausibility that they do not have in the case of foreign investment in manufacturing. I say plausibility rather than validity, for while as such the primary production activities leading to exports may exert few developmental effects, they do finance imports which can become very powerful agents of development as we shall see below.

Since interdependence in the input-output sense [10] is so largely the result of industrialization, we must now attempt to trace the various ways in which manufacturing and the accompanying linkage effects make their appearance. In this connection, we shall utilize another one of Chenery's findings, namely that more than ninety percent of all input-output flows can usually be arranged in a triangular pattern.[11] Circularity—i.e., the fact that coal is needed for steel-making and steel for coal mining—is undoubtedly present in the structure of a country's production, but apparently to a much smaller degree than would be suspected upon looking at an input-output table that has not been "triangularized." In other words, there is no compelling *technological* requirement for the simultaneous setting up of various industries, an interesting complement to our case against the existence of such a requirement on economic grounds.

In a triangular arrangement of the input-output matrix, there is a "last" sector whose output goes entirely to final demand and which takes in inputs from a number of other sectors; the second-to-last sector sells its output to final demand and to the last sector and buys

10. This qualifying clause is needed, as it is possible to have extensive division of labor, and therefore interdependence in final demand, in an economy that shows very little "structural" interdependence.

11. Chenery and Watanabe, "International Comparisons," pp. 7–10.

inputs from some or all other sectors except from the "last"; and so on, until we come to the "first" sector whose output goes to all the subsequent sectors and possibly also to final demand, but which does not use any inputs from other sectors.

Industrialization can of course *start* only with industries that deliver to final demand, since *ex hypothesi* no market exists as yet for intermediate goods. This means that it will be possible to set up only two kinds of industries:

1. those that transform domestic or imported primary products into goods needed by final demands;

2. those that transform imported semimanufactures into goods needed by final demands.

To the pioneer industrial countries only the first course was open, and this explains the towering importance of a few industries (textiles, iron and steel, pottery) during the early stages of the Industrial Revolution. In today's underdeveloped countries the textiles, food processing, and construction materials industries based on local materials are still of great importance, but, to a very significant extent, industrialization is penetrating these countries in the second manner, through plants that perform the "final touches" [12] on almost-finished *industrial* products imported from abroad. Examples are the many converting, assembly, and mixing plants, the pharmaceutical laboratories, the metal-fabricating industries, and many others. This trend has many advantages: it often provides an investment outlet for small amounts of capital that might not easily become available for ventures which require the pooling of the resources of many investors, and it makes it possible to start industrial undertakings without the heavy risk that comes in underdeveloped countries from having to rely on the output of unreliable domestic producers.

In this way underdeveloped countries often set up "last" industries first—i.e., these are "last" industries considering the input-output flow of the advanced countries: what in these countries are inputs from the other sectors are replaced in underdeveloped countries by imports. Such industries could be termed "enclave import industries," in analogy to the enclave export activities that were previously mentioned. For here again we have an undertaking that at least in its

12. This term was used by Hayek in his discussion of the "stages of production." Cf. *Prices and Production* (London, Routledge, 1931), p. 70.

beginning is antiseptically linkage-free; materials are imported from abroad, some value is added to them through mixing, assembling, packaging, etc., and the finished product is rushed to the final consumers. The enclave nature of these industries is sometimes emphasized by the location of the plant at a point as close as possible to the most convenient port of arrival of the imported materials, and again this type of venture has proven particularly attractive to foreign capital—many of the branch plants owned by foreign corporations specialize in this kind of operation.

But there is a considerable difference between the enclave export and enclave import activities. The former have great trouble in breaking out of the enclave situation. Usually some forward linkage effects can be utilized—ores and cane sugar can be refined before being shipped. But the scope for such operations is strictly limited. With respect to import enclave industries, the situation is radically different: they set up backward linkage effects of practically infinite range and depth.

In fact, much of the recent economic history of some rapidly developing underdeveloped countries can be written in terms of industrialization working its way backward from the "final touches" stage to domestic production of intermediate, and finally to that of basic, industrial materials. In this way, industrialization has even proven to be a powerful stimulus to the development of agriculture. By providing a reliable market, processing industries originally based on imported agricultural materials such as cotton textiles and beer have stimulated in Colombia the domestic production of cotton and barley. In Brazil, likewise, "modern cotton, peanut and cereal processing plants sometimes preceded the expansion in agricultural output. Similarly the very sizable investments in cotton, sisal and cocoa ginning and pressing plants, gave evidence of the way in which industrial and commercial capital has been ready to seek out profitable opportunities to strengthen the country's raw material base." [13] Backward linkage effects are important not only from secondary back to primary production, but also from tertiary back to both secondary and primary production. The experience of Sears, Roebuck and of some

13. *The Development of Brazil,* Report of the Joint Brazil-United States Economic Development Commission, Institute of Inter-American Affairs (Washington, 1954), p. 12.

successful supermarket ventures in Latin America are cases in point.[14]

In most of these cases, imported goods have been gradually replaced by domestic production which has been called forth by the existence of a large and stable market. Of considerable importance are the backward linkage effects that are the combined result of the existence of several "last stage" industries. The minimum economic size of many intermediate and basic industries is such that in small markets a variety of user industries needs to be established before their combined demand justifies a substitution of imports of intermediate and basic goods by domestic production.

A Model of Capital Formation Based on Backward Linkage

In view of the importance of backward linkage as a development mechanism, it may be interesting to construct a growth model where this mechanism would act as a prime mover.

As backward linkage is brought into play by increases in demand, we shall suppose that autonomous growth is taking place as a result of some net capital formation, improvement in efficiency, and rise in exports. But let this be a slow growth, far below the ceiling set for an economy by its potential ability to generate savings and to attract foreign capital. We then assume that backward linkage unfailingly triggers additional net capital formation whenever the imports of some commodity pass the "threshold" of minimum economic size. The situation may be analyzed in the following terms using familiar input-output concepts:

Let there be n activities the first k of which are not carried on within our country at the beginning of the development process. The outputs of these activities which are carried on abroad are imported into the country to be used (1) as inputs in the $n-k$ activities that are carried on within the country; and/or (2) directly as final demand deliveries. This yields an input-output table which differs from the usual type in that imports have been disaggregated. If we assume that

14. R. Wood and V. Keyser, *Sears, Roebuck de México*, S.A., National Planning Association, Washington, 1953. Experience of Sears, Roebuck in other Latin American countries has been similar to that described in this pamphlet. The International Basic Economy Corporation (IBEC) of New York has reported favorable effects of its supermarkets on agricultural production in Venezuela.

imports take place only in commodities that are not produced domestically, then we can represent the table as follows:

	Intermediate Demands from: $1 \cdots k$	$k+1 \cdots\cdots n$	Final Demand	Total Demand
1	$O \cdots O$	$M_{1,k+1} \cdots M_{1n}$	M_{1F}	M_1
2	$O \cdots O$	$M_{2,k+1} \cdots M_{2n}$	M_{2F}	M_2
Outputs from $\quad k$	$O \cdots O$	$M_{k,k+1} \cdots M_{kn}$	M_{kF}	M_k
$k+1$	$O \cdots O$	$X_{k+1,k+1} \cdots X_{k+1,n}$	$X_{k+1,F}$	X_{k+1}
n	$O \cdots O$	$X_{n,k+1} \cdots X_{nn}$	X_{nF}	X_n
Value added	$O \cdots O$	$X_{V,k+1} \cdots X_{Vn}$	—	—
Total input	$O \cdots O$	$X_{k+1} \cdots X_n$	—	$X+M$

The first k columns of the matrix are filled with zeros because they correspond to the inputs of the first k activities which, in accordance with our assumption, have not as yet come into being within the country considered.

We are interested in the growth of the various import categories through time and in the consequences of their growth for capital formation. The imports M_1, $M_2 \ldots M_k$ are determined by specifying final demands; this gives us directly the final demand component of the M's (M_{1F}, $M_{2F} \ldots M_{kF}$), and indirectly, via the inverse matrix, the intermediate import demand components.

Suppose that we know in this way the growth of the M's through time, and that we know also for each M the domestic production threshold, i.e., the minimum economic size at which domestic production is undertaken. Let the outputs defining these thresholds be T_1, $T_2 \ldots T_k$, and the corresponding capital requirements K_1, $K_2 \ldots K_k$. At the beginning of the growth process all the M's are smaller than the corresponding T's. But with the growth in final demands, a point will come at which some M_j will be equal to or larger than T_j and thereupon the economy will make the investment K_j. In each period, induced capital formation is therefore equal to the sum of those K's for which this occurs. In this way, one can derive an induced investment pattern that is likely to exhibit strong ups and downs even on the assumption of a perfectly smooth path for the growth of demand.

It is conceivable that this model could be of considerable help in accounting for the sudden spurt of investment relative to income—Rostow's "take-off" point—that appears to characterize the growth process of a number of countries. On our assumptions, a sudden spurt could easily occur in newly industrializing countries. But once domestic production has been established in a large number of lines, capacity can be adjusted far more gradually to increasing output. Therefore, as the industrial base of a country expands, capital growth in response to gradual increases in final demands is likely to be steadier than in the early stages of a country's development.

Empirical studies designed to determine the probable capital requirements of an economy that would develop in accordance with the model just outlined could be of considerable interest. Such studies might permit us to discover certain typical oscillations of the investment impulses which underdeveloped countries are likely to receive along their growth path.

The model could conceivably be put to a different and more intriguing use. Instead of estimating how much capital formation is "triggered" when the final demands are rigidly specified in advance, we could think of influencing capital formation by modifying observable trends in the growth of final demands. For instance, we could wish to maximize backward linkage effects and the concomitant capital formation, and we would then want to manipulate final demands with this end in view. Such manipulation would, of course, have to remain subject to certain reasonable constraints such as:

1. that there is a ceiling for the annual rate of growth of total imports; in view of the assumption of fixed coefficients, this condition automatically places a ceiling on the growth rate of all domestic outputs into which imports enter at all;

2. that the departure of the *manipulated* final demands in either direction from the *expected* demands (i.e., those that would obtain without interference) are kept within certain boundaries.

Whether or not such a maximization problem can receive a general solution, some interference, through tariffs, excise taxes, and subsidies, with the developing consumption of a country may be justified if it can be demonstrated that a certain growth pattern of consumption would exert far more powerful backward linkage effects than the pattern that is likely to develop in the absence of interference. This holds even though one discards the unrealistic assumption that invest-

115

ments will necessarily and always be undertaken as soon as the threshold is passed. The important point remains that investment decisions are made much easier once this is the case.[15]

To give one example: the minimum size of an automobile body stamping plant varies sharply for different types of automobile. It is much higher for today's typical American car with its huge fenders that merge with the body than for automotive vehicles requiring smaller and simpler stampings. By fiscal policies that favor the latter type of vehicle a country may be able to advance by several years the point at which the establishment of a stamping plant within its territory becomes feasible and attractive to investors.

The rationale for interference with the market mechanism and consumers' preferences which we have just given is particularly strong in slow-moving economies where industrial growth is incipient. If, in such countries, capital formation can be called forth merely by rearranging and concentrating the pattern of imports, then such interference may often be deemed a price well worth paying for an increase in the country's pace of industrialization. In rapidly developing countries, on the other hand, where inflation is rampant, we may use our knowledge of these backward linkage effects for the opposite purpose: namely to ward off the bunching of investment demands that might occur at certain stages of the development process as a result of too many "thresholds" being crossed at the same time.

Combining Backward and Forward Linkage

Backward linkage effects are much neater than forward linkage effects. If it is rather daring to assume that a certain investment will take place as soon as domestic demand reaches the "threshold," it would be downright absurd to set up any model that would presume to indicate which kind of metal-fabricating industries would come into existence at what point of time in the wake of the establishment of a basic iron and steel industry. As was already indicated earlier in this chapter, forward linkage could never occur in pure form. It must always be accompanied by backward linkage, which is the result of the "pressure of demand." In other words, the existence or anticipation

15. Kafka has called attention to the related idea that the distribution of income will affect the pattern and timing of a country's industrialization; see "Some As-

of demand is a condition for forward linkage effects to manifest themselves.

While forward linkage cannot therefore be regarded as an independent inducement mechanism, it acts as an important and powerful reinforcement to backward linkage for the reasons listed earlier in this chapter. Investment decisions that are taken as a result of both backward and forward linkage are caught, as it were, in a pincer movement and must be prized by us since they are sure to be particularly easy-to-take ones.[16]

How are such pincer movements engineered in the course of economic development? They are somewhat difficult to visualize on the basis of the traditional concept of "stages of production" where the successive stages are farther and farther removed from final consumption. But this concept is unrealistic as has been shown by input-output analysis. Many industries produce intermediate goods for other industries and serve final demand at the same time. Thus it is quite possible for industry A to be established as a result of final demand for its products crossing the threshold, and then for B to follow suit not only because of demand factors but also because B intends to use A's products as a principal input. Such a development has a particularly dynamic quality because it necessitates an expansion of industry A, which was originally set up only in response to final demand and must now satisfy new industrial customers as well. In other words, while the existence of industry A helps to induce the establishment of industry B, this establishment in turn induces the building of new capacity for A.

This kind of *pincer cum feedback* effect can only be obtained with the help of industries that, in the triangularized matrix of interin-

---

pects of the Theoretical Interpretation of Latin-American Economic Development," paper given at the Rio Roundtable of the International Economic Association, 1957, p. 19 (mimeographed). For any one level of income there will always be commodities whose domestic production could be started, and others whose production would cease to be profitable, if the distribution of income were more equal, or more unequal, than it actually is. Theoretically, it is therefore possible to define, at any given level of income, a distribution of that income which maximizes backward linkage effects.

16. The approach toward the establishment of an industry through backward and forward linkage illustrates the similarity of economic development to a jigsaw puzzle—if a piece is surrounded from several sides, it is easier to fit it in. See p. 82.

dustry transactions, are located at some distance from the top rows. This means intermediate or "basic" industries whose products are distributed as inputs through many other industrial sectors besides also going directly to final demand. It is clear now that such industries should be given preference over the "last" industries, if they are at all economically feasible.

There are other reasons why the most "efficient" or "dynamic" way to work one's way through the triangularized matrix may not be by a gradual trickling down from the top. The ability of underdeveloped countries to start industrialization in this fashion by giving the "last touches" to imported materials is no doubt an advantage inasmuch as it permits industries to be started even in areas where markets are small and technical knowledge and organizational know-how are scarce. But it is also a disadvantage, for it builds up resistances for every new step in the trickling-down process. In dealing with backward linkage effects, we have thus far taken it almost for granted that as soon as domestic demand passes the threshold of minimum economic size, domestic production will be undertaken. But while some forces no doubt make for this course, counterforces are also at work. The industrialist who has worked hitherto with imported materials will often be hostile to the establishment of domestic industries producing these materials. First, he fears, often with good reason, that the domestic product will not be of as good and uniform quality as the imported one. Secondly, he feels that he might become dependent on a single domestic supplier when he could previously shop around the world. Thirdly, he is concerned about domestic competition becoming more active once the basic ingredients are produced within the country. Finally, his location may be wrong once the source of supply of the materials he uses is thoroughly altered.

For all these reasons, the interests of the converting, finishing, and mixing industries are often opposed to the establishment of domestic sources of supply for the products that they convert, finish, or mix. It takes a fairly violent shock—usually resulting from balance-of-payments or inflationary disturbances—to divert such industries from their defense of the status quo.

Therefore, excessive gradualism in introducing industry by successive small bits of value added may not pay off. Whereas the first steps are easy to take by themselves, they can make it difficult to take the next ones. An industrialization that proceeds in this way is a particularly quiet and uninspired affair, almost at the antipodes of Schumpeter's creative entrepreneur. The founding of a new industry in an advanced industrial country is always a job full of excitement and travail that brings with it new development stimuli in many directions: sources of supply for needed materials must be located or their production in accordance with new specifications must be organized; there is much experimenting with alternative techniques and layouts. When the same industry is set up twenty or thirty years later in an underdeveloped country, the operation in itself is already bound to be far less "exciting," since the technological problems are by then largely solved and the industry is past its phase of fastest technological progress. If, in addition, the industry is of the "enclave import" type, i.e., entirely based on converting imported materials, the national economy is deprived, at least at this stage, of the *unsettling* effects of industrialization that are so beneficial for further development. Borrowing a term from the theory of the multiplier, we may say that these imports of semifinished materials that are always ready to rush in from abroad whenever an industrial project is being considered are real *leakages* of development effects.

Certainly, but for the process of starting with the "last touches," many industries could never be undertaken at all in underdeveloped countries; once this is recognized, however, much is to be said for biting off *as large pieces of value added at a time* as the underdeveloped country can possibly digest.

CHAPTER 7

Industrialization: Further Characteristic Aspects

The Role of Imports in Inducing Industrial Development

THE PRECEDING analysis helps to throw some new light on the relationship between foreign trade, particularly imports, and economic development.

Imports play a dual role in the course of development. First, as we shall see, they bring with them powerful development stimuli. And yet this creative role is being performed in a manner worthy of ancient tragedy: once the stimuli have become sufficiently strong to result in effective development moves, the specific commodity flows from which they emanated in the first place are destined to wither and die. No wonder that modern commodity flows do not enjoy being tragic heroes: they fight for survival, and, having called forth development stimuli, attempt to block their fruition in what is usually a losing battle. Hence the dual character of imports. The latter, obstructionist role has received far more attention on the part of underdeveloped countries than the former, and an indiscriminate protectionist policy has usually resulted. For this reason, I shall stress here the positive contribution of imports to development; it needs to be fully understood if economic and commercial policies are to be effectively shaped to promote development.

In the course of the discussion of backward linkage effects, the role of imports in slowly paving the way for domestic production as the domestic production threshold is being approached has already been brought out. The matter can be put quite simply. One of the real difficulties of development is lack of knowledge of, and uncertainty about, the market.[1] This uncertainty is often compounded by disbelief of the local capitalists and entrepreneurs in the potentialities of the

1. See Aubrey, "Investment Decisions in Underdeveloped Countries" in *Capital Formation and Economic Growth* (Princeton, 1955), pp. 397–440.

domestic market. The upper classes always tend to think that the poor are perfectly happy that way, that they have limited wants, that they would not really know what to do with additional income except possibly spend it on alcohol. Naturally such an appraisal of one's countrymen's consumption aspirations is not likely to be a spur to investment activity. It still leaves the door open for the setting up of industries that replace essential mass consumption goods turned out by handicraft methods, but as will be seen later in this chapter such investments are perhaps none too plentiful aside from textiles, and none too certain in outcome. In fact it is the difficulty of this situation that has led some economists to the theory of balanced growth which, as we have seen, gives up the existing economy of the underdeveloped country as hopeless and proposes to set up a new self-contained economy next to it.

Although there is no need for all this despondency, domestic investors often feel that they must see to believe the unbelievable. Some of them have learned by this time to look abroad and to infer from foreign experience where new ventures can be successfully started. But imports still provide the safest, most incontrovertible proof that the market is there. Moreover, they condition the consumer to the product, breaking down his initial resistance. Imports thus reconnoiter and map out the country's demand; they remove uncertainty and reduce selling costs at the same time, thereby bringing perceptibly closer the point at which domestic production can economically be started.[1a] This point is of course again determined by the minimum size of plant, as well as by cost and location factors that jointly define the "domestic production threshold."

The process is strongly reminiscent of the ancient tale in which an ogre diligently feeds his victims and eats them one by one as they reach an appetizing degree of fatness. The ogre is usually thwarted at some point and the hero is saved, through his cunning or through divine intervention. For instance, in the Hansel and Gretel variant, the children fatten well enough on the candy of the house, but trick

1a. At times this mechanism is in evidence even in the industrial countries. A recent example is the reported decision of the major United States producers of automotive vehicles to enter the small car field, in the wake of the successes achieved by Europe's small car manufacturers in discovering and developing a sizable demand in this country. (Cf. *New York Times,* March 9, 1958.)

the witch who keeps them prisoners by making her feel thin wooden sticks instead of their fingers, thus managing continually to flunk the fatness test.

In our tale, the victims are the various commodity imports of a developing country, and this country plays the role of the ogre since it "swallows" these imports one by one as the volume passes our domestic production threshold. With all countries keeping foreign trade statistics, the imports can hardly hope to save themselves by *pretending*, in Hansel and Gretel fashion, that they are lean when in reality they are fat. Therefore, the imports of manufactures that are most likely not to be replaced by domestic production are those that remain in fact small (relative to the domestic production threshold).

The gradual swallowing up of manufactured imports is certainly everyday experience in developing countries. The defenders of traditional international trade theory lament it because they view it as a loss of real income caused by interferences with the price mechanism. The protectionists and advocates of industrialization are delighted by it because they see in it liberation from exploitation by the industrial countries. But both parties have failed to see the connection between the two phases, i.e., the manner in which the growth of imports induces domestic production.

Traditional theory could hardly be expected to see a connection that could also be formulated as follows: countries tend to develop a comparative advantage in the articles they *import*. This paradox is of course largely a play on words, since "comparative advantage" refers here not to the usual comparison between the actual production processes of various commodities as carried on in different countries but to the choice which a country makes in starting to produce one commodity rather than another. Nevertheless, our reasoning has some new implications for international trade theory. It has long been recognized that the basis of the international division of labor is constantly changing, and that therefore new commodity flows will always emerge. But we are now going a little farther than that. We affirm that trade flows themselves play an important role in inducing these shifts: if a country does not produce commodities A and B and if it is importing A in more rapidly increasing volume than B, then it is likely to undertake domestic production of A long before that of B and is acting quite rationally in doing so. This does not merely mean that the international division of labor will change by the emergence of new tastes and techniques. More radically we find that changes are bound to occur even with constant tastes and techniques and that the chances of survival of any given commodity flow toward underdeveloped but developing countries are inversely proportional to its current rate of expansion.

This conclusion follows easily once we assume the existence of unemployed resources of labor and capital in underdeveloped countries and recognize imports as the catalytic agent that will bring some of these resources together for the purpose of exploiting the opportunities they have revealed.

At the beginning of the twentieth century, when it first became clear that industrialization was not necessarily going to be confined to a few Western countries, a German economist asked worriedly: "Is export of machinery economic suicide?" [2] To the extent that the establishment of industries in underdeveloped countries is considered lethal for the older industrial countries, this question did not really go to the heart of the matter. For, as we see now, the "suicide" is already in the making while the industrial countries are still gaily and profitably exporting finished consumer goods, and exports of machinery represent just the final pulling of the trigger. Actually it would be more correct to compare the exporting of certain manufactures to the imparting of a lesson which is finally learnt as home production is started in the heretofore importing country: when a tutor has successfully accomplished his job, and has as a result made it possible for the pupil to dispense with him in a particular subject, we do not consider that he has committed suicide.

The advocates of protection and industrialization have also been reluctant to notice the connection between imports and industrialization. They were probably far too intent on blaming imports for the economic backwardness of their countries to recognize that imports fulfill the very important function of demand formation and demand reconnaissance for the country's entrepreneurs. As a result underdeveloped countries, always ardently protectionist, have often adopted a policy that is self-defeating from the point of view of their avowed

2. Karl Dietzel, *Ist Maschinenausfuhr wirtschaftlicher Selbstmord?* Berlin, 1907. For a review of these early fears, see my *National Power and the Structure of Foreign Trade* (Berkeley, 1945), pp. 146 ff.

objective: by restricting imports too severely, they have been shutting out the awakening and inducing effects which imports have on industrialization.

If our analysis is correct, then an economic policy designed to encourage industrialization ought to be one thing after new domestic industry has come into being and quite another before the infant has been born. During this *prenatal*[3] stage, the opposite of the infant industry treatment is called for if the confinement is to be accelerated. In fact, if it is desired to prepare the ground for the creation of a particular industry, then it might be advisable to restrict *other* imports so as to channel import demand artificially toward the commodity whose eventual domestic production is to be fostered.

The essential conclusion for commercial policy is that infant industry protection should not be given *before* the industry has been established but should become available, if at all, only once this event has taken place. A particularly apt instrument of this kind of conditional protection is the granting of tax privileges to new industries. It is also possible to design tariffs in such a way that they enter into force only upon the foundation of industrial establishments that supply a certain minimum percentage of domestic demand for the to-be-protected items, but this is obviously a comparatively clumsy device.

Another corollary of which the spokesmen for underdeveloped countries are often insufficiently aware is the strategic role played by exports in economic development. Economic policy of underdeveloped countries often treats exports like a stepchild, either because foreign interests are involved in the production of export commodities under "enclave" conditions or for revenue reasons. If it is grudgingly recognized that exports are essential for the financing of imports, then reference is usually made to the imports of raw materials, machinery, and equipment needed to support productive activities and investments that are already under way. The importance of imports in creating and mapping demands and in paving the way for the *next* development move is usually disregarded and thus leads to an underestimate of the crucial contribution of exports. In other words, there is no real alternative between export promotion and import substitution. The former may often be the only practical way of achieving the latter.

We have stressed here the "creative" role imports can play in the

3. This term was suggested to me by Alexander Gerschenkron.

development process, a role that has been almost entirely overlooked. As we said at the beginning of this chapter, imports play this role *malgré eux* and while they prepare the terrain for domestic production they also resist its coming. They create powerful commercial interests bent on perpetuating so highly profitable a business. At the same time, loyalties toward the foreign articles arise among the consuming public, which in most underdeveloped countries is affected by "domophobia," i.e., by a mistrust and disbelief in the quality of domestic as compared to foreign products.[4] Also, banks become used to extending credit primarily for the comparatively short-term financing needs of the import trade. Finally, the countries where the imports originate may exert political or economic pressures so as to prevent or retard the loss of valuable markets.[5] Protectionists have long been busy pointing out and fighting against these and other obstacles to industrialization. These obstructionist forces exist even though their strength is easily overestimated because they are identified with vocal interest groups and existing action patterns—in short, with the status quo. But they certainly are able to engage in protracted rearguard fights.

In fine, the process by which imports induce domestic production cannot be expected to be perfectly smooth. The kinds of disturbance that may sometimes be required to help the process along are discussed in Chapter 9.

The Reason for Dualistic Development

By bringing out the role of imports in inducing new industries, and by underlining, in the previous chapter, the importance of backward linkage, we have examined two characteristic features of the contemporary industrialization process. A third feature, closely related to the other two, is the prolonged coexistence and cohabitation of modern industry and of preindustrial, sometimes neolithic, techniques. It is often said that the underdeveloped but developing countries are apt to pass from the mule to the airplane in one generation. But a

---

4. To the extent that this is a purely irrational attitude, the imposition of corrective fiscal devices would be justified. See G. Haberler, *The Theory of International Trade* (New York, 1936), p. 283.

5. See my "Effects of Industrialization on the Markets of Industrial Countries" in *The Progress of Underdeveloped Areas*, pp. 270–83.

closer look at most of these countries reveals that they are, and appear to remain for a long time, in a situation where *both airplane and mule* fulfill essential economic functions. This "dualistic" character of developing countries is to be noted not only with respect to methods of production and distribution; it exists also in attitudes and in ways of living and doing business. Lewis describes it well:

> We find a few industries highly capitalised, such as mining or electric power, side by side with the most primitive techniques; a few high class shops, surrounded by masses of old style traders; a few highly capitalised plantations, surrounded by a sea of peasants. But we find the same contrasts also outside economic life. There are one or two modern towns, with the finest architecture, water supplies, communications and the like, into which people drift from other towns and villages which might almost belong to another planet. There is the same contrast even between people; between the few highly westernised, trousered, natives, educated in western universities, speaking western languages, and glorying in Beethoven, Mill, Marx or Einstein, and the great mass of their countrymen who live in quite other worlds.[6]

In part, dualism results of course from the sudden irruption of twentieth-century techniques into primitive societies which can adapt only gradually. But there is reason to believe that certain preindustrial economic activities have today a far better chance to survive than was the case during the rise of industry in Western Europe. The forces of industrialization tend at present, far more than formerly, to *leave the preindustrial sectors alone* for a prolonged period rather than attacking them frontally. We shall now explore the reasons for this tendency.

Probably one of the principal economic characteristics of any country where industrial development is incipient and spotty is the existence of two distinct wage levels, one applicable to the industrial sector and the other to the preindustrial sectors. The latter comprise most

6. "Economic Development with Unlimited Supplies of Labour," p. 147. For a general discussion of the concept of dualistic development, see J. H. Boeke, *Economics and Economic Policy of Dual Societies,* New York, 1953; the criticism by B. Higgins, "The Dualistic Theory of Underdeveloped Areas"; and J. M. van der Kroef, "Economic Development in Indonesia: Some Social and Cultural Impediments," who in turn criticizes some of the points made by Higgins; both articles are in *Economic Development and Cultural Change, 4* (Jan. 1956).

of agriculture, trade, and services (except banks and insurance companies) as well as handicraft and small-scale industry.

With mobility far from perfect, the dual wage level reflects different marginal productivities of labor in the modern and preindustrial sectors of the economy, but it is also explained by social security and minimum wage legislation which is usually enforced and enforceable only in the larger industrial units, by the high cost of living (particularly of housing) in the growing industrial cities, and by persistent preferences for the traditional and more independent pursuits in agriculture, small trade, and small industry.

While labor is cheaper in the underdeveloped sector of the economy, capital is typically more expensive, also for a variety of reasons: access to the banks is difficult and interest charges are much higher; machinery, equipment, and tools are bought at retail rather than imported directly from the foreign manufacturer at important savings, etc.

To illustrate what happens to industrial development in countries under these conditions, a familiar diagrammatic technique may be employed.[7]

In Figure 5 the ordinate measures capital, and the abscissa labor input, both in physical units. We assume two distinct wage and capital cost levels and therefore the expenditures corresponding to identical labor and capital inputs are different in the industrial and preindustrial sectors. For the purpose of the argument, it is supposed that one homogeneous good is to be produced and that two processes are available, the industrial one which is comparatively capital-intensive and necessarily uses "expensive" labor and "cheap" capital, with the expansion path OA, and the labor-intensive preindustrial process which uses "cheap" labor and "expensive" capital and is shown by the expansion path OB. We shall now draw a constant-expenditure line for different combinations of labor and capital reflecting the dualistic situation we are describing. Let DC be such a line for the industrial processes and sectors. If labor and capital costs in the preindustrial sectors are 50% and 150%, respectively, of what they are in the industrial ones, then we derive a corresponding constant-expenditure

7. For recent applications to related problems, cf. R. S. Eckaus, "Factor Proportions in Underdeveloped Areas," *American Economic Review*, 45 (Sept. 1955), 539–65.

line *RE* for the preindustrial processes by making *CE* equal to *OC* and *OR* equal to twice the length of *RD*.

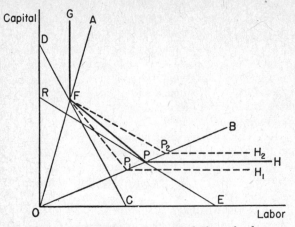

Fig. 5. Choice of technology with dual cost levels

On these assumptions, any combination of labor and capital shown by points on lines *DC* and *RE* requires the same expenditure, it being understood that line *DC* refers to industrial and line *RE* to preindustrial conditions. If the industrial process is used, it is possible to produce with this expenditure the quantity of output corresponding to *OF*, and the same expenditure yields the output corresponding to *OP* in case the preindustrial process is used. Now, if production *OF* happens to be equal to production *OP*, in other words if the constant-product line is represented by *GFPH*, it is a matter of indifference whether the commodity in question is produced by one process or the other. If, on the other hand, the constant-product line going through *F* is correctly shown by GFP_1H_1, the preindustrial process is less expensive and will be adopted. On the other hand, if the constant-product line is GFP_2H_2, then the labor-intensive process is more expensive for the same output than the industrial process and the latter will be used.

Of course, the neatness with which the diagram shows under what conditions the industrial process can or cannot compete with the preindustrial one is blurred in the real world. As the preindustrial wage is ordinarily implicit, and as operators in this area will take considerable squeezing of their earnings before they actually stop production, the potential investor in modern industrial processes is not confronted with a point such as P against which he must successfully compete, but with a range of such points along the OB line. He must therefore be sure that he can compete with the preindustrial operators not only on the basis of present prices but even on the basis of prices that may be considerably lower.

In some industries, the ability of modern techniques to emerge victorious from the competitive struggle is not subject to any doubt. The classical example here is, of course, the textile industry, particularly spinning.

But there are a number of sectors in which the appearance of advanced industrial methods is seriously handicapped by the possibility of competition from independent, small-scale producers. Examples that come to mind are the manufacture of furniture, shoes, apparel, bricks, ceramics, cigars (as opposed to cigarettes), baskets (holding back the development of modern forms of wrapping, bagging, and packaging), some metalworking, as well as large parts of the food-processing and construction industries. Most services, in particular retailing, are also in this category. In truck and bus transportation, the dual wage situation and the relatively small size of the needed capital investment make for organization along traditional small-business lines in preference to modern large-scale operations, and consequently the service provided retains a distinctly preindustrial flavor in spite of the modern equipment used.

Now all these activities stand today a fairly good chance of being "left alone" for a considerable length of time because there exists a *third* category of investment outlets: namely industrial processes which are entirely outside the technological and capital capabilities of the local handicraft and small workshop industries. These are the processes characteristic, for instance, of chemicals, petroleum refining, basic iron and steel, cement, pulp and paper, but also of many modern consumer goods, from radios and light bulbs to toothpaste and aspirin.

With respect to this pattern of industrialization, today's underdeveloped countries enjoy a definite advantage over nations where modern manufacturing first developed. In the latter nations, as is well known, the industrial revolution introduced fundamental technological innovations into iron, textile, and pottery manufacturing, with immediate adverse impacts on the well-diversified handicraft and small-scale industries that had previously supplied these products.[8] In today's underdeveloped countries, on the other hand, industrial progress can concentrate on a wide range of useful and desirable products that are entirely new to the economy. As a result, the traditional handicraft and cottage industries are given a valuable respite which can be utilized to improve the efficiency of their operations and the quality of their output.

It must be understood that if this opportunity is not taken advantage of, industrial methods will eventually infringe upon the handicraft sector. As the economy grows in size, industrial methods will reveal themselves superior to the preindustrial ones in more and more areas, in spite of the dual-wage situation. But the absence of sharp competition by modern industry during the first stages of development should make it possible to save a strong handicraft and small workshop tradition where it exists. It is well known that small and inexpensive additions of capital equipment, made available at easy credit terms and combined with technical education and cooperative marketing, may considerably improve the performance of these industries.[9] By providing them with a new margin of protection against encroachment by big industry, successful efforts in this direction would also make it possible progressively to reduce the wage gap. Clearly, this is a more promising approach than the always futile attempt to freeze existing situations through legislative action. For many countries, this approach also seems wiser, and may be more efficient in setting the stage for unified development, than a policy of letting "nature take its course," i.e., passive resignation to the squeeze of many old trades and skills which so obstinately refuse to die.

The preference of investors in developing countries for new-product industries throws some light on the problem of the appropriate degree of capital-intensity of new ventures in these countries. Much attention has been given by economists—though not much yet by engineers—to the question of adapting modern technology to countries where

8. Cf., e.g., J. L. and B. Hammond, *The Rise of Modern Industry* (London, 1937), Pt. II.

9. Cf. Aubrey, "Small Industry in Economic Development." For encouraging evidence from Indonesia, see K. Nagaraja Rao, "Small Scale Industry and Economic Development in Indonesia," *Economic Development and Cultural Change, 4* (Jan. 1956), 159–70.

labor is cheap and plentiful and where the introduction of certain labor-saving (as opposed to capital-saving or product-improving) innovations may not be justified. While the search for evidence of such adaptation apparently has been somewhat disappointing, it would be wrong to conclude that differences in factor endowments and costs relative to those of industrial countries are not exerting profound effects on the pattern of development in underdeveloped countries. But these differences are perhaps more importantly reflected in the outright *absence* of modern methods from a number of branches of commerce and industry than in the always difficult transformation of technical processes in those branches into which modern industry is selectively moving.[10]

In this sense, our analysis accounts, along orthodox lines of economic efficiency, for the priority that underdeveloped countries are frequently found to give to capital-intensive industries with a highly advanced and complicated technology.[11] It would probably be wasteful for such an economy to invest its scarce capital resources in duplicating lines of production that are already being carried on, even though inefficiently. A better use for capital would almost certainly be in the establishment of new-product industries. But in such industries capital-output ratios are likely to be typically high whereas they tend to be comparatively low in industries that would produce goods and services similar to those turned out by existing small-scale operators.

In other words, the most efficient use of capital in underdeveloped countries is not in capital-intensive industries *qua* capital-intensive; it is in industries that open new product horizons for the economy and these industries are likely to be more capital-intensive than others with which the country can dispense for the time being because the needs served by them are satisfied by existing handicraft and cottage industries. Therefore, what looks like a puzzling preference for capital intensity on the part of capital-poor countries in effect turns out to be the incidental result of a perfectly commonsense way of husbanding capital.[12]

10. See, however, p. 152, n. 25.
11. See Ch. 8 for an entirely different line of reasoning that leads to the same conclusion.
12. Spengler has shown that product-adding innovations will ordinarily result in enlarging the supply of effort more than product-replacing innovations. See his

Thus, while dualism no doubt brings with it many social and psychological stresses, it has some compensating advantages and represents in a way an attempt by the economy of an underdeveloped country to make the best of its resources during a transitional phase. While developing countries may be anxious to put this phase behind them, they ought to realize that in doing so they need not necessarily follow the path of those nations that industrialized in an earlier period.

"Product-Adding vs. Product-Replacing Innovations," pp. 249–80. The introduction of product-adding innovations in the pioneering industrial countries is of course equivalent in underdeveloped countries to the establishment of new-product industries. Spengler's analysis reinforces our argument: in comparing the social productivity of an industry whose output is to replace existing handicraft products with that of a new-product industry, it would be wrong to focus only on the comparative capital intensity of the two industries. Account should be taken of the fact that the former industry will replace existing economic activities whereas the new-product industry may represent, to a considerable extent, a net addition. Thus even though the capital-output ratio of the product-replacing industry considered by itself is lower than that of the new-product industry, the net social productivity of capital may be higher in the latter.

CHAPTER 8

Efficiency and Growth of the Individual Firm

The Need for Built-In Spurs

THE PRECEDING chapters explored the ways in which economic progress is communicated by one sector, one industry, or one firm to another. By thus judging the developmental merit of a project in terms of the likelihood that it will induce a series of other ventures, we have taken it for granted that the project itself is "here to stay." This assumption will be dropped in the present chapter, in which we will inquire into some of the conditions under which new ventures, once established, may be expected to prosper as efficient and dynamic units of the economic system. We are still searching for inducement mechanisms: but instead of gauging the probability that project A will call forth project B, we will now be concerned with the manner in which the growth of a given project becomes "self-induced," i.e., with its own development path.[1]

In any underdeveloped country one can always hear many a—duly embroidered—tale about ventures that were so hastily undertaken and so badly planned that they had to be written off as a total loss while still under construction or shortly thereafter. But more demoralizing even than such obvious failures is the spectacle of enterprises that, after a hopeful start, have stagnated and deteriorated. Examples of such deterioration are always at hand: the pasteurizing plant whose milk one is strongly recommended to boil thoroughly before drinking; the first-class hotel that three months after a triumphant opening has become third-rate; the "supermarket" which slowly

1. The terms "project," "firm," "venture," "enterprise" are used interchangeably in this chapter. We are thinking not only of private industrial or commercial firms, but of any economic unit which enjoys a considerable degree of autonomy, whether it is publicly or privately owned and managed.

takes on again the familiar aspects of the much decried open-air affairs.[2]

The difficulties commonly experienced by new enterprises in underdeveloped countries have often been noted and so has the adverse effect of disappointments and miscarriages on entrepreneurial expectations and therefore on further development. However, Western observers, having diagnosed the disorder, have usually not bothered about ways and means of improving the performance of individual ventures from within, but have looked for efficiency-inducing and survival-guaranteeing pressures from without.

This is in fact what we have done ourselves thus far. We could argue that all that is needed to ensure the success of any venture is for it to represent a link in one of our development sequences. It is clear that the projects that are best at calling forth other ventures are also those that are most likely to do well themselves. Paradoxically, a road that is not traveled is likely to deteriorate sooner than one that has to support heavy traffic: the former will surely be neglected whereas there is some hope that the latter will be maintained. Similarly, once an industry causes other industries to be established through forward or backward linkage, it will be needed by these industries as a supplier or a market and its chances of survival and continuous expansion will be better than before.

That growth *around* a venture creates favorable conditions for the health and growth of that venture can hardly be doubted. But if we let

2. The present-day interest in economic development has led economic historians to re-examine the early stages of the industrialization process in Western Europe. In such studies the usual focus is on identifying key factors responsible for this unique instance of successful development. But actually industrialization proceeds in many countries today whether or not they are endowed with all of the factors, attitudes, and beliefs found to have been present in, say, eighteenth-century England. Therefore, historical studies of the conditions under which efforts at industrialization have turned out to be abortive may yield more valuable lessons. The attempts by Muhammad Ali to implant textile and other industries in Egypt during his reign (1805–49) would seem to be an excellent instance. For some intriguing data on this episode, see David S. Landes, "Bankers and Pashas" in *Men in Business,* ed. William Miller (Cambridge, Mass., 1952), pp. 23–70; Moustafa Fahmy, *La Révolution de l'industrie en Egypte et ses conséquences sociales au 19ᵉ siècle* (1800–1850), Leiden, 1954; and particularly Helen Anne B. Rivlin, *The Agricultural Policy of Muhammad Ali in Egypt* (to be published), ch. 7.

things go at that we would limit ourselves to one side of a two-way relationship. The successful performance of an individual venture is needed for the launching of complementary projects just as much as the coming into existence of the latter is healthy for the original venture. Moreover, in underdeveloped countries a venture may have to live as a lonely outpost for a considerable time before it is joined by others through linkage effects. And even after it has been joined, it remains severely exposed to the investment-corroding forces which we mentioned earlier [3] and whose action must now be more fully understood and taken into account.

Any attempt at solving the difficulties of new ventures in underdeveloped countries entirely through pressures from without must appeal to some progressive influence that is supposed to be already at work in the society where the venture operates. But this procedure means that the difficulties with which we are concerned are assumed away rather than solved. A striking instance of this procedure is, as we have seen, the balanced growth theory, which holds that a venture will be successful if it comes into the world as a member of a complex of firms lending each other mutual, complementary support.

A similar criticism must be made of the usefulness in underdeveloped economies of the, in a sense, opposite mechanism that is frequently relied on for "placing the managers . . . under the proper pressures to perform for society": [4] competition. In developed industrial countries competition, actual or potential, is no doubt powerfully conducive to keeping firms efficient and progressive. But in urging underdeveloped countries to rely on this mechanism, we would again assume away some of the most typical difficulties they face and give them the unrealistic advice to jump over an important stage in their growth —the stage where in many lines the market cannot support more than one firm, where regional monopolies abound because of poor transportation facilities, and where collusive agreements or strongly entrenched custom hold back the emergence of genuinely competitive marketing.

Thus, complementary and competitive relationships with other firms cannot be relied on exclusively or even primarily to set up ef-

3. See Ch. 2.
4. Clark Kerr, "Productivity and Labor Relations," Reprint No. 96, Institute of Industrial Relations (Berkeley, 1957), p. 8.

fective pressures to perform for the individual firm. Such pressures must also be generated within the firm itself. To understand how this may be achieved it is necessary to review the typical shortcomings that undermine the efficient functioning of many firms in underdeveloped countries. A list of such shortcomings, which is meant to be purely illustrative, would contain the following items:

1. Absence of a sufficiently vigorous "growth mentality," reflected in:
   a. failure to plow back profits adequately, tendency toward "milking" firms;
   b. failure to keep up with technological progress abroad;
   c. preference for a stagnating enterprise that stays "within the family" over expansion that is bought at the cost of partial surrender of control.

2. Difficulties in administration, management, and "human relations," shown in such symptoms as:
   a. excessive centralization of decision-making and inability or unwillingness to delegate authority;
   b. ineffective staff work and coordination;
   c. failure to pay adequate salaries to key personnel in spite of high turnover and recognized scarcity;
   d. failure to impart to subordinates a feeling of participation and spirit of initiative;
   e. neglect of personnel relations and morale;
   f. neglect of public relations.

3. Difficulties in carrying out functions not directly connected with the central production process, evidenced in:
   a. defective advance planning (engineering studies, market research, provision for finance);
   b. defective cost accounting and control in general;
   c. defective maintenance.[5]

5. For some evidence on these points, see U. N. Economic Commission for Latin America, *Labour Productivity of the Cotton Textile Industry in Five Latin American Countries*, New York, 1951; S. D. Mehta, *The Indian Cotton Textile Industry: An Economic Analysis* (Bombay, 1953), pp. 72–85; F. H. Harbison and I. A. Ibrahim, "Some Labor Problems of Industrialization in Egypt," *Annals of the American Academy of Political and Social Science* (Philadelphia, 1956), pp. 114–24. Naturally, these shortcomings can also be found in advanced industrial countries. It is merely suggested here that their relative importance is greater in underdeveloped countries.

These deficiencies can be accounted for in several ways. In part, they are of course due to inexperience in the management of large-scale organizations. But one wonders if this is all, in view of the persistence of some of these traits. Several among them (e.g., 1a, 1c, 2a, and 2b) are directly related to the analysis of the development process which was proposed in the first chapter. The difficulties in cooperative decision-making which derive from an exclusively ego-focused image of change, and which were shown to be a major obstacle to development, do of course affect the day-to-day administration of existing firms and ventures as much as, if not more than, their actual promotion. The lack of a vigorous growth mentality and of effective staff work and personnel relations can be viewed as natural concomitants of a management whose principal members do not yet quite believe in the possibility of mutual gains—nonzero sums—in social and economic "games."

In the second place, the pattern of values and attitudes with which underdeveloped countries set out today on the path to modernization and industrialization is probably less suited to the successful accomplishment of these tasks than the pattern which prevailed in Western Europe at the beginning of the Industrial Revolution. Without stirring up the old dispute about the primacy of beliefs and attitudes, it will perhaps be granted that certain values and institutionalized behavior patterns that are conducive to successful development such as Max Weber's rationality and discipline, or Parsons' universalism and functional specificity,[6] or McClelland's achievement motivation[7] must be induced in most of today's underdeveloped countries by the process of development itself, whereas it can be argued that in some Western European countries and the United States these behavior patterns were already strongly entrenched before the start of the process.

Finally, we have the special problems of the latecomers. Derived

6. Talcott Parsons, "The Professions and Social Structure," *Essays in Sociological Theory Pure and Applied* (Glencoe, Ill., 1950), pp. 185–99; for an application of these categories to development problems, see Marion J. Levy, "Some Sources of the Vulnerability of the Structures of Relatively Nonindustrialized Societies to those of Highly Industrialized Societies" in *The Progress of Underdeveloped Areas*, pp. 113–25.

7. See Ch. 1, n. 3.

development, as Wallich has called it,[8] is less inspiring a task than it was in the pioneering countries or in those that came later but strained to overtake the pioneers in the shortest possible time. Such ambitions are beyond the horizon of most of today's latecomers. All they can do is tread ploddingly a trail that others have blazed long ago. Moreover, industries are usually established only when their technology has already settled down, and, as we have seen, they are often based on the importation not only of all of the equipment, but also of many semifinished materials and parts, so that the entrepreneurial function of combining production factors appears to be a comparatively routine one. In fact, the task of adaptation always remains, but is often underestimated just because everything *appears* to be so cut and dried. This is one of the reasons why new ventures are often undertaken without adequate planning and attention to specific environmental factors.

It is even possible that derived development is exposed to some additional, subtle obstacles of a psychological nature. While overtly considerable effort is made in a country to introduce modern methods and techniques, a vague resentment may yet exist at the same time against the new ways, a secret hope that the equipment or the methods will not work out in "our milieu"; and these feelings may well lead to actions that will bring about the unconsciously desired result, namely the breakdown of the newly introduced techniques. Anthropologists have noted the phenomenon of "defensive ignorance" or of "rejection pattern" practised by certain communities that are actively warding off foreign influences.[9] Here we are concerned with a subsequent stage in which ostensibly the new techniques are brought in with eager enthusiasm. But in actuality an *ambivalent* attitude prevails: one expects miracles and at the same time one hopes they won't happen, so that one may say, with a sense of relief: "These foreign contraptions are no good after all." This attitude is most obvious with respect to technical assistance programs. The excessive enthusiasm with which

8. H. C. Wallich, "Notes toward a Theory of Derived Development," paper prepared for the Havana Meeting of Central Bank Technicians, 1952, to be published in *The Economics of Underdeveloped Countries,* ed. Indian Institute of Economic and Social Research, Allahabad.

9. Wolf, "Types of Latin American Peasantry," p. 459; and Ralph Beals, "Notes on Acculturation" in *Heritage of Conquest,* p. 229.

foreign missions and experts are greeted at their arrival in a country is part of this ambivalent pattern: when unreasonable expectations are raised about the possible accomplishments of a mission, the letdown and disappointment which one also hopes for are virtually guaranteed to follow. In effect, instead of a rejection pattern we have here one of acceptance qualified by (unconscious) sabotage. In the case of modern machinery and equipment, it may account for the defective maintenance, for the inadequate efforts to train and retain skilled mechanics to serve the machines, and even for the neglect of the nontechnical aspects of production. For here again there is a tendency vastly to exaggerate the perfection and self-sufficiency of the machine and to overrate the extent to which it solves all production problems —an attitude that leads to many a breakdown.[10]

It turns out that the difficulties besetting the proper functioning of new enterprises are the same as those that affect their promotion, *plus a few more.* Therefore we have met with a new kind of imbalance likely to arise in underdeveloped countries: at a certain stage of their growth, the ability to *promote* new ventures may outstrip the ability to *run* them efficiently. Herein lies a further justification for undertaking a careful search for mechanisms that will induce efficiency and growth within the new ventures and which will help to minimize and, through learning processes, eradicate the failings that have been noted.

The Maintenance Problem and a Suggested Solution

Up to now we have insisted on certain handicaps of the latecomers; but there are compensating advantages. Even though they are constrained by the availability of natural resources, by the narrowness of their domestic market, and by the techniques developed in the advanced countries, today's developing countries can choose from a far

10. Psychoanalysis has shown how a situation of ambivalence is characterized by (a) reaction formation, i.e., the fact of showing and feeling consciously the opposite of what is repressed and felt unconsciously, and (b) the return of repressed hostility in some, usually disguised, form with the aim of bringing about the defeat or destruction of the object of ambivalence. The attitude here described— exaggerated enthusiasm and the raising of excessive expectations—realizes both these phenomena jointly, as though to kill two birds with one stone. I am indebted to Dr. Samuel P. Hunt for discussing this matter with me.

wider variety of ventures and techniques than could the industrial nations. In part it has been this situation that has given rise to the search for *investment criteria*. The discussion started out with the hope of producing a workable formula for development planners anxious to know which of the various projects should be selected. But, as was already indicated, such hopes were soon to be dashed as the subject became increasingly complex with every new contribution.

Fortunately we are able to sidestep this discussion. Maximization of output is for us a final outcome of successful development rather than a proximate objective; and the criteria we are now looking for are those that will permit us to judge new ventures, products, and processes in terms of their probable contribution to "self-inducement."

The most obvious, but also the most platitudinous advice to give to underdeveloped countries in this connection is to pick only projects whose output is assured of a rapidly growing market. Certainly, the increase in demand is a powerful energizing influence that creates a growth mentality even when there was none in existence to begin with and that places strong pressures on managers to improve the organization of the production process. The expansion of demand leads to growth of the enterprise and thus provides an element of "excitement" and opportunities of advancement for all personnel. Finally, it may also cause competition to appear and would thereby provide a further stimulus to performance.

But actually it is clear that this criterion sins against the rule which we had set ourselves in the last section, namely, that our self-inducement mechanisms, to be genuine, must not appeal to progressive forces that act on the firm from the outside and thereby make everything easy. This is exactly what we have done by assuming the existence of a strong and growing demand somewhere. The kind of question we are interested in here is rather: given potential demand of equal strength in several lines, which kind of undertaking will be best able to elicit this demand and develop it further through the quality of its product, the shrewdness of its distribution and publicity, and in general the excellence of its management? More generally, given the difficulties already discussed, *what are the kinds of jobs underdeveloped countries are likely to be particularly good (or bad) at?*

We shall use induction in attempting to answer this question and

look closely first at one of the difficulties: the lack of proper maintenance. This is perhaps one of the most characteristic failings of underdeveloped countries and one that is spread over the whole economic
landscape. Eroding soils, stalled trucks, leaking roofs, prematurely
run-down machines, unsafe bridges, clogged-up irrigation ditches—
all testify to the same pervasive and paradoxical trait: the inadequate
care for existing capital in capital-poor countries.

The basic difficulty about maintenance of capital—as opposed to
operation on the one hand and to repair on the other—is that it is a
preventive activity which must be performed at fairly long intervals
that are neither known with precision nor signaled by the capital
itself. In primitive societies the need for imparting temporal precision
to tasks that by nature are postponable within rather wide limits is
often satisfied through ritual. Thus, the beginning and end of the
principal phases of the agricultural work cycle are ceremoniously
ordered and routinized by means of seasonal festivals, "first-furrow"
ceremonies, and the like.[11] For maintenance to be effective, people
must be similarly made to act *as though* it had to be undertaken at
precise intervals, suppressing their better knowledge that deferment
by a day, a week, or a month may not matter; they must organize this
fiction, submit to it, and set up a signaling system to enforce it. In
other words, maintenance is predominantly an administrative process
if we so define an activity whose performance is not directly invited or
compelled by the production process or the product itself, and as
such it requires an especially high degree of organizational ability.

Once maintenance is recognized as a special problem, the most
obvious course would be to undertake only projects which do not
require it. This seems to have been indeed a preferred solution of the
great architects and engineers of the past, whether we think of the
Egyptian or Aztec pyramids, of the Roman highways, the *caminos
reales* in Latin America, the Etruscan, medieval, or Chinese walls.

However, this solution has several drawbacks: in the first place, it
is extremely expensive in real resources (even though slave labor be
used) and is therefore available only for a few key structures; secondly,

11. See Stanley Hart Udy, Jr., *The Organization of Production in Non-Industrial
Cultures*, unpublished dissertation, Princeton Univ., Department of Economics and
Sociology (1957), p. 224.

it is inapplicable in any event to machines with moving parts that require maintenance; and thirdly, it perpetuates the problem by considering the difficulty of *learning* maintenance insuperable.

An opposite type of solution now suggests itself: instead of rendering maintenance entirely unnecessary, is there not something to be said for enterprises in which maintenance is of supreme importance? We are thinking of industries and processes where lack of maintenance carries stiff penalties in the form of serious breakdowns and accidents instead of simply leading to a slow deterioration in the quality and quantity of output or to brief outages of single machines that do not disrupt the whole production schedule. It is this *compulsion to maintain* that is, for instance, characteristic of the operations of integrated, "continuous-flow" processes such as petroleum refining and other chemical transformations. In transportation, a high degree of compulsion exists for airlines—nonmaintenance here means certain disaster—while highways can be left to deteriorate for a long time until they become actually impassable, and even then the consequence is inconvenience and impairment of income distributed among many people rather than massive loss of life and property. In the case of railroads, the compulsion to maintain is less strong than for airlines, but probably stronger than for highways, as the accidents resulting from nonmaintenance are more serious. Our hypothesis that underdeveloped countries will do best in activities where maintenance is inescapably imposed is in this instance nicely borne out by observation: the performance of airlines in these countries is usually quite creditable, that of the railroads mediocre, and the highway system is frequently in a parlous state of disrepair.

The foregoing observations suggest that underdeveloped countries may well make a surprising success of ventures with a complicated technology which *must* be maintained in top working order. It is in these industries that the *maintenance habit* can be acquired and from there spread to the rest of the economy. On the other hand, the "simple" industries which the poorer countries are often admonished to set up first may be precisely those that will exhibit a strong tendency to deterioration. For while here lack of maintenance does not have immediate drastic consequences (and is therefore likely to be indulged in), it does in the longer run have a serious adverse impact on efficiency and morale.

Developing countries cannot, of course, abstain from building highways or from establishing textile mills on the ground that such ventures are exposed to deterioration. But an awareness of the special risks to which this type of investment is exposed can only be advantageous in that it may lead to the adoption of processes especially oriented toward our difficulty. A good example is provided by road construction in Colombia as explained by the consulting engineer who was in charge of supervising the road construction and rehabilitation program financed by the International Bank:

> We made one major concession in our planning to the recognized maintenance organization problem, and it sounds odd, at first thought. We encouraged the construction of low-type bituminous surfaces on relatively low-travelled routes, where this use would not ordinarily be justified in this country. We assumed that, with the increasing truck and bus industry in Colombia, local pressure would be applied to the Ministry of Public Works to repair the deep holes which will develop in cheap bituminous pavements if maintenance and retreatment is delayed, and that such pressure would be greater than if a gravel and stone road is allowed to deteriorate. Gravel and stone surfaces disappear at the rate of 20 to 40 tons per kilometer per year, and its loss may not be detected until the base is damaged. In other words, neglect of a bituminous surface is more obvious than neglect of a gravel or stone surface.[12]

The mechanism invoked here is, in addition, a striking example of reliance on nonmarket forces—pressure by the highway users on the Ministry of Public Works—for corrective action in a disequilibrium situation.

Generalizing the Solution

The reasoning used in the consideration of the maintenance problem can be applied to other problems in investment planning. For instance, if there is a tendency for new ventures to be undertaken without sufficient advance consideration of the technical, economic, and social conditions essential to their success, an argument can be made in

12. From a letter to the author from Forrest Green, Professor of Highway Engineering at Purdue University.

favor of enterprises that imperiously require careful advance planning because of the complex nature of the investment and the amount of money and prestige committed. Thus, under certain circumstances, it may be rational for governments in underdeveloped countries to concentrate on "show-pieces": when a government undertakes the construction of a large hydroelectric station or of a steel mill, it simply cannot afford to let such ventures go wrong—it places itself under a far stronger compulsion to "deliver" than if it were to spend the same funds on a large number of small projects. The large ventures are therefore likely to be planned much more carefully than the small ones and this factor ought to qualify any comparison of their respective "marginal social productivities."

Similarly, if it is a fact that enterprises in underdeveloped countries are exposed to forces making for a deterioration in the quality of their output because of lack of competition, lack of maintenance of equipment, or for other reasons, then something may be said for considering seriously the establishment of industries where the latitude or tolerance for such deterioration is particularly low—precision instruments, for instance. The field for this type of action may be limited because of the many other elements, particularly with respect to market size, that enter into investment decisions. But it is interesting to note that the firm requirement of high standards of quality is an element in favor of, rather than, as would usually be believed, against, the introduction of this type of production into underdeveloped countries. Since they would tend to do badly the jobs that may be done either well or badly, it is clear that these countries would have a comparative advantage in jobs that must be done well if they are to be done at all.

To use a parallel from individual behavior: a person whose attention is apt to wander is likely to drive quite well in heavy city traffic, but is in great danger of landing in a ditch as soon as he reaches an "easy" country road.[13]

13. This example makes it clear that what we have in mind is definitely *not* a challenge-and-response mechanism. Our driver does well in city traffic not because of the "challenge" of the task but simply because, given his constitution, it is actually on balance *easier* for him to drive properly in the city than in the country—the city traffic requires greater technical mastery, but this increase in the difficulty of driving is outweighed by the fact that intense traffic helps him

But instead of searching for additional analogous situations, it is perhaps of greater interest to attempt a generalization of our analysis. The special problem presented by maintenance resided in its not being directly related to the production process so that its timing and periodicity result from arbitrary arrangements rather than from signals sent out by the process or the product itself. In fact, in order to organize maintenance on an efficient basis, we generally resort to arrangements that *simulate* the sending out of such signals either by the calendar or by the machine itself, as when we have our car lubricated when the speedometer passes a mileage number with three zeros—we act *as though* the car asked to be lubricated at this point. This suggests that efficiency can be reinforced by signals, indications, and hints given off by the production process, and that the absence of such hints creates a special difficulty which will be particularly hard to overcome in underdeveloped countries.

In looking at the production of goods and services from this point of view, the impact on labor efficiency of machine-paced as opposed to operator-paced operations first comes to mind. It appears likely that an untrained labor force will perform better in machine-paced operations, not so much because of a tendency toward slacking when the machine does not compel the work, as because machine-paced operations provide for steadiness of pace and regular brief rest periods which the inexperienced self-paced worker has difficulty in observing.[14]

In general, it is well known that output per worker varies far more in operator-controlled than in machine-controlled operations.[15] The

in the task of focusing his attention. I suspect that quite a few of Toynbee's challenge-and-response mechanisms can be reinterpreted in a similar way, and, in the process, rendered more intelligible.

14. Cf. U. S. Department of Labor, *Hours of Work and Output,* Bulletin No. 917, Washington, 1947. This bulletin reports on the differential effect on workers' productivity of increases in daily work hours during wartime. One of its conclusions is (p. 11): "Where the workpace is controlled by the machine, thus affording the operator some brief rest periods while waiting for the machine to perform its operation, the increase in output is more nearly proportional to the increase in hours [than in operator-paced operations]."

15. Adam Abruzzi, *Work, Workers and Work Management* (New York, 1956), pp. 14, 201; and Bela Gold, *Foundations of Productivity Analysis* (Pittsburgh, 1955), pp. 188 ff. In *The Instinct of Workmanship* (New York, Macmillan, 1914), pp. 306–7, Veblen gave a masterly description of machine-controlled operations:

situation is therefore, once again, similar to the one involved in maintenance: if, for a number of reasons, labor productivity tends to be low in underdeveloped countries, this tendency is given much more room to assert itself in operator-controlled operations. Therefore, these countries will tend to do comparatively better in industrial operations that are primarily machine-paced.

Since machine-paced operations are typically more capital-intensive than operator-paced ones, our argument qualifies the advice to adopt labor-intensive processes usually given to capital-poor and labor-rich countries. This advice rests on the assumption that the productivity of labor in underdeveloped countries will not deteriorate relative to developed countries as technology becomes more labor-intensive. But since the scope for poor performance becomes wider when more labor-intensive processes are used, this assumption may be untenable.

This argument for capital-intensive technology in underdeveloped countries will be considered in more detail later in this chapter. Let us first give it greater generality by moving from the individual factory operation to the production process as a whole. This is necessary in any event to explain satisfactorily why labor productivity is likely to be low in operator-paced operations; for low labor productivity is most typically the result of poor management.[16]

Certain types of modern technology perform a crucial function in aiding management in the performance of new, unfamiliar, and perhaps somewhat uncongenial tasks. By predetermining to a considerable extent what is to be done where and at what point of time, the machines and the mechanical or chemical processes they perform reduce these difficulties immeasurably in comparison with a situation where work schedules depend exclusively on the convergence and

---

"The share of the operative workman in the machine industry is typically that of an attendant, an assistant, whose duty it is to keep pace with the machine process and to help out with workmanlike manipulations at points where the machine process engaged is incomplete." Veblen opposed this machine worker to the craftsman but did not see that a large area in modern industry is reserved to the self-paced operator with power tools and operator-controlled machines.

16. The close relationship between organizational and managerial skills, on the one hand, and labor productivity on the other, has been shown by Frederick Harbison, "Entrepreneurial Organization as a Factor in Economic Development," *Quarterly Journal of Economics*, 70 (Aug. 1956), 364–79; cf. also Tulsi Ram Sharma, *Location of Industries in India*, 3rd ed. (Bombay, 1954), p. 220.

coordination of many human wills and actions. The productivity effects of technology have been so spectacular that its role in assisting management and thus enhancing efficiency has gone largely unnoticed. Ever since Adam Smith, it has been realized that the division of labor induces mechanical inventions. But the inverse relationship also deserves to be stressed. The technical processes carried out by machinery provide factory operations with a basic structure and rhythm which in effect deal out functions and determine sequences. If it is correct, as Chester Barnard has said, that "processes of decision . . . are largely techniques for narrowing choice," [17] then the use of modern technology in manufacturing is one of the most powerful of such techniques.

The degree to which modern technology facilitates coordination varies from one industry to another. In some industries, the technology consists of a basic process around which work falls into place almost naturally; examples are smelting, petroleum refining, cement, brewing, and many others. In other industries, such as construction and much of metalworking, as well as in most service industries, work is not patterned around one or several key technical processes. As a result, sequences are far less rigidly compelled, it is impossible to identify any one process as central, and tasks are typically defined in terms of their *direct* contribution to the achievement of the goal—the final product—rather than in terms of the roles performed in different phases of the production process. In these "product-centered" industries technology therefore makes much less of a contribution to the coordination of efforts unless it succeeds, by organizing "flow," in imitating the conditions prevailing in the "process-centered" industries. Thus, the efficiency-enhancing and coordination-promoting property of modern technology tends to be much more pronounced in process-centered than in product-centered industries.

It is possible to classify a plant (or industry) into one or the other

17. Chester I. Barnard, *The Functions of the Executive* (Cambridge, Mass., 1938), p. 14. Note also the following description of assembly problems in M. E. Salveson, "On a Quantitative Method in Production Planning and Scheduling," *Econometrica, 20* (Oct. 1952), 562: "In an assembled commodity, if there are n component parts there will be theoretically $n!$ different sequences in which the parts can be assembled together. . . . In any real situation, it would be prohibitive to enumerate all of these different sequences and select the one which is optimum. . . . Instead an engineering type of analysis is used to select some one sequence of assembly according to which the assembly methods and tooling are laid out."

category by asking the question whether its physical assets have a definite capacity.[18] If a positive answer can be given, as is the case with a blast furnace, a refinery, or a brewery, we have a process-centered situation: with a certain equipment, it ought to be possible to produce so many tons or gallons per day. In the product-centered industries as, for example, in the case of a construction firm or a repair shop, it is not possible to make this kind of statement: outputs here are often heterogeneous and even if the problem of adding them up can be satisfactorily solved, capacity is far less rigidly set by the physical assets alone or it is a far less useful benchmark because actual output seldom reaches more than a fraction of theoretical capacity. This test illuminates another aspect of the manner in which technology in process-centered industries acts as an aid to management: the rated capacity of the plant provides managers with a performance goal and an objective criterion of failure or success, provided demand is adequate. This is a very valuable mechanism in underdeveloped countries where, as we know, competition is often not a sufficiently strong spur to good performance.

Thus there are various ways in which capital enhances the efficiency of management and therefore of labor. This function of capital is of particular importance in underdeveloped societies where the tasks of coordination and of cooperation in large-scale organizations meet with special difficulties.

That there exists a strong social need for this stimulating and co-ordinating function is suggested by the fact that, in the absence of modern technology, it is frequently performed, particularly in co-operative work, by other devices such as singing [19] or magic and ritual. Among the Trobriand Islanders, according to Malinowski, "magic is a systematizing, regulating and controlling influence in garden work. The magician, in carrying out the rites, sets the pace, compels people to apply themselves to certain tasks, and to accomplish them properly and in time. . . . There is no doubt that by its influence in ordering,

18. This test was suggested to me by Alan S. Manne.

19. Georges Friedmann, *Industrial Society* (Glencoe, Ill., 1955), pp. 157–9, and sources there cited. Cf. also C. J. Erasmus, "Cultural Structure and Process: The Occurrence and Disappearance of Reciprocal Farm Labor," *Southwestern Journal of Anthropology, 12* (Winter 1956), 452.

systematizing and regulating work, magic is economically invaluable." [20]

A particularly striking example of the elaborate way in which the function is performed in a primitive society is given by Raymond Firth in his description of the role of ritual in canoe-building and net-making in Tikopia.[21] He shows in minute detail how "certain types of ritual make for conformity of the work to a time-schedule and so help to safeguard the task from miscalculation and inertia." The ritual acts not only as a "unifying factor for the assembly of labor" and as a "general stimulus to the productive process," but also as a specific guide in the course of this process since "the traditional sequence of rites of necessity involves a corresponding sequence of technical operations."[22]

Finally, Firth shows that "with similar environmental, technical and social conditions, work of this kind [i.e., work involving cooperation in large-scale activities] is performed with less regularity, secures a smaller labor force and is integrated less effectively where it is not accompanied by such ritual." His conclusion is that the extra degree of capital intensity implicit in the time-consuming performance of ritual is fully justified, since without it output would substantially decrease and deteriorate.[23]

The parallel is complete with the special stimulating role which modern technology performs and which because of inexperience in management and difficulties in cooperation is particularly needed in underdeveloped countries. Here also some additional capital intensity may sometimes be well worth while if it "safeguards the task from miscalculation and inertia" and prevents decay.[23a]

20. B. Malinowski, *Argonauts of the Western Pacific* (London, Routledge, 1922), p. 60.
21. *Primitive Polynesian Economy*, London, Routledge, 1939.
22. Ibid., pp. 183, 179, 125, and 181.
23. Ibid., pp. 182–4.
23a. Our argument can be given further support from a different direction, but through closely analogous considerations. Besides inducing efficiency, capital-intensive forms of production are likely to prove stimulating to new capital formation. That some economists have claimed too much in this connection is shown in A. O. Hirschman and Gerald Sirkin, "Investment Criteria and Capital Intensity Once Again," *Quarterly Journal of Economics*, 72 (Aug. 1958). But, as is also

Capital-Intensive Technology?

Let us formalize our argument. We have given some reasons for believing that production functions are not the same for developed and underdeveloped countries, even though the underlying technological possibilities are identical. The marginal rate of substitution of labor for capital is larger in underdeveloped countries as, with the loss in managerial and labor efficiency consequent upon the adoption of less capital-intensive methods, more labor is needed than in developed countries to make up for a given decrease in capital.

Employing the usual diagram, with labor and capital measured respectively along the abscissa and the ordinate, the constant-product curves for a given output of any good may be expected to coincide for industrial and underdeveloped countries only along their most capital-intensive segments. Thereafter the curves will follow different paths, with the isoquant of the underdeveloped country—curve AU in Figure 6—lying somewhat to the right of the isoquant AI that applies in the industrial country. Only the latter is a genuine technical-possibilities curve.

With this situation, it becomes immediately evident that identical relative factor prices in both countries should result in the adoption of more capital-intensive processes in the underdeveloped country than in the industrial one.[24] This is shown by comparing the points of tangency P_1 and P_2 of the two parallel lines DE and FG. More realistically, if we assume by drawing the line MN that relative factor prices are more favorable to labor in the industrial country, this does not necessarily mean that techniques should be less capital-intensive in the underdeveloped country. In spite of this country's lower ratio of labor costs to capital costs, the point P_1 shows that it should use

---

pointed out in this paper, a presumption exists that "capital-intensive capitalists" are more accumulation-minded than land- or labor-intensive property owners, if only because of the threat of obsolescence of their machines and equipment. In other words, the argument in favor of capital-intensive technology can be strengthened by taking into account the differential effect of various types of technology on *savings out of profits*. In underdeveloped countries, where capitalists must learn to plow back profits, this differential effect is likely to be of particular importance.

24. Capital intensity is here understood to be measured by the capital-output, rather than by the capital-labor, ratio.

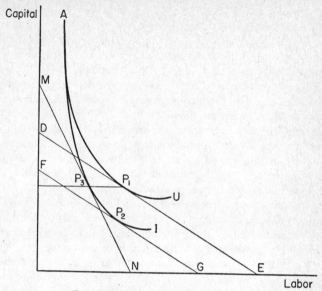

Fig. 6. Divergent production functions

the same amount of capital as the industrial country which will now aim at the point of tangency of *MN* with isoquant *AI*, i.e., at P_3.

Having stated the argument, we must qualify it. In the first place, it is quite possible that Western technology has only a few processes to offer, and that, even after taking into account the factors here discussed, all of them are too capital-intensive for the underdeveloped countries in view of their low wages and disguised unemployment. This would be the case if, in the figure, the isoquant *AU* existed not as a continuous curve but as a limited number of points, all of them located northwest of P_1.

Secondly, we have rather arbitrarily equated process-centered industries with capital-intensive technology. This would be correct if process-centered industries were necessarily made up entirely of machine-paced operations. Actually, this need not be the case. A process-centered industry will typically contain a *central* mechanical or chemical process which takes place in a series of machine-controlled operations, but all movements toward and away from that process— of handling materials and internal transportation—could well be man-rather than machine-paced.[25] As long as plant operations *as a whole* are process-centered, the fact that the peripheral operations—which often represent a considerable fraction of total cost—are man-controlled need not affect efficiency since the central process still would indirectly set the pace of *all* operations in the plant.

Conversely, product-centered processes are not necessarily of low capital intensity. The production of made-to-order machines with the help of highly complex machine tools is a case in point.

Nevertheless, in combination, the criteria developed here do point toward certain highly capital-intensive pursuits as particularly well suited for underdeveloped countries. The list includes thus far: large-scale ventures, activities that must be maintained in top working order, that must observe high quality standards for their output, machine-paced operations, and process-centered industries. For the time being, these criteria can of course be considered only as hypotheses. Empirical verifications should not be too difficult to undertake. If we are correct, labor productivity differentials between an underdeveloped and an industrial country should be much larger in certain industries (e.g., metal fabricating) than in certain others (e.g., cement) even when essentially similar techniques are used in both countries.[26]

25. It seems that this is what happens in Soviet industry. See David Granick, "Economic Development and Productivity Analysis: The Case of Soviet Metalworking," *Quarterly Journal of Economics*, 71 (May 1957), 205–33, for interesting evidence on the use of labor-intensive methods, principally in auxiliary operations such as handling of materials, inspection, and repair. For similar evidence from underdeveloped countries, see V. V. Bhatt, "Capital Intensity of Industries," *Bulletin of the Oxford Institute of Statistics*, 18 (May 1956), 179–94.

26. Leontief's celebrated findings about the comparatively high labor content of United States exports could be considered corroborative evidence (see his "Factor Proportions and the Structure of American Trade: Further Theoretical and Empirical Analysis," *Review of Economics and Statistics*, 38 [Nov. 1956], 386–407, and literature there cited). Conversely, our analysis provides an explanation of Leontief's statistics, related to the one he has proposed himself. It has been suggested that underdeveloped countries may find it easier to approach the efficiency standards of the advanced industrial nations in capital-intensive, process-centered, than in labor-intensive, product-centered industries. Therefore, as worldwide industrialization progresses, the comparative advantage of the advanced industrial countries may come to lie increasingly with certain types of labor-intensive goods and services. This can best be illustrated by a fanciful hypothesis. Let us imagine that certain labor-intensive services such as maintenance of roads, buildings, and machinery could become objects of international trade at moderate

Production versus Administration Tasks

The new criteria which have been suggested here are designed to help in locating new activities that can be successfully undertaken in underdeveloped countries. In other words, they do not imply any judgment with respect to activities that have long been carried on in these countries, such as handicraft and small industry. As was seen in Chapter 7, the kind of industrial development to which our criteria point actually improves the chances of small industry for survival and growth in the course of development.

With respect to new activities, our criteria obviously cannot pretend to replace the usual considerations that make up investment decisions: size of market, locational advantages, and the like.[27] But they add a new dimension to these decisions.

Frequently it will be advisable or necessary to establish enterprises that do not meet our criteria. But in such cases something might still be gained from being aware of the handicaps under which these firms are likely to operate, for it should lead to particular care in the selection of management, personnel, and techniques.

Actually, it will be very difficult to classify projects neatly into those that do and those that do not meet our criteria. For the several characteristics that would make up the *ideal* firm from the point of view of our criteria are most unlikely to be found together in more than a very few projects. Therefore, many firms will have split personalities. For instance, manufacturing firms may well combine product-centered and process-centered operations, as is the case in certain assembly operations or when large, isolated process-centered plants, such as sugar and petroleum refineries, have their own machine shops.

But wherever production of physical goods takes place at all, the operators are being helped in their efforts by the tangible nature of their task. The help is particularly substantial in the case of process-

transport costs. I have no doubt that in this eventuality the older industrial nations would specialize in the export of such services, quite possibly importing steel and cement in exchange!

27. The best treatment and practical illustration of these matters is found in W. A. Lewis, "The Industrialization of the British West Indies," *Caribbean Economic Review*, 2 (May 1950), 1–61, and *Report on Industrialization and the Gold Coast*, Government Printing Department, Accra, Gold Coast, 1953.

centered and machine-paced operations, but it is also present in product-centered work. Even though the necessary coordination of efforts has here to be "invented" by the production manager without the powerful hints that a basic process provides, the image of the final product still acts both as a spur to everybody's efforts and as an objective test of achievement or failure.

Any production activity has these three assets: the target is clear-cut, we know it can be reached, and success in doing so is subject to an objective test. These elements are, for instance, fully present in such entirely product-centered operations as the repair of a machine or vehicle.

As soon as we move from the sphere of production to that of administration, tasks lose their definiteness and achievement its "testability." It is therefore to be expected and is indeed widely confirmed by observation and experience that efficiency will be higher in the plant- than in the office-operations of industrial firms.[28] By the latter we mean such functions as production control, planning, finance, personnel and public relations, distribution and advertising, and general housekeeping. The comparative elusiveness of these tasks is combined with a tolerance for poor performance which is unmatched by any production job. It is almost proverbial for production men to complain that they would have been fired long ago if they turned in as poor a performance as some of the people behind a desk. This special tolerance of "desk jobs" for poor performance makes them also the prey and point of penetration of the forces that remain unconvinced of the need for exertion and achievement: friends and relatives find here an excellent refuge from which to make a last-ditch stand for their right to a quiet, incompetent existence.

It is now easy to understand why functions that are completely divorced from the actual production of goods and services tend to be the real stepchildren of progress in underdeveloped countries. National character and history are usually appealed to in explaining the malfunctioning of the political and administrative processes which stands so often in sharp contrast to real achievements in industrial and agricultural production. Seldom is it realized that these processes are intrinsically harder to master than production jobs. On the contrary,

28. United Nations, *Labor Productivity of the Cotton Textile Industry in Five Latin American Countries* (New York, 1951), passim.

amazement is expressed that a country pretends to set up modern industries when basic problems of public administration have not yet been solved. But this is only one of the many instances where what seems a cart-before-the-horse sequence turns out to be the efficient one in underdeveloped countries: efficient public administrators, admittedly so much needed, can perhaps best be trained in the arts of management by being first exposed to the powerful "teaching aids" which are standard equipment in any industrial production process.

CHAPTER 9

The Role of Disturbances

THE ANALYSIS of development processes and sequences which has been presented in the preceding chapters will now be used to reinterpret certain disturbances that affect underdeveloped countries. The most typical among these disturbances are inflation and balance-of-payments difficulties, on the one hand, and population pressures on the other. Our principal task will be to understand how these difficulties and pressures arise in the course of development, and how they in turn affect the course of economic growth.

Inflation

Types of upward pressure on prices. Several writers have remarked on the fact that the underdeveloped but developing countries of today appear to be much more subject to inflation and balance-of-payments difficulties than were the countries which passed through their early stages of economic growth in the nineteenth century. Henry Wallich, in a stimulating paper, explains this difference by referring to a basic change in attitudes. Development in today's underdeveloped countries is primarily consumption-oriented, whereas it was production-oriented during the past century. "In a production-oriented society, the logical way of looking at [economic progress] is to visualize the benefits coming from one's productive effort. In a consumption-oriented society, . . . social demand, working through political and trade union levels, seeks to extract from the economy more than what, through domestic production and international trade, it can be made to yield." [1]

A similar explanation is implicit in Nurkse's appeal to the "demonstration effect": [2] the attraction exerted on the consumers of underdeveloped countries by the high standard of living of the advanced

1. Wallich, "Notes toward a Theory of Derived Development."
2. Nurkse, *Problems of Capital Formation*, pp. 58 ff.

countries, and by the goods available there, makes them desire the fruits of economic progress, but does not prepare them for the sacrifices necessary to obtain them.

Other explanations of persistent inflationary pressure have run in terms of excessive investment rather than excessive consumption or insufficient savings. In fact, since it is usually impolitic or difficult to change the latter two quantities in the short run, attempts to deal with inflation usually concentrate on restricting investment, and the country is told that it is having inflation and foreign-exchange difficulties because it is "trying to do too many things at the same time." In this version, some writers speak about the permanent tendency of present-day governments in underdeveloped countries to undertake overambitious development plans and projects.

Inflation and an excess of imports over exports mean, of course, that a country's consumption and investment demands outrun the total available product at current prices, and the various accounts of the process that we have just recalled do little more than restate this fact in sociopsychological terms. But the explanation is perhaps not so simple as that; for if it resided entirely in unrealistic aspirations, in the refusal of these countries to live within their means, then the phenomenon would not be so severe, recurrent, and protracted as it has been. After all, societies have been known to learn from their experiences and to take effective steps against lesser evils than the systematic debasement of their currencies. Why should the banking system be allowed to keep expanding credit at too fast a rate? Why should the finance minister always lose out to the spending ministers or the central bank president to the finance minister? On the individual level also, the effect on savings of the "revolution of aspirations" is likely to be as indeterminate as that of a change in interest rates: a higher level of aspirations may lead to more spending out of a given income or to more savings with a view to future spending or to an increase in work preferences and enterprise.

Thus the explanation of inflation in terms of psychological propensities is not entirely convincing; it is in fact somewhat reminiscent of the long-discarded theories that attempted to explain the trade cycle by alternating waves of optimism and pessimism.

The view of the development process which has been presented in the preceding chapters leads to a different approach: it permits us to show how inflationary impulses are communicated to the economy by *certain types of development sequences* rather than indiscriminately by the general desire for development.

We have argued that economic development typically follows a path of uneven growth; that balance is restored as a result of pressures, incentives, and compulsions: that the efficient path toward economic development—and therefore the one that will often be instinctively taken if we can rely on the "principle of least effort"—is apt to be somewhat disorderly and that it will be strewn with bottlenecks and shortages of skills, facilities, services, and products; that industrial development will proceed largely through backward linkage, i.e., will work its way from the "last touches" to intermediate and basic industry.

A mere description of this type of growth process conveys an almost physical sensation of inflationary shocks being administered to an economy. Individual price rises and the profit opportunities they signal are indeed an essential part of the process, one of the prime movers in the mechanism of unbalanced growth. With short-run supply elasticities typically quite low, rises in some prices are bound to be substantial. Such advances in individual prices are not, of course, sufficient reason for a general rise in prices. But with any given level of skill and determination of a country's monetary and fiscal managers, general price stability will be easier to maintain when individual prices are subject to small random shocks than when strong price-raising forces are operating at various conspicuous growing points of the economy.

It may be objected that similar forces must have been at work during the earlier developmental stages of today's leading industrial countries. But, in the first place, these forces were perhaps less powerful, and secondly they were matched by other forces which made for periodic price declines and which are far weaker in the underdeveloped areas of today. The first point is somewhat speculative. But a comparison between today's underdeveloped countries and the Western societies on the eve of industrialization has led many observers to conclude that cultural and institutional obstacles to change are more important in the former than they were in the latter—hence a relatively greater need to rely on active inducement mechanisms, such as price rises, to call forth investment decisions. When entrepreneurs anticipate rising and complementary demands, an economy can economize on the use of price signals; when they are somewhat more sluggish and inclined never to act except on the basis of incontrovertible evidence that a lot of money can indeed be made in this or that venture, then the use of price signals will be far more widespread and intensive.

The greater use of price signals also makes for less of a stabilizing effect on prices with the completion of a given project. As one product appears on the market, new shortages and "entrained wants" arise, so that the downward pressures that could come with the opening up of new productive units are swamped by upward pressures emanating from the unanticipated needs revealed in the course of the production or use of the newly produced commodities.[3]

The downward pressures on prices are likely to be comparatively weak in industrial latecomers for another reason. These countries are usually establishing industries that have already passed through the most active phase of their technological progress, which leads to large cost and price reductions and/or quality improvements. At most, they are benefiting from this progress as importers,[4] but the effect of

3. Cf. Ch. 4.
4. This point has a bearing on the controversy about the terms of trade of underdeveloped countries. As is known, such authors as Singer, Prebisch, and Lewis have argued that gains in productivity tend to result in lower prices in the underdeveloped countries and in higher factor incomes in the industrial countries. Hence it is concluded that the gains from technical progress tend to accrue primarily to the industrial countries. Let us assume for the sake of the argument that *average* increases in productivity are reflected in rising factor incomes rather than in declining prices in the developed countries. Yet in these countries productivity gains are much faster in some lines than in others and therefore some prices will fall while others will rise. Now, when the underdeveloped countries industrialize, they are likely to pick first those industries whose technical progress has become stabilized. The foreign exchange thus released will then be shifted toward other industries. Developing latecomers will thus be able constantly to redirect their foreign purchases toward the most rapidly progressing industries of the advanced countries. In this way, they will concentrate their imports on those goods that, despite a stable *general* price level in the advanced countries, will show price declines or quality improvements. This is of course an argument in favor of industrialization—but it shows that the exchange of primary products against manufactures, even on the basis of the special Singer-Prebisch-Lewis assumptions, need not be a losing proposition for the primary producing countries provided they industrialize and are thus enabled to shift the composition of their purchases of manufactures.

a fall in import prices on the general price level is likely to be less pervasive and contagious in its psychological repercussions than the effect of a fall in prices of domestically produced goods.

Another characteristic feature of today's pattern of industrialization works in the same direction. Industrialization takes place at present far more than in the nineteenth century through the process of introducing entirely new products into the economy rather than through the replacement of handmade by machine-made goods. The latter process, dominant in the early stages of industrial development in the Western world, is marked by competitive price cutting in the area where machine production is attempting to assert itself. In contrast, the introduction of a new product which has no close substitutes is not likely to have any such localized impact; rather, price and output effects are going to be widely diluted among all the goods and services that compete for the customer's peso or rupee.

In addition, the small size of the market of many underdeveloped countries does not permit the establishment of more than one or two producers in many industries, and price competition *within* the new industrial sectors is therefore frequently conspicuous by its absence.

Thus the forces that are likely to act today on individual commodity prices in newly developing countries are going to make the task of avoiding inflation particularly difficult.

The preceding analysis shows that the task of monetary policy is not an easy one in today's underdeveloped countries. Since relative price rises are bound up with important development processes and must therefore be allowed to take place, general price stability can be successfully maintained only if monetary policy actually causes some prices to fall. Moreover, to enforce such a "neutral" policy, a decrease in the money supply may at times be required as for example in the case when holders of wealth in liquid form decide to reduce their liquid assets in order to take advantage of some of the investment opportunities signaled by price rises.

The price-price spiral. We have argued that underdeveloped countries are likely to make particularly lavish use of relative price rises as signals for entrepreneurs. Rises in individual prices result from complementarities and shortages and have the function of calling forth investments and increased output. The sectional price rises may be more or less successful in this endeavor, depending on the longer-run supply elasticities. Also, they may or may not lead to a general inflationary rise in prices, depending on the skill and determination of the monetary and fiscal managers.[5]

This gives us four possible types of price and output behavior in the course of uneven or unbalanced growth:

1. The best of all possible worlds is achieved when inflation is resisted while new investment and output are being induced.

2. The worst of all possible worlds prevails if the sectional rise in prices does lead to general inflation but not to increased output in the sector that is being signaled.

3. An intermediate situation is created when the signaling is successful in eliciting more production, but also leads to a generalized rise in prices.

4. Another intermediate situation is the opposite one, namely, overall stability but no response to the sectional price signals. Except when the commodities whose prices rise are of very small importance, this seems so unlikely an outcome that we may neglect it.

Under 2 and 3, this classification draws a distinction between two types of inflation: the former is obviously an unmitigated nuisance whereas the latter may sometimes constitute a necessary evil. This distinction between a sterile and pointless inflation cum stagnation, on the one hand, and an inflation that is not "all bad" has of course often been made, but usually the criterion has been the extent to which inflation results in "forced saving," i.e., permits an actual lifting of the volume of investments to a higher and more efficient level. Our criterion would be rather whether or not in the course of inflation certain basic imbalances which arose in the course of growth (and which led to sectional price increases followed by a generalized rise in prices) are

5. Recently some interesting efforts have been made to analyze the process of inflation when different supply elasticities prevail in different sectors of the economy. In these constructions, inflation is taken as a datum while we are primarily investigating how inflation is *induced* through the supply problems that arise in a developing economy. Nevertheless, the two inquiries touch on similar problems and I have profited in particular from the article by John H. Adler, "Deficit Spending and Supply Elasticities," *The Indian Journal of Economics*, 37 (July 1956), 15–38; cf. also S. P. Schatz, "Inflation in Underdeveloped Countries: A Theoretical Analysis," *American Economic Review*, 47 (Sept. 1957), 571–93.

being overcome. This will happen only if investment is undertaken in the signaled sectors, and here there is an obvious point of contact between the two criteria.

Actually it is of course a gross oversimplification to consider only the three or four possibilities mentioned thus far. To scan a more continuous range of conceivable outcomes, let us resume our analysis from the point at which we posited a rise in prices of some A-goods relative to the prices of some other B-goods. This increase determines simultaneously two reactions during any given period:

1. a certain increase in the rate of output of A-goods, depending on the elasticity of supply;

2. a certain change (decrease or increase) in the prices of B-goods; this reaction, which could also be defined as an elasticity, may be termed the *inflationary pull* exerted by A-prices on B-prices.

There is some equilibrium output of B for every ratio of A-prices to B-prices; when this point of "structural balance" is reached, there will be no further special incentives for expanding the production of A relative to B.

Under these conditions, the rise in A-prices will set off a contest between two forces: if the supply elasticity is high and the inflationary pull is low, structural balance is likely to be restored before inflation has been able to gather much or any strength; but if the supply elasticity is low and the inflationary pull is high, then the price advantage of the commodities whose output needs to be expanded will disappear before structural balance has been restored, so that these prices will go up again and thus cause one or several subsequent rounds of inflation.

It may be noted that this latter "sterile" type of inflation will not necessarily be faster moving than an inflation that solves the economy's supply problems as it moves along, for new imbalances may well arise once the old ones are solved and it is quite possible for both supply elasticities and inflationary pull to be high. But there is a real difference between an economy that solves *new* supply problems in every round of inflation and one in which it is the same supply problem that is constantly causing prices to resume their upward course.

A typical area in which the deleterious combination of low supply elasticity and high inflationary pull is apt to appear is that of agriculture. Rising agricultural prices will often not be very effective *by themselves* in calling forth additional output, because incentives to increased cultivation are weakened by existing land tenure systems and other institutional rigidities, and because knowledge of improved farming methods or the extension of such knowledge is inadequate. At the same time, a rise in agricultural prices is most "effective" in pulling up other prices because of their effect on wages, which is particularly strong in low-income economies.

A similar situation will often be found to obtain if some type of unbalanced growth within the economy drives up the price of foreign exchange. If the country relies on the exports of a few primary products, its foreign exchange earnings may respond but little to a fall in the exchange rate. On the other hand, the higher price of imports may affect importantly the costs of manufacturing as well as the prices of many consumer goods and may also have a serious psychological impact.

Knowledge of the sectors where price rises are inefficient in inducing additional output, but all too efficient in communicating themselves to the other sectors of the economy, is useful in indicating priority fields for action by public authorities. Such action would attempt to improve basic supply elasticities. In agriculture this might be achieved through research and extension services, through rural education, improvements in transportation and marketing, and, if necessary, through agrarian reforms and large-scale investment in irrigation, drainage, and colonization schemes. In exports, active promotional efforts are required, including studies of foreign markets and of exportable domestic resources and products.

In some areas, then, we dare not rely on price movements, or on price movements alone, as inducement mechanisms. Fortunately the strategy of unbalanced growth does not stand or fall with the efficacy of price signals. Alternative methods for restoring balance between sectors whose uneven growth creates economic tensions will be considered below.

The analysis of inflation in underdeveloped but developing countries which has been presented here differs considerably from the usual one: it points to a "price-price spiral," akin to the wage-price spiral familiar from recent experiences in advanced industrial countries, as a permanent source of inflation, one that is more insidious, ubiquitous, and harder to deal with than an excess of demands for investment and consumption over available resources. It is not denied, of course, that the latter explanation is correct at times. In particular, there is always the possibility that a demand inflation is superimposed on an inflation of the price-price spiral type.

Nevertheless, anti-inflationary policies must certainly be re-examined if excess demand is not considered to be the only or even the principal villain.[6] In the first place, we can then understand why both the commercial banks and the central bank are often taken aback by the admonition that they must not finance an investment boom. All they are doing, they will maintain, is adjusting existing credit lines to the higher prices that have come to rule for some commodities. We see now that this opinion may not be as naïve as we usually tend to think. The role of the banking system in a price-price spiral inflation is far more passive than in a demand inflation. The banks merely permit their clients to pass on all price increases, in the interest, so they argue, of maintaining economic activity at previous levels, not of expanding it. The carrying through of restrictive policies under these conditions is likely to meet with considerable resistance; and the risks of starting a downturn in economic activity rather than a mere scaling down of excessive investments are correspondingly greater. Also, there is a permanent need for flexible selective credit policies designed to help in expanding the production of those goods whose price rise is setting off inflationary developments.

Balanced growth and inflation. In our view, inflation in underdeveloped countries arises principally from the supply imbalances that are characteristic of the growth process. By way of a footnote we shall now draw on the "pure" balanced growth theory—which deals with the demand side—to supplement the analysis.

Let us assume—for just one moment—that the balanced growth theory is correct, i.e., that development must take place simultaneously over a great number of industries if the output of any one industry is

6. The points made here are related to the recent discussion about the effectiveness of traditional monetary policy instruments under conditions of cost- rather than demand-inflation in the economically advanced countries. Some pertinent questions in this respect were raised by R. Ruggles in "Recent Price Increases and their Relation to Administered Prices," U. S. Senate (85th Congress), Subcommittee on Antitrust and Monopoly, *Hearings on Senate Resolution 57* (Washington, 1957), Pt. I, pp. 136–8.

to find a market. Let us assume also, this time in accord with our opinion, that the achievement of balanced growth is beyond the capabilities of the country's citizens and government. Caught between this impotence and the likelihood of failure in single ventures, the government ought perhaps to give up altogether any ambition to contribute to its country's development. But suppose it is stubborn: is there anything left that it might do? There is, of course. Instead of choosing a project whose output must be disposed of through sale, but which in accordance with the balanced growth doctrine will prove to be unsalable, the government may pick projects whose output is not expected to be sold or which are not expected to break even. Such projects will not therefore become *obvious* failures if their capacity remains un- or underutilized. For example, under the stipulated conditions, governments that insist on "doing something" might engage in vast public works and social overhead capital programs including some that are unproductive and therefore highly inflationary.

Holding the balanced growth theory to be incorrect, we do not really believe that governments are caught in the kind of dilemma just described. But we must admit that many of them act as though they were thus caught since they in effect restrict themselves entirely to public works in their attempts to promote development. This does not mean, of course, that they have gone through and accepted the reasoning of the preceding paragraph. Let us look for another explanation. The preference of governments for investment in public works and utilities could conceivably be due to the influence of Western liberal doctrine about the appropriate roles of public authorities and private initiative in economic life. However, this also seems improbable, for the doctrine is based on the assumption that private initiative is at all times buoyant, ready to assume risks, opportunity-perceiving, and efficient. It is therefore so obviously inapplicable to underdeveloped countries that its preachings could hardly have achieved success in so many instances for so long had a more basic motivation not been at work.

The fact is perhaps that governments do not need to be pushed very hard *not* to engage upon new developmental activities whose output must be marketed. For while such ventures may well prosper (in disobedience to the balanced growth doctrine) they may also cause embarrassing losses; and governments are not at all anxious to submit their performance to the test of the market. It therefore takes an un-usually enterprising and risk-accepting government to engage in novel manufacturing activities instead of going on with its port and highway projects. Highways never fail, and, as they are usually not maintained, they can even be built over and over again, thus turning out to be ideal outlets for governmental funds, involving no risk and a bare minimum of mental effort in general.

Governments therefore tend to share with the balanced growth doctrine an aversion to ventures that would introduce new or cheaper products into the economy; this aversion may even lead them to highly inflationary spending or unproductive public works. By throw-ing the weight of its influence against governmental activities in manu-facturing, United States policy would therefore not only be pursuing a course whose political wisdom is highly questionable; it would also support governments in a course that is apt to be both unimaginative and inflationary.

Balance-of-Payments Pressures

Supply imbalances and the demand for imports. The usual view of inflation as being caused by excess demand is paralleled by the account of balance-of-payments trouble in terms of inflationary pressures. Part of the excess demand spills over into imports. That inflation always has balance-of-payments repercussions is certain. But there may be more to the persistent balance-of-payments difficulties of underdeveloped countries. It is at least conceivable that these difficulties appear directly, as a result of some typical growth sequences, rather than exclusively as a reflection of domestic inflation.

One such sequence is suggested by our analysis of the growth process. In an open economy the imbalances characteristic of develop-ment are not reflected immediately in higher prices for those goods and services that can be imported. If shortages appear in such goods, they will be ordered from abroad. As long as foreign exchange re-serves can be drawn upon, the additional demand can be filled without any rise in prices. From this point of view, balance-of-payments pres-sures take place *in lieu of, rather than on top of,* price rises. Should we consider such behavior of the economy as a diversionary and ad-justment-delaying maneuver, rather than as a positive signaling device? It must be granted that as long as the balance-of-payments pressure takes the form of a decline in reserves at a fixed exchange rate, private operators are not going to feel any immediate strong incentive to correct the situation.[7] But we recall that we do not confine ourselves to considering the action of market forces. Governments can normally be expected to pay some attention to changes in their foreign exchange holdings and are likely to take action to prevent exchange rate depreciation or tighter exchange controls which they know to be inevitable unless they are able to correct the situation. Exchange rate depreciation would of course bring market forces back into operation. But during the period in the course of which foreign exchange reserves —or foreign aid allocations—are being drawn down, inducement mechanisms working through market forces (i.e., price rises) are largely suppressed, and are replaced by the action of nonmarket forces.

Under what circumstances would such an arrangement be desirable? The previous analysis of inflation provides a clue. When price signals would be ineffective or slow in calling forth additional production, but would exert a rapid and strong inflationary pull on other prices, there is clearly much to be said for not using price rises as an adjustment mechanism. The respite granted by an import surplus can then be extremely valuable, provided it is utilized by the public authorities to push through some of the reforms required to increase supply elasticities. In such situations we find a principal rationale for financial assistance from abroad in the course of development.

The foreign exchange illusion. Pressures on a country's international accounts are now already seen to be part and parcel of the process of unbalanced growth. In fact, the balance of payments is particularly vulnerable in the course of development, because of what might be termed the "foreign exchange illusion." *Within* an economy, operators take account of certain supply limitations that are obvious to them; they change their plans, refrain from placing orders which they know cannot possibly be filled or which they expect to produce unacceptable price rises. This is of course noncompetitive behavior, but it is none the less common for that; it acts in effect as a brake on the speed with

7. The well-known money-flow and income repercussions of a balance-of-payments deficit are unlikely to provide even a partial cure for the specific sectoral imbalances which we assume here to lie at the root of the deficit.

which supply imbalances lead to individual price rises. The latter are the typical reaction to supply imbalances and shortages only if there are many buyers who bid against each other or, in case there are only a few buyers, if these shortages are hidden from them and have to be revealed precisely by the rise in prices. This is one of the reasons why prices are far more volatile in agriculture than, say, in machinery within the same country.

Now the ignoring of supply limitations is virtually complete with respect to imports. For here, with a single country taking up only a small portion of the world supply of the commodities it imports, the ability of other countries to furnish additional quantities at existing prices is hardly ever in question. As a result, the user of imported products immediately reacts to an increase in his needs by putting through more orders, and the importer transmits them abroad with gay abandon, not realizing that the *real* supply limitation consists in the ability of the country to earn additional foreign exchange through exports. This supply limitation is never perceived in advance and must therefore be brought home to the economic operators entirely through rises in the price of foreign exchange or through exchange controls resulting from excess demands for foreign currencies.

These considerations apply with particular strength to countries that start out with the "final touches" and develop from then on through backward linkage. For as long as a country imports the principal industrial materials it uses in manufacturing, its industries will expand their operations, assuming the existence of a horizontal supply curve for their material inputs. Only when a country depends on its own basic industry do the intermediate and "last stage" operators discard this blithe assumption and make their own expansion plans somewhat contingent on the likelihood that they will be able to secure a stable flow of needed materials from domestic sources. Moreover, once established, basic industry will be able to claim its share in the flow of investment funds so that an increase in demand for the products of the intermediate and "final touches" industries will from then on lead to a balanced expansion in capacity throughout the industrial structure rather than to one that places new burdens on the balance of payments.

Here we have, then, another argument for accelerating the establishment of basic industries in developing countries. Their presence brings into view some of the supply limitations that would otherwise remain hidden by the "foreign exchange illusion"; and it makes for an allocation of investment that is much less likely to land the country in constantly renewed balance-of-payments difficulties.

"Exportability" of fast-growing outputs as a condition of external balance. The balance-of-payments pressures that have been examined have this in common: they result from specific output-input imbalances and disproportionalities that arise in the course of growth rather than from the usually assumed grand imbalance between the investment required for attaining a certain rate of growth and domestic savings.[7a] In other words, we interpret the excess of investment over domestic savings that occurs when there is a balance-of-payments deficit as an incidental result rather than as the fundamental characteristic of the process. The question may then be asked: granting that such disproportionalities are likely to imperil balance-of-payments equilibrium, why do they always work in the same direction, namely in that of an *import* surplus? This systematic bias may be held to indicate that a savings-investment imbalance is after all present as a basic causative factor, and, consequently, the need for our additional hypotheses would be in question.

However, the type of analysis we have pursued leads us to propose a different explanation of the bias: whether rapid growth of specific outputs gives rise to import surpluses depends on what will be called the "exportability"[8] of these outputs. If exportability is high, growth will not lead to balance-of-payments pressures and may actually be accompanied by export surpluses. If, on the other hand, the possibility of rapid growth is largely confined to activities whose outputs are characterized by low exportability—and this happens to be the case in most underdeveloped countries today—then the development process will be punctuated by recurrent tendencies toward an import surplus.

7a. That balance-of-payments difficulties may be due to structural factors rather than to the inability or unwillingness of developing countries to live within their means is also shown by G. M. Alter in "The Servicing of Foreign Capital Inflows by Underdeveloped Countries," paper presented at the Rio Roundtable of the International Economic Association, 1957 (mimeographed).

8. Apologies are offered for the introduction of this term, whose meaning is clarified below.

These considerations, which we shall now attempt to elucidate, may provide a clue to an understanding of why foreign capital and aid are so important for the growth of most underdeveloped countries today, even though the leading industrial countries of the world were able to develop largely without the benefit of foreign capital.

Let us distinguish between a sector R whose output can be rapidly expanded and a sector S where increases in output can be achieved only much more slowly. The difference between sectors R and S stems from a simple empirical fact: the accumulation of technical knowledge does not occur at the same rate for all economic activities, and receptivity to innovations also varies widely among different sectors, so that at any one time the *scope* for growth is much larger in some activities than in others. If all the activities producing inputs for the activities making up sector R also belong to sector R, then, savings and demand permitting, the growth potential of the sector can be fully utilized without any strains or stresses. However, such a situation is possible only if the economy is split into two entirely independent sectors, a most unlikely state of affairs.

If there is interdependence between the two sectors, outputs from some S-activities will be required as inputs into R-activities. If we assume that *all* of the outputs of these S-activities are used up in the R-activities, that technical coefficients are fixed, and that there is no foreign trade, the result is obvious: the rate of growth of the R-activities would be brought down to that of the S-activities.[9] Relaxing the first two assumptions makes it possible to conceive of a less depressing outcome; nevertheless, the R-activities would continue to experience some difficulties in fully utilizing their growth potential. These difficulties would of course set up a variety of pressures to improve the productivity of the S-activities in question and are thus likely to call forth eventually what is known as induced technical progress and induced change in general.

An escape from these difficulties becomes possible if foreign trade is brought into the picture, i.e., if the procurement of needed inputs

9. We may include in the S-sector those primary activities that, for lack of natural resources, cannot take place in the country. This is the limiting case since the potential growth rate is zero for the outputs of these activities within the country; if they are required as inputs into the R-activities, imports are obviously the only solution.

for the R-activities can be supplemented from foreign sources of supply. In this eventuality the scope for rapid growth of the R-activities would be fully exploited—on one condition: that the balance-of-payments problem can be solved.

It is for this reason that it becomes crucial to examine what we called before the exportability of the R-sector outputs.

Exportability depends on three main factors:

a. on the ability of a country to supply, at competitive prices, goods already in use abroad;

b. on the country's production of goods that are new to other countries and that because of their obvious usefulness or attractiveness will not only claim a share of these countries' existing incomes but *raise their demand for income*,[10] i.e., will make them substitute work for leisure and bring incentives into play to increase productivity; and

c. on the extent to which the country's R-sector corresponds to the other countries' S-sectors so that *they* need its output to realize the growth potential of their own R-sectors.

Of these three factors, the latter two are by far the most important in a protectionist world; they are the ones that keep international trade going. But it can now be seen that the exportability of the outputs of the R-sector in today's underdeveloped countries is bound to be far lower than that prevailing in the advanced industrial countries. For the R-sector in underdeveloped countries is predominantly made up of industries that have already been built up in the advanced countries; the exportability of the products of these industries could be based only on the weak support derived from factor *a*, whereas the exportability of the R-sector outputs in the advanced countries could always count heavily on factor *b*, and, inasmuch as they are exporting capital goods for rapidly developing industries abroad, on factor *c*.

It may be asked why the underdeveloped countries could not rely on this factor *c* for keeping themselves supplied with foreign exchange; why, in other words, they cannot derive from their traditional primary exports the wherewithal to keep their expanding R-activities supplied with the needed inputs from abroad. The answer is that the only secure way in which a country can finance the imports it needs to exploit the growth potential of its R-activities is by being able to sell abroad a

10. See Spengler, "Product-Adding vs. Product-Replacing Innovations," for a comprehensive treatment of this point.

pórtion of the output of *these same activities:* only then will the spurts in imports caused by the growth pattern of the *R*-activities be *systematically* offset (save for lags) by spurts in exports. Any offsetting by other exports is to a considerable extent a matter of luck. Some nations, such as Japan, with the expansion in silk exports during the phase of her rapid industrialization,[11] and some of the industrializing petroleum producers today, were or are lucky in this way. But, ordinarily, the latecomers in industrialization will have trouble obtaining the imports they require for rapid growth in the self-liquidating fashion of the pioneer industrial countries who could—and can—always find foreign markets for the output of their newest inventions and creations.

Our analysis has three corollaries. In the first place, failing luck, a sustained effort may help. Underdeveloped countries certainly ought to be particularly active in investigating all possibilities for export promotion, from raw materials to handicraft items, and their fiscal and foreign exchange policy should not compound the difficulties of the situation as it sometimes has been doing.

Secondly, it appears that the need of the industrializing latecomers is less for a "supplement of real resources" than for *some specific additional imports, no matter whether they are obtained by trade or by aid.* This conclusion permits a correct appraisal of the long-term purchase agreements currently being negotiated by Russia in a number of underdeveloped countries. Since we always think in terms of savings and investment and are convinced that the underdeveloped countries are primarily in need of a "supplement of real resources," we have a tendency to underrate the attractiveness of these arrangements as compared to offers of aid.

Finally, we must briefly consider a possible objection to our analysis on the ground that any of the balance-of-payments pressures which have been described will surely bring with them price and income effects tending to restore equilibrium. This is true, but there is a great deal of difference between countries where imports and exports are securely locked together in a combined expansion process and those

11. "Japan's decision to industrialize mainly succeeded because at the time there was a very keen American demand for silk, owing to the outbreak of the silkworm disease in Europe." D. T. Lakdawala, *International Aspects of Indian Economic Development* (London, Oxford Univ. Press, 1951), p. 11, quoted in C. P. Kindleberger, *Economic Development* (New York, McGraw-Hill, 1958), p. 252.

which must continually invoke a variety of adjustment mechanisms to balance their foreign accounts. Usually differences in balance-of-payments vulnerability are explained in terms of varying degrees of smoothness with which these mechanisms work. We have suggested here that the explanation could also lie in the greater or lesser need to bring corrective forces into play at all.

Growth-inducing effects of fluctuations in foreign exchange earnings. Whether or not a country receives balance-of-payments assistance, the foreign exchange available to it is likely to fluctuate. Variations in foreign exchange earnings as a result of fluctuations in the prices of their principal exports are in fact the principal form in which cyclical movements are transmitted to or generated in the underdeveloped areas.

As was already hinted in Chapter 7 (p. 118), such fluctuations are not necessarily a setback to a country's development: a temporary fall in foreign exchange availabilities permits it to overcome the resistances against the beginning of import-substituting production that are felt during periods of foreign exchange abundance even after domestic production thresholds have been crossed. These resistances are much weakened and the incentives to start domestic production become very strong when balance-of-payments difficulties appear.

That fluctuations in foreign exchange availabilities may, up to a point, accelerate economic development can be shown in the following way. Take first the years during which foreign exchange earnings are ample and import restrictions nonexistent. During this period an underdeveloped country expands its traditional imports and develops a taste, a market, and a need for a number of hitherto unknown and unappreciated commodities. As more imported incentive goods become available, backward-sloping supply curves of effort are being "unbent" and economic operators become more market-oriented in their work habits and production efforts. A number of "thresholds" are being crossed, but production is not started because of the opposition of the importing interests, the difficulties of competing with them, and the lack of interest of public authorities.

Come the lean years and imports are restricted in one way or another: the entrepreneurs then know from the previous phase that the size of the home market for some of these imports warrants the building up of domestic manufacturing, and such projects now are strongly supported by public opinion because the absence or high price of the previously imported commodities is felt as a deprivation; in fact, in this phase, the domestic importers themselves, or the foreign exporting interests, often turn producers of the goods they previously shipped into the country.[12] One might even point out that import restrictions lead to a kind of "forced saving" that will be helpful in financing the new ventures. For, in view of the absence of close substitutes, the would-be, but temporarily frustrated, purchasers of these imported commodities are not likely to replace them entirely by consumption of domestic goods and services.[13]

We are clearly taking here an optimistic view of the balance-of-payments disturbances affecting underdeveloped countries. The opposite interpretation is far more current: focusing on the availability of capital, this view shows how in time of prosperity and foreign exchange abundance countries have the means but not the will to industrialize, and the will but not the means during the ensuing phase of depression and foreign exchange scarcity. The history of economic progress in many underdeveloped areas during the great depression and two World Wars [14] shows that our analysis is not inconsistent with the facts; and while we would certainly agree that extreme fluctuations in foreign exchange earnings are far from desirable and may produce stagnation rather than development, we can easily account for such an outcome in terms of our own analysis. For the positive effects to be felt, the goods imported during prosperity must become part of a consumption pattern sensed as "normal." If they are considered a

12. A survey conducted by the Department of Commerce in 1952 among United States manufacturing companies with plants abroad showed that two out of five companies had started their foreign operations in order to *maintain* a market in which they had become established, mainly when loss of this market was threatened by tariffs or other import barriers. See E. R. Barlow and I. T. Wender, *Foreign Investment and Taxation* (Englewood Cliffs, N.J., 1955), pp. 116–17 and 146–51. Also R. F. Mikesell, *Promoting United States Investment Abroad*, National Planning Association (Washington, 1957), ch. 3.

13. Cf. W. F. Stolper, "The Volume of Foreign Trade and the Level of Income," *Quarterly Journal of Economics, 61* (Feb. 1947), 285–310.

14. H. Mendershausen, "The Pattern of Overseas Economic Development in World War II" in *Economia Internazionale, 4* (Aug. 1951), 745–71, in particular 752–5.

windfall and an extravagance they will not be judged a firm enough foundation for the building up of domestic industry.

In a sense, our thesis is an elaboration of the Duesenberry-Modigliani assumptions about consumer behavior; applied to underdeveloped countries we find that they have important implications for development and production. In a developed country with balanced international accounts, Duesenberry's "fundamental psychological postulate" [15] that during a period of falling incomes consumers will strain to maintain the highest standard of living attained in the past, will manifest itself exclusively in a reduced propensity to save. But the peak standard of living is surely identified with a certain pattern of spending one's income on desirable goods and services. Now, in underdeveloped countries, when real incomes decline as a result of smaller imports, the peak standard of living previously enjoyed cannot be protected just by saving less; in fact, savings may paradoxically increase as a result of what is essentially the same behavior pattern, if consumers find that the availability of desirable goods has fallen more than their incomes. In such a situation, the desire to recapture the past can be successful only if it causes entrepreneurs to produce domestically at least some of the goods that were previously imported.

The preceding argument is not designed to advocate strong fluctuations in foreign exchange receipts for underdeveloped countries. All it says is that such fluctuations may set in motion certain valuable development mechanisms. In other words, if an underdeveloped country could count on a perfectly stable or a regularly rising foreign exchange income, something might be said for inducing a spending pattern that would result in drawing down exchange during one period and in accumulating it during another. But in the real world our problem has been traditionally how to cope with excessive fluctuations in foreign exchange income as a result, for instance, of violent ups and downs of commodity prices, and it seems unlikely that we will ever need to adopt policies that would simulate, as it were, instability in export receipts. Nevertheless, an understanding of this development mechanism cannot fail to be of interest to the policy maker, if only because it permits him to gauge correctly the forces spontaneously

15. J. S. Duesenberry, *Income, Saving and the Theory of Consumer Behavior* (Cambridge, Mass., 1949), p. 84.

making for industrialization at different phases of the foreign exchange cycle.

Population Pressures

Few topics in the theory of economic development have evoked such unanimity as population growth. With increases in per capita income widely accepted as the objective of development or as the best available approximation to it, population is firmly relegated to the denominator of the expression which we want to maximize and any increase in numbers can only be considered a setback on the road to development. Such expressions as the population growth that "swallows up" increases in output in whole or in part, such images as walking up a downward moving escalator,[16] and the virtually obligatory quotation from Lewis Carroll: "Here it takes all the running you can do, to keep in the same place,"—all testify to the universal assumption that the exclusive effect of population growth is to frustrate economic development. Some writers are of course aware of the fact that demographic stagnation or declining population growth were high on the list among the explanations for the falling behind of France as a major political and economic power, and were one of the three pillars of the stagnation thesis in the United States. But any disturbing ideas on that account could be quickly discarded by the reassuring, if somewhat shapeless, thought that the problems of developed and underdeveloped countries are entirely distinct.

In the face of such unanimity, we shall present with considerable reluctance some reasons which make us think that population pressures are to be considered forces that may stimulate development. We are fully aware that this is a dangerous thought—dangerous not so much for the world at large as for the reputation of the author; and in order not to expose ourselves too long to the heavy fire which will certainly be opened on us, we shall dispose of what we have to say with the utmost brevity.

Let us start out by again invoking Duesenberry's "fundamental psychological postulate," which says that people will resist a lowering in their standard of living. If they do this as a result of a cyclical depression why should they not also react in some way against their

16. Singer, "Economic Progress in Underdeveloped Countries," p. 7.

incomes being squeezed by an increase in population? Our first proposition is therefore that *population pressure on living standards will lead to counterpressure, i.e., to activity designed to maintain or restore the traditional standard of living of the community.* Leaving the validity of this proposition for later consideration, we shall assume for the moment that this counterpressure is partially or wholly successful in restoring per capita incomes. Thus far, then, the psychological postulate yields at best a mechanism of equilibrium, i.e., of stagnation rather than development.

But the situation is not really the same after this process, for in its course the community has *learned,* through wrestling successfully with new tasks. Our second proposition is therefore that *the activity undertaken by the community in resisting a decline in its standard of living causes an increase in its ability to control its environment and to organize itself for development.* As a result, the community will now be able to exploit the opportunities for economic growth that existed previously but were left unutilized.

In short, the learning a community does when it reacts to population pressures increases the total stock of its resources much as investment adds to total productive capacity. To revert to the images mentioned earlier: walking up downward escalators or running in the same place is excellent exercise and practice for people who need to improve their walking or running performance. Anyone who has watched attempts by public and private bodies to cope with the traffic, water supply, electric power, housing, school, and crime problems of a growing city can have little doubt that the qualities of imagination and organization developed in these tasks of *maintaining* standards of living in the face of population pressures are very similar to those that are needed to *increase* per capita incomes. The basic determinant of development which we have called the "ability to invest" is decisively enhanced in the course of the struggle to accommodate more people.

Returning to our first proposition, we cannot claim that it is more than a variant of an old idea. Many writers, Malthus among them, have remarked on the incentive effects of the need to provide for one's wife and children. Others have examined the stimulating effect of population increases, not on the individual's "natural indolence," but on society's. In this respect, much that is incisive has been said, in particular by the Belgian sociologist and philosopher Dupréel who has traced the many ways in which an increasing population leads to improved performance of the administrative, political, and cultural processes.[17] But while these direct positive influences and actions of population growth on individual motivations and economic and political developments are of interest, we think it more useful to stress the *reaction* mechanism that is set up when population growth depresses, or is about to depress, living standards, for the recognition of this reaction mechanism permits us to go beyond the following, somewhat unsatisfactory summary of the problem by Schumpeter: "Sometimes an increase in population actually has no other effects than that predicted by classical theory—a fall in per capita real income; but at other times it may have an energizing effect that induces new developments with the result that per capita income rises."[18] By viewing the "energizing" effect as potentially induced by the "classical" effect, we can at least attempt to reduce the complete indeterminateness of this statement.

Our affirmation that a society will attempt to react to the "dilution" of total income that comes with larger numbers is of interest only if the reaction can be successful, i.e., if there is some "slack" in the economy that can be taken up. This assumption is of course contrary to the basic hypothesis of the neo-Malthusian models, *viz.* "all productive forces are fully utilized, i.e., there are no unemployed resources—the supply of land and capital is fixed."[19] This formulation is not even sufficiently strong if we wish to stipulate that it is impossible to squeeze more output from the available resources without a prior increase in per capita incomes out of which new savings can be extracted. We must then also suppose that production is *optimally* organized, that all existing technological and organizational knowledge that does not require capital outlays is fully applied. Obviously, even in densely populated underdeveloped areas, such a situation will be exceedingly rare.[20]

17. E. Dupréel, "Population et progrès" in *Deux essais sur le progrès*, Brussels, 1928.

18. J. Schumpeter, "The Creative Response in Economic History," *Journal of Economic History*, 7 (Nov. 1947), 149.

19. Alan T. Peacock, "Theory of Population and Modern Economic Analysis," *Population Studies*, 6 (1952–53), 115.

20. Malthus can be quoted in support of this view: "There are few large countries, however advanced in improvement, the population of which might not

The panorama changes abruptly if it is granted that a margin of possible improvements exists, and if, more generally, we revert to our diagnosis of underdevelopment as a state where labor, capital, entrepreneurship, etc. are potentially available and can be combined, provided a sufficiently strong "binding agent" is encountered (Chapter 1). Then an increase in incomes is by no means the only way of starting the economy on an upward course. Nevertheless, there is some question whether population pressure can be considered an "inducement mechanism" in the sense in which we have used this term. How will it cause the possible improvements to be made? How will it call forth the latent resources of the economy?

Among the inducement mechanisms we have studied, from the various complementarity effects on down, population pressure must rank as the least attractive one. In the first place, it works through an initial decline in per capita income rather than through, e.g., an uneven expansion in output. Secondly, it is less reliable than the other mechanisms we have considered. In our previous, vaguely similar mechanism, i.e., losses in foreign exchange income leading to industrialization, we could point to several solid links in the reaction chain: specific, now unsatisfied, needs; "forced savings" of a kind; the interest of the heretofore importers or foreign suppliers, etc.[21]

In the case of population pressures, on the other hand, we are provided only with an aspiration to return to the status quo ante, but generally not with specific means or intermediate reaction links for doing so. Nevertheless, in some of the following situations, the passage from aspiration to reality becomes plausible or is more readily visualized than in others.

-----

have been doubled or tripled, and there are many which might be ten or even a hundred times as populous, and yet all the inhabitants be as well provided for as they are now, if the institutions of society and the moral habits of the people, had been for some hundred years the most favourable to the increase of capital, and the demand for produce and labour." A Summary View of the Principle of Population, reprinted in Introduction to Malthus, ed. D. V. Glass, London, Watts, 1953, pp. 151–2.

21. Note that this mechanism is in turn less reliable than the one utilized in Duesenberry's construction. In the case of a sudden absence of a desired good because of balance-of-payments difficulties, consumers cannot protect their previous standard of living just by saving less as Duesenberry's consumers are wont to do in a depression.

1. The probability of a strong reaction is greater if the population increase comes as a sudden shock. A community may not feel impelled to "make a stand" when population increases and declines in living standards are slow, just as workers will sometimes experience greater difficulty in maintaining their real wages in the face of creeping inflation than when prices rise a good 20% a year. For this reason, the dramatic decline in mortality rates and the consequent massive increase in numbers that is taking place today in underdeveloped areas holds greater promise of a vigorous reaction than the far slower increases of previous epochs.

2. A population increase is likely to be more action-stimulating if it is combined with increased urbanization and therefore leads to obvious needs and pressures for more overhead facilities, such as housing, schools, and public utilities.

3. Again, the reaction may be facilitated if population growth takes place in underdeveloped countries which as a result of the increase in numbers pass minimum production thresholds in a number of important industries, as compared to more populous countries where these thresholds have long been passed or to much smaller countries where they remain far away.

4. The reaction may be easier to accomplish if the increase affects primarily the upper classes of society, or at least the upper classes along with the lower classes, for the need to provide for one's children is in this case more likely to take the form of increased entrepreneurial activity.

5. Finally, the closer a country actually is to the rigid assumptions of the neo-Malthusian models which we mentioned above, i.e., the more fully and perfectly its resources are already utilized, the less room there is for any reactions outside of the most direct ones—namely, birth control and postponement of marriage. Precisely because of the assumption of fixed resources, this reaction to population pressures has virtually monopolized the attention of demographers. From our point of view, the "preventive checks" are only one of the many forms which the reaction mechanism can take. Under present conditions, in fact, it is in many countries more difficult to visualize population pressures resulting in effective birth control measures than in improvements of agricultural techniques and in stepped-up capital formation in industry and public utilities. In any event, our second proposition applies here also, even though perhaps somewhat indirectly: for a peo-

ple that is induced to exercise foresight to the point of adopting effective birth control techniques is again learning that one's environment can be controlled and changed and will therefore be better equipped for coping with the tasks of development.

All in all, population pressure still qualifies as an inducement mechanism in the sense that it presents the developmental forces within a society with an opportunity to assert themselves. It supplies "the motive and the cue for passion" (though admittedly it fails to provide many cues for action). Thus it seems wrong to say that population pressures act as an obstacle to development. There are circumstances under which these pressures are unsuccessful in performing their stimulating role just as relative price increases are at times ineffective in calling forth increases in the supply of the "signaled" commodities.

The view that has been presented is consistent with the fact that population pressures have demonstrably been an integral part of the development process in all countries that are economically advanced today. It would surely be most unrealistic to look at the population increases in Europe in the nineteenth century and at those in, say, Brazil and Mexico today as a depressing influence on economic development. But if this is granted, then we must ask the partisans of the classical view to explain why population growth, like some of the lesser Homeric gods who throw their support to the winning side at the height of battle, suddenly becomes a stimulant to economic development after having long played the role of obstacle. In our view, no such switch ever occurs; rather we are able to account by a single hypothesis for a stream of events within which we might distinguish three periods: during the first, per capita incomes do not increase, but countries, in reacting to population pressures, acquire the abilities to launch undertakings that will lead to genuine economic growth; during a second period, per capita incomes begin to rise, with economic growth continuing to draw strength from population growth; and only at a later stage does economic growth wean itself from population growth and becomes self-sustained.[22]

What conclusion can be drawn from the preceding remarks for population policy in underdeveloped countries? Certainly not that they should institute a system of generous family allowances. In the first place, we have already stated our view that population pressures

22. With population still growing in all economically progressive countries, we actually have no conclusive empirical evidence about the existence of this stage.

181

are a clumsy and cruel stimulant to development. Actually, under-developed countries are today abundantly supplied with this stimulant, whether they want it or not, as a result of the universal and rapid decline in mortality rates. Secondly, we consider the spread of birth control as one important form which the reaction to population pressure can take, and one that, if it occurs, brings with it basic attitude changes that are favorable to development.

Our policy conclusions, then, are somewhat anticlimactic. Any practical usefulness of our reasoning lies in the fact that it leads to a less alarmist attitude toward the population problem than is displayed by the current literature with its "traps" and the need for a huge jump to break out of them. This kind of reasoning derives of course from the comparisons of population growth with output growth rates. A highly sophisticated version of this approach is given by Leibenstein; he demonstrates that if a country has a population growth rate of, say, one per cent per year, it is not sufficient for it to achieve an output growth rate in excess of one per cent; for when output and therefore income rise, population may rise even more; so that to overtake population growth for good, the country may have to achieve a rate of output growth that is a multiple of the initial rate of population growth; and it must achieve this rate not gradually but in one jump, for at any intermediate point the country's rate of income growth will be dragged down again to its low-level starting point.[23]

Our approach leads us to take a far calmer view of the situation. We have shown that if a country is at all able to offset, be it even partially at first, the effect of the population increase, then we may have confidence that, through the learning acquired in this process, it will be able to do progressively better in marshaling its productive forces for development so that eventually output growth will overtake population growth. If a community makes a genuine effort to defend its standard of living in the face of population pressures, it need not be afraid of imaginary traps, for cumulative growth is then already in the making: just as income can rise in advance of consumption, so can economic progress get under way before being registered in per capita income increases.

23. Leibenstein, *Economic Backwardness and Economic Growth,* pp. 170–2. See also Ch. 2, n. 16.

CHAPTER 10

Interregional and International Transmission
of Economic Growth

"Growing Points" and Lagging Regions

To COMPLETE our survey of inducement mechanisms, we shall examine in this chapter how growth can be communicated from one region or one country to another. In this inquiry we may take it for granted that economic progress does not appear everywhere at the same time and that once it has appeared powerful forces make for a spatial concentration of economic growth around the initial starting points. Why substantial gains may be reaped from overcoming the "friction of space" [1] through agglomeration has been analyzed in detail by the economic theory of location. In addition to the locational advantages offered by *existing* settlements others come from nearness to a *growing* center where an "industrial atmosphere" has come into being with its special receptivity to innovations and enterprise. It was largely the observation of the latter connections that suggested to Marshall the concept of external economies.[2]

Whatever the reason, there can be little doubt that an economy, to lift itself to higher income levels, must and will first develop within itself one or several regional centers of economic strength. This need for the emergence of "growing points" or "growth poles" [3] in the course

1. This term was used by Robert M. Haig in "Toward an Understanding of the Metropolis," *Quarterly Journal of Economics, 40* (1926), 184–5.
2. A good survey of Marshall's views and of other contributions to this subject is in Eric A. Lampard, "The History of Cities in the Economically Advanced Areas," *Economic Development and Cultural Change, 3* (Jan. 1955), 81–137, particularly 92–101.
3. "Pôle de croissance" is the term used for both regional and sectoral growth leadership in the expanding and instructive French literature on the subject. See, e.g., Perroux, "Note sur la notion de 'pôle de croissance'"; *Matériaux pour une analyse de la croissance économique*, Cahiers de l'Institut de Science Eco-

of the development process means that international and interregional inequality of growth is an inevitable concomitant and condition of growth itself.

Thus, in the geographical sense, growth is necessarily unbalanced. However, while the regional setting reveals unbalanced growth at its most obvious, it perhaps does not show it at its best. In analyzing the process of unbalanced growth, we could always show that an advance at one point sets up pressures, tensions, and compulsions toward growth at subsequent points. But if all of these points fall within the same privileged growth space, the forces that make for transmission of growth from one country, one region, or one group of persons to another will be singularly weak.

The ability and tendency of growth to round itself out for a long time within some subgroup, region, or country while backwardness retains its hold elsewhere has often been noted. If the tendency manifests itself along clearly marked geographic lines, the result is the division of the world into developed and underdeveloped countries and the split of a country into progressive and backward regions. On the other hand, progress and tradition may dwell in close spatial proximity by simply fastening on different human groups and economic activities that exist side by side; this state of affairs, often encountered in developing countries, has been aptly termed "dualism" and has already been examined in our analysis of the industrialization process (Chapter 7).

With respect to different social or income groups a similar phenomenon may be noted: once one group has shown its readiness to acquire new wants and its ability to afford the products satisfying them, it will be catered to by a multitude of firms all tailoring their output to the type of per capita buying power and to the size of the market that have been revealed. It takes innovators like Ford and Giannini to strike out beyond this charmed circle, just as it seems to take a special kind of boldness to establish a new basic industry or to perceive the development potentials of the more backward regions of a developing country.

Thus investors spend a long time mopping up all the opportunities around some "growth pole" and neglect those that may have arisen or

nomique Appliquée, Série D, No. 8, 1955; J. R. Boudeville, "Contribution a l'étude des pôles de croissance brésiliens," Cahiers, Série F, No. 10, 1957.

could be made to arise elsewhere. What appears to happen is that *the external economies due to the poles, though real, are consistently overestimated by the economic operators.*

The reason for this tendency—perhaps implicit in the phrase "nothing succeeds like success"—must be sought in the realm of social psychology. The progressive sectors and regions of an underdeveloped economy are easily overimpressed with their own rate of development. At the same time, they set themselves apart from the less progressive operators by creating a picture of the latter as lazy, bungling, intriguing, and generally hopeless. There seems to be a cliquishness about progress when it first appears that recalls the same phenomenon among adolescents: the girls who menstruate and the boys who shave have an acute sense of their superiority over those who cannot yet claim such achievements. The tendency to magnify the distance that separates one group or region from another shows up in the derogatory use of the term "indio" in some Latin American countries to designate whoever is economically or socially one's inferior. Similarly, the average Italian, in whose country economic progress has long been closely associated with latitude, is always ready to declare that Africa begins just south of his own province.

Thus the successful groups and regions will widely and extravagantly proclaim their superiority over the rest of their country and their countrymen. It is interesting to note that to some extent these claims are self-enforcing. Even though the initial success of these groups may often be due to sheer luck or to environmental factors such as resource endowment, matters will not be left there. Those who have been caught by progress will always maintain that they were the ones who did the catching; they will easily convince themselves, and attempt to convince others, that their accomplishments are primarily owed to their superior moral qualities and conduct. It is precisely this self-righteousness that will tend to produce its own evidence: once these groups have spread the word that their success was due to hard work and virtuous living, they must willy-nilly live up to their own story, or at the least will make their children do so.[4] In other words, there is reason to think that the "protestant ethic," instead of being

---

4. Observation would seem to confirm that the behavior of second generation businessmen is far more compulsively "businesslike" than that of the pioneer generation.

the prime mover, is often implanted *ex post* as though to sanctify and consolidate whatever accumulation of economic power and wealth has been achieved. To the extent that this happens, a climate particularly favorable to further growth will actually come into existence in the sectors or regions that have pulled ahead, and this will confirm the economic operators in their preference for these regions and make it somewhat less irrational.

The less developed groups and regions also make unwittingly a contribution to the process which we can only sketch here. Faced with the sudden improvement in the fortunes of some of their own compatriots, they will frequently retort to the claims of superiority of these *nouveaux riches* by accusing them of crass materialism, sharp practices, and disregard for the country's traditional cultural and spiritual values. While such charges are directed with particular relish at minorities, whose importance in the process of development is well recognized, purely indigenous entrepreneurial groups are by no means exempt from them. In this way these groups are, as it were, converted into minorities in their own country,[5] often estranged from the rest of their compatriots, and ostracized by the traditional elites. Such a development is particularly likely when the first stages of commercial and industrial progress are localized in a center other than the capital city. In this case, the rift between this center and the capital may well widen cumulatively over a long period of time. The very fact that the leading families of such cities as Barcelona, São Paulo, Medellín, and Guayaquil lived far away from, and often in conflict with, the centers of politics, public administration, and education made for a dogged concentration of succeeding generations on business pursuits rather than for absorption of the most talented by other careers that carry more prestige in a traditional society. This situation may again lead

5. A good example is supplied by the inhabitants of Antioquia, a province of Colombia. The Antioqueños have been outstandingly enterprising in bringing virgin lands under coffee cultivation and in establishing industries, mostly in their capital of Medellín. Their racial, religious, and cultural characteristics do not differentiate the Antioqueños from the other Colombians, but having taken such a prominent part in the country's development, they are *now* considered practically as a separate group; and even though it is unsupported by any evidence (see J. J. Parsons, *Antioqueño Colonization in Western Colombia* [Berkeley, 1949], p. 62), the conviction is widespread that they are really of Jewish, or at least of Basque, origin!

to a clustering of investment around the initial growing point, which is healthy for the consolidation of economic growth at its beginning but may represent irrational prejudice and clannishness at a later stage.

Trickling-Down and Polarization Effects [5a]

No matter how strong and exaggerated the space preference of the economic operators, once growth takes a firm hold in one part of the national territory, it obviously sets in motion certain forces that act on the remaining parts. In examining these direct interactions, we shall call "North" the region which has been experiencing growth and "South" the one that has remained behind. This terminology is suggested by the fact that a large number of lagging areas, at least in the Northern Hemisphere, appear to be located in the southern parts of the countries to which they belong. The term "South" as used here does not include *undeveloped*—i.e., largely unsettled—areas.

The growth of the North will have a number of direct economic repercussions on the South, some favorable, others adverse. The favor-

5a. Footnote added in proof: The argument of the following sections was outlined originally in my article "Investment Policies and 'Dualism' in Underdeveloped Countries," *American Economic Review*, 47 (Sept. 1957), 550–70. I now find that Gunnar Myrdal has addressed himself to similar problems in *Economic Theory and Under-Developed Regions* (London, 1957), particularly in chapters 3 to 5, and has had recourse to the same conceptual tools that are employed here: his "backwash" and "spread" effects correspond exactly to my "polarization" and "trickling down" effects. Nevertheless, there are considerable differences in emphasis and conclusions. Myrdal's analysis strikes me as excessively dismal. In the first place, he fails to recognize that the emergence of growing points and therefore of differences in development between regions and between nations is inevitable and is a condition of further growth anywhere. Secondly, his preoccupation with the mechanism of cumulative causation hides from him the emergence of the strong forces making for a turning point once the movement toward North-South polarization within a country has proceeded for some time. Finally, the picture he paints of international transmission of growth is also too bleak in my opinion as he overlooks that the polarization (backwash) effects are much weaker between nations than between regions within the same country. However, I fully agree with Myrdal on the importance of political forces in effecting a North-South rapprochement within a country and on the need for the emergence of such forces on the international level to help narrow the gap between the developed and the underdeveloped countries. I have anticipated here the discussion contained in the remainder of this chapter.

able effects consist of the *trickling down* of Northern progress: by far the most important of these effects is the increase of Northern purchases and investments in the South, an increase that is sure to take place if the economies of the two regions are at all complementary. In addition, the North may absorb some of the disguised unemployed of the South and thereby raise the marginal productivity of labor and per capita consumption levels in the South.

On the other hand, several unfavorable or *polarization* effects are also likely to be at work. Comparatively inefficient, yet income-creating, Southern activities in manufacturing and exports may become depressed as a result of Northern competition. To the extent that the North industrializes along lines in which there is no Southern production, the South is also likely to make a bad bargain since it will now have to buy Northern manufactures, produced behind newly erected tariff walls, instead of similar goods previously imported from abroad at lower prices.

A most serious, and frequently observed, polarization effect consists in the kind of internal migration that may follow upon the economic advances of the North. Instead of absorbing the disguised unemployed, Northern progress may denude the South of its key technicians and managers as well as of the more enterprising young men. This type of migration may actually be undesirable not only from the point of view of the South but also from that of the country as a whole, for the loss to the South due to the departure of these men may be higher than the gain to the North. This possibility is inherent in the contact between the expanding North and the stagnant South: in the North new jobs must be manned and, at least in the skilled grades, the wage and salary scale will reflect relative scarcities and productivities; whereas in the South skilled work and better-than-average performance will often be poorly remunerated either because they are simply not recognized or because they are not valued very highly [6] or because they carry nonmonetary rewards. Thus actual pay differentials between North and South are likely to overstate considerably the real productivity differentials in the most productive and skilled grades. In addition, of course, mobility is highest in these same lines so that it becomes almost a certainty that the South will lose to the North first

6. Even societies that actively discourage better-than-average performance (see p. 12) are unable to abolish it altogether simply because of innate differences.

and foremost its more highly qualified people. And, along with skill and enterprise, what little capital the South generates is also likely to migrate northward.

In spite of this bleak picture, we would still feel confident that in the end the trickling-down effects would gain the upper hand over the polarization effects if the North had to rely to an important degree on Southern products for its own expansion. For instance, if the North specializes in manufactures and the South in primary production, the expanding demand of the North ought to stimulate Southern growth. But things may go less smoothly. It is likely, in particular, that the short-run supply elasticity is low in the South so that the terms of trade will move against the North.[7]

In this case, three possibilities arise. In the best of worlds, the rise in Southern prices would fairly soon prove effective in raising production. Another possible, though far less satisfactory, outcome would consist in the slowing down of Northern progress resulting from rising labor and material costs. But such a development is unlikely as long as the North is not entirely dependent on the South. The third possibility is therefore for the North to alter its method of procuring needed primary products. Faced with the upward trend in Southern prices and exasperated by the unreliability of Southern production, Northern operators may draw on imports from foreign areas or may replace Southern products by developing their own primary production. In this way, *checks to the trickling-down effects* may well come into play, and as a result the South could be left in a far worse backwater than before. For once the North possesses within itself a large and productive agricultural area or is able to supply its needs in primary products from abroad and through domestic synthetic production, the South will be largely cut off from beneficial contact with Northern development, while remaining exposed to the adverse polarization effects. Under these conditions—which are or were fairly typical of such backward regions as Brazil's Nordeste, Colombia's Oriente, and Italy's Mezzogiorno—the stage would be set for a prolonged split of the country into a progressive and a depressed area.

7. This situation has been fully analyzed by H. G. Johnson for the case in which a developing industrial country trades with a stagnant agricultural country; see his "Economic Expansion and International Trade," *Manchester School of Economic and Social Studies*, 23 (May 1955), 96–101.

Eventually, economic pressures to remedy such a situation are likely to assert themselves again. Industry will become congested in Northern cities and its expansion will be hampered by the insufficient size of the home market resulting from the depressed income levels in the South. Also, economic policy makers will be impelled to take a close look at Southern development potentials whenever balance-of-payments or other supply difficulties make it clear that the country is harming itself by its failure to utilize fully its Southern resources.

In other words, if the market forces that express themselves through the trickling-down and polarization effects result in a temporary victory of the latter, deliberate economic policy will come into play to correct the situation. Actually, of course, economic policy will be an important influence throughout the process. The nature of this influence will be analyzed presently.

The Regional Distribution of Public Investment

The most obvious manner in which economic policy affects the rates of growth of different parts of a country is through the regional allocation of public investments. Three principal patterns of allocation can be distinguished: dispersal, concentration on growing areas, and attempts to promote the development of backward areas.

In contrast to widespread impressions, the most pervasive tendency of governments of underdeveloped countries in making their investment decisions is not so much the obsession with one showpiece as the dispersal of funds among a large number of small projects scattered widely over the national territory.

While this pattern is *dominant* only in countries where dynamic economic growth has not yet taken hold, it can be said to exert a steady pull in practically all underdeveloped countries. The most obvious reason is that public investment decisions are easily the most political ones among the economic policy decisions taken by governments. Whether to build a road here rather than there, whether to construct a power plant that is to supply towns A, B, and C, rather than D, E, and F—these are questions that have decisive local political impact.

Thus, as all governments regardless of their democratic character desire and need support from all sections of the country, the temptation is strong to scatter the investment effort far and wide. Disconnected roads are built at many points; small Diesel power plants and aqueducts are installed in many towns; even low-cost housing programs which should obviously concentrate on relieving critical shortages and on slum clearance in the big cities are often similarly dispersed.

More fundamentally, the tendency toward wide dispersal of investment funds may be due to what was called in Chapter 1 the group-focused image of change, i.e., to the fact that economic progress is conceived as a force which ought to affect equally all members and sections of the community. Wherever this idea prevails, governments are unprepared and unwilling to make the choices about priorities and sequences that are the essence of development programs. When the feeling is widespread that something is wrong with even temporarily preferred treatment for some regions, the government may find it politically dangerous not to take this factor into account.

Finally, the dispersal pattern can be explained by certain shortages usually affecting underdeveloped countries. The elaboration of the many small projects into which public investment is typically split up when this pattern is dominant requires comparatively little engineering and planning talent, whereas the larger projects in electric power, transportation, or basic industry require far more such talent than is usually available to the government. This is why entirely too much has been made of the argument that development is held back not by the scarcity of funds, but by a scarcity of "bankable," i.e., well-conceived and engineered, projects. The question which should come first, the project or the funds, is really of the chicken-egg variety. Obviously funds can be spent only on clearly defined projects. But without definite expectations that funds—from domestic or foreign sources— will be forthcoming, the considerable cost of engineering and economic studies and the administrative effort required to gather the necessary staff and to obtain the assistance of foreign consultants will most likely not be undertaken. The promise of foreign funds—provided the studies prove the project feasible and worth while—is particularly important if this effort is to be made, as a large project usually results in one region's obtaining for the time being a substantial advantage over all others. This is an investment decision which a national government may find it difficult and imprudent to make unless it has the feeling—and the excuse vis-à-vis the other regions—that international development capital is not to be had at all on other terms.

Moreover, the study and preparation of a large-scale project implies in itself—especially in countries where there is the rhetorical tradition of confusing the word with the deed, and the announcement of plans with their realization—a commitment to the region which is going to be principally benefited. Governments are therefore reluctant to start such studies unless they feel reasonably sure that they will be able to "deliver." Unless they have assurances in this regard, they would be politically much better off to let sleeping projects lie.

The International Bank for Reconstruction and Development has often defended itself against charges of insufficient lending by the argument that there were not enough "bankable" projects available.[8] But in fact the Bank has frequently acted in accordance with the point of view just outlined—i.e., it has helped in the preparation of such projects by virtually committing itself in advance to the financing of their foreign exchange costs, including even the cost of the preliminary engineering surveys.

In this way the availability of international development capital may make for a shift from dispersal of public investment toward concentration on a few key projects. The "demonstration effect" of similar projects undertaken in other countries also works in this direction. But the most important force opposing the tendency toward excessive dispersal of public investment is the growth pattern characteristic of rapidly developing countries. Development often begins with the sudden, vigorous, and nearly spontaneous growth of one or a few regions or urban centers, resulting in serious shortages of electric power and water supply, as well as in housing and transportation bottlenecks. Thus, urgent demands for several types of capital-intensive public investment appear and must be given the highest priority whether or not

8. Statements to this effect can be found in several of the Bank's annual reports; e.g.: "Perhaps the most striking single lesson which the Bank has learned in the course of its operations is how limited is the capacity of the underdeveloped countries to absorb capital quickly for really productive purposes. . . . The Bank's experience to date indicates that the Bank now has or can readily acquire sufficient resources to help finance all the sound productive projects in its member countries that will be ready for financing in the next few years, that can appropriately be financed through repayable foreign loans and that cannot attract private capital." *Fourth Annual Report* (Washington, 1948–49), pp. 8, 13.

they correspond to the government's sense of distributive justice and to its pattern of regional political preference. The public investment in overhead capital in turn makes possible further growth of industry and trade in the favored areas and this growth requires further large allocations of public investment to them.

Determined as it is by the volume of private investment and the general rise in income in the developing areas, public investment clearly plays here an "induced" role, and investment choices are often remarkably and unexpectedly obvious. It is not always easy, however, to have these obvious choices adopted, partly because of the continuing desire of governments to revert to the policy of scatter, and partly because a new pressure soon makes itself felt—namely, to accelerate development in the areas that have fallen behind.

A situation in which the bulk of public investment is continuously being sucked into the comparatively developed portions of the national territory cannot in the long run be considered satisfactory by governments because of compelling considerations of equity and national cohesion. In fact, the attempt to change drastically the distribution of public investment in favor of the country's poorer sections often comes at a point that seems premature to the foreign observer or adviser for the simple reason that the more rapidly advancing sections do not strike *him* as so outstandingly prosperous. It is, however, quite understandable that the attempt should be made long before these sections have come anywhere near fully developing their potential. Moreover, the poorer sections of the country, where careers in industry and trade are not promising, often produce, for this very reason, a majority of the country's successful politicians and thereby acquire influential spokesmen in the councils of government.

It is possible that the transition from the second pattern—concentration of public investment on spontaneously growing areas—to the third—attempt to ignite development in the heretofore stagnant areas through "autonomous" public investment—is facilitated by certain peculiar properties of public investment. Usually the second phase results not in a mere shift from scatter to concentration of a given investment total, but in a considerable enlargement of the total amount of funds required for public investment. These funds are secured through the introduction of new and higher taxes or through other *permanent* revenue-raising devices.

On the other hand, it is probably reasonable to assume that the need for the investment of public funds in the country's spontaneously growing areas is particularly great in the initial stages of development, as basic utilities are created and rapidly expanded. After development has proceeded for some time, the need for public investment in relation to private investment tends to decline and in any event an increased portion of public investment can be financed out of earnings of previous investments. This kind of change in the composition of investment is implicit in the term "social *overhead* capital."

As the taxation and other measures which have financed the original spurt in public investment continue to yield revenue, some funds may thus become, if not unemployed, at least less compellingly employed than previously. This is likely to be immediately sensed by the officials responsible for apportioning public investment and provides an excellent opportunity to those among them who want to change its geographic composition in favor of the less developed sections.

Thus, while public investment policy may accentuate at one stage the North-South split, it can be counted upon to stage at least an attempt to heal the split should it turn out to be prolonged. For this reason governmental intervention is particularly prevalent in the development of the backward areas within underdeveloped countries. In fact, the government will, to the best of its ability, attempt to counteract in part the polarization effects that result from the operation of market forces: to counterbalance the northward emigration of capital and talent, an even larger flow in the opposite direction will be organized; to offset the locational advantages of the North, governments may offer special tax advantages or create similar external economies in the South through public investments.

Naturally, the channeling of large-scale expenditures toward the underprivileged areas of a country contains the danger of misguided investment to a much higher degree than where spontaneous growth has already staked out fairly well the areas in which public investments are urgently required. The most obvious and least "risky" course [9] is to endow the South with just as good a system of transportation, electric power stations, and other social overhead capital facilities as are available in the North. But we have already explained that this may not be the most efficient method of inducing growth in

9. See pp. 165–6.

the South because of the weakness of its entrepreneurship and the purely "permissive" character of the inducement mechanisms set in motion by these investments. Although some investment in public utilities may be indispensable, the essential task is to endow the South with some ongoing and actively inducing economic activity of its own, in industry, agriculture, or services. For this reason, the building of a steel mill in Colombia's Oriente and the founding of the new Brazilian capital in the long neglected "interior" will probably turn out to be effective governmental development moves in spite of initial mistakes, difficulties, and setbacks.

Interregional and International Transmission Compared

Our discussion has made it clear that the interregional transmission of growth cannot be expected to proceed smoothly. Obstructionist forces have been seen to be at work alongside those that make for integration, in the economic and political fields. It is tempting then to apply an a fortiori argument to the *international* transmission of growth: if interregional transmission is beset with obstacles, is it not natural to conclude that international transmission will be even more difficult?

While the disparity in the development levels of different countries would seem to support such a conclusion, it is not at all justified by the arguments we have used in demonstrating the difficulties of interregional transmission of growth. Some of these arguments rather point to the somewhat unsettling thought that the various "Souths" might be better off if they were sovereign political units, i.e., that in some respects growth may be more easily transmitted from one nation to another than from one region to another within the same country. We will first explore these "economic arguments for separatism" and then show in what respects transmission mechanisms are after all more effective between regions than between sovereign countries.

The case for separatism. In general it may be expected that because of the closer contact and more intensive interaction that exist among regions of the same country than among sovereign nations, both trickling-down *and* polarization effects will be found to be stronger in interregional than in international economic relations.

195

The case for separatism will therefore consist largely in showing that the polarization effects will be far less damaging to a country than to a region. This is certainly the case for the mobility of factors of production. We have seen that within a country this mobility can be highly prejudicial for the South, and conceivably even uneconomic from the point of view of the country as a whole. If the South were an independent country, mobility would certainly be far lower and the Southern development potential would be less impaired.

Another polarization effect consisted in the debilitating influence of Northern competition on Southern economic activities satisfying domestic or export demands. Again, this effect would be virtually absent between independent countries. With respect to the latter, countries compete in international markets on the basis of comparative advantage, regions within a country on the basis of absolute advantage. Suppose that North and South, considered independently, both have a comparative advantage in cane sugar, but that production is more efficient in the North. Then, if each were an independent country, they would both specialize in sugar, with real factor returns being lower in the South. But if North and South are united in one country, sugar production would be expanded in the North and may be abandoned in the South even though the maintenance and expansion of sugar exports could represent the valuable beginning of a "growth pole" for the South.

The same reasoning holds for industrialization. It has frequently been pointed out that, if there is any substance to the various arguments for protection, they must apply just as much to a region as to a country; but the region cannot ordinarily protect its industries except through exemption from minor local taxes. Also, within a country (or in relations between a country and its colonies) Northern industrialists may often effectively prevent or delay the development of industry in the South; in relations between sovereign countries, attempts in this direction have sometimes been made, but obviously have far smaller chances of success.

Finally—and related to the previous points—the absence of economic sovereignty with respect to such matters as currency issue and exchange rate determination may be a considerable handicap for the development of a region.

The preceding argument is reminiscent of Viner's celebrated thesis that a customs union between two countries may lead to a less, rather than more, efficient allocation of resources.[10] To prove this proposition, Viner invoked only the "trade-diverting effects," i.e., the possibility that the partners of a customs union will now buy from each other what they could previously obtain more cheaply—and what can be more efficiently produced—in third markets. This argument is also applicable to our problem, but the polarization effects relating to factor mobility and North-South competition in exports and industry are perhaps more important in a developmental situation.

The case for surrender of sovereignty. We must now come to the other half of our story. As the polarization effects will be stronger when there are no frontiers to cross, so will the trickling-down effects. The advance of the North is bound to lead to purchases and investments in the South. All complementarities that exist within a country will be readily exploited. Regional specialization patterns will emerge and are not likely to be tampered with even when they are based more on historical accident than on comparative resource endowments. Not so between sovereign countries. Here potential complementarities are likely to be taken advantage of in a far more selective and spotty fashion, not only because of the "friction of space" but because of the many other frictions that are encountered as soon as frontiers are crossed. Protectionist movements and reactions to balance-of-payments difficulties will set up strong obstacles to the emergence of a finely articulated division of labor and will always threaten it if it should arise.

The trickling-down effects will still be powerfully effective in promoting development of countries with resources that are highly prized by the industrial countries. But if a country has nothing particularly essential or attractive to offer, it may remain excluded for a long time from any important participation in world trade when, as a region integrated into a larger country, it might have contributed quite nicely to interregional trade.

In our treatment of interregional transmission of growth we saw the principal danger of an emergence of a North-South problem in

10. Viner, *The Customs Union Issue* (New York, 1950), ch. 4. For a systematic discussion of the issues raised by Viner, see J. E. Meade, *The Theory of Customs Unions,* Amsterdam, 1955.

the low supply elasticity characteristic of the South and in the consequent loss of interdependence as the North extricated itself from dependence on Southern products in a variety of ways. In international relations these checks to the trickling-down effects are stronger, just as the trickling-down effects themselves are weaker, than in interregional relations. Within a country, the loss by the South of its markets in the North will be resisted: not entirely unselfish efforts will be made by Northern interests to help the South overcome its supply difficulties which, if unresolved, will make it necessary for the North to look elsewhere. And, as has already been pointed out, even if a temporary lapse in North-South trade occurs, such efforts are likely to be resumed whenever balance-of-payments or other supply difficulties press upon the country.

In relations between advanced and underdeveloped nations, one of the major forces making for the growth of the latter is the need of the advanced nations for certain, usually primary, products of the underdeveloped areas. But if the foreign producers for one reason or another are unable to fulfill the rapidly growing requirements of the industrial centers, they cannot expect to be treated with the same patience and periodic consideration that they would receive if they were part of the industrial countries themselves. Domestic or other foreign sources of supply will be tapped or synthetic production will be undertaken largely on the basis of economic calculations, whereas political and social considerations will importantly affect similar decisions in North-South relations and are likely to help the South retain its role as a supplier of the North.

In this fashion we are brought back to the political forces making for the transmission of growth. These forces help definitively to redress the balance of our argument away from separatism. Within a country, as we have seen, there will come a point when a determined effort will be made to pull the underdeveloped regions within that country out of their stagnation. The ultimate reason for the confidence one may have in the emergence of such an effort is the solidarity that binds different parts of a nation together and the ability of each part to make itself heard and to bring pressures to bear on the central government. In spite of much progress in recent years, international solidarity of this kind is unfortunately still in its infancy.

We conclude that, on balance, the forces making for interregional transmission of growth are likely to be more powerful than those making for international transmission.

Optimal Institutional Arrangements

The reader may wonder why we examined in so much detail whether it is better for an underdeveloped area to be a region or a nation. Few areas can choose. Nevertheless, the realization that growth is transmitted more easily between nations than between regions from the point of view of some of the mechanisms we have analyzed, while the opposite holds for others, makes it tempting to think about the possibility of optimal institutional arrangements. If only we could in some respects *treat a region as though it were a country* and in some others *treat a country as though it were a region,* we would indeed get the best of both worlds and be able to create situations particularly favorable to development.[11]

Let us look first at the regions. Their advantage consisted largely in their greater exposure to the trickling-down effects and in their ability to call for help from the larger unit to which they belong. Their disadvantage seemed to lie principally in their exposure to polarization effects, in their inability to develop production for exports along lines of *comparative* advantage, and in the absence of certain potentially development-promoting policy instruments that usually come with sovereignty. A nation attempting to develop its own backward regions should therefore provide certain "equivalents of sovereignty" for these regions. The most important of such equivalents is a reaction against the feelings of despondency and self-denigration so often encountered in the South, and the mobilization of its energies through regional institutions and programs. The need for this approach has been felt in several countries where regional development corporations and banks have been set up. Effective aid to the establishment of industries in the South may call also for national income tax deductions (equivalent to tariff protection) and some autonomy in bank credit policy. To permit production to proceed on the basis of com-

11. We assume that the areas we are talking about have a substantial untapped development potential. There are of course many regions and perhaps even some countries whose natural resources are so poor or depleted that their best hope lies in becoming empty spaces—or at least far emptier than they are now.

parative advantage, Southern exports could be—and have at times been—stimulated through preferential exchange rates. Under such conditions, it might be held that imports into the South should be subject to compensating surtaxes, but this complication can be avoided on the ground that the South could satisfy many of its needs more cheaply in world markets if it were not prevented from doing so by the protection of Northern industries.

It is in line with our analysis that a policy of closing the gap between the South and the North requires the use of instruments that would ordinarily be thought to be disruptive of the very integration they are designed to achieve. While it is the purpose of these instruments to cut down the strength of the polarization effects, great care must be taken, of course, not to interfere with the efficacy of the trickling-down effects. Thus, the economic policies just outlined are designed to insulate the South sufficiently so that it may undertake certain industrial and export activities in competition with the North; but, at the same time, the complementary relationships that make the South a supplier of the North must be preserved and intensified.

For *international* transmission of growth, the optimal institutional arrangements would be of the opposite kind. The task here is to keep the polarization effects as weak as they normally are among independent nations, but to increase the strength of the trickling-down effects. In other words, the underdeveloped countries ought to retain the developmental advantages of sovereignty: obstacles to the emigration of skills and capital and a measure of independence in tariff, monetary, and foreign exchange policy. At the same time, they must be more closely integrated into the world economy through arrangements that make for more rapid growth and greater stability in their export markets. In addition, their development could of course be greatly accelerated if the community of nations disposed of a political mechanism similar to the one that within a nation makes eventually for a redistribution of public investment funds in favor of the South.

The world is already groping for formulas that would combine in this way the advantages of sovereignty with those of integration.[12] For the time being, these efforts are largely the incidental results of

12. Attempts of sovereign countries to assess themselves for costs incurred in joint programs are reviewed in Thomas C. Schelling, *International Cost-Sharing Arrangements*, Essays in International Finance No. 24, Princeton, 1955.

a struggle for power. Yet it is obvious that they would be intensified rather than abandoned if this struggle were to cease tomorrow. It seems a pity, therefore, that we in the United States insist so loudly that the bold and pioneering steps we are taking to help the underdeveloped countries are dictated by military necessity or are "straightforward business transactions." [13] Must we thus pave with apologies the road to what can be one of mankind's highest achievements? But perhaps it is inevitable that progress along this road should be reluctant. For, as Bergson has said, "the moral, original and fundamental structure of man is made for simple and closed societies . . . man outwits nature when from the solidarity of these societies he steps into human fraternity." [14]

13. Gunnar Myrdal makes some interesting observations on this point in *An International Economy* (New York, 1956), ch. 9.

14. *Les deux sources de la morale et de la religion* (Paris, 1934), pp. 53–4.

CHAPTER 11

Conclusion: Functions of Government
and Foreign Aid

IN THE PRECEDING CHAPTERS we have indicated whatever specific conclusions for economic policy followed from the treatment of each topic. There is no need to recapitulate these findings in detail. But the results of our inquiry into the development problem permit some brief summarizing and concluding comments on the role of government and on the function of foreign capital and aid.

The Two Functions of Government

In an unforgettable movie Charlie Chaplin, as glazier, employs Jackie Coogan to throw stones into shopwindows, whereupon he providentially passes by and obtains the job of repairing the damage. The ingenious twist consists here in combining, *under a single command*, the disequilibrating and the equilibrating functions. From our point of view, the story's only blemish—which, incidentally, accounts for its hilarious quality—is the fact that the unbalancing act is destructive rather than constructive. Otherwise, we find in it a perfect illustration of what we conceive as the two principal roles of governmental economic policies in the course of the development process. To be effective, they also must initiate growth through forward thrusts that are meant to create incentives and pressures for further action; and then they must stand ready to react to, and to alleviate, these pressures in a variety of areas. No matter how important the role of the state in the economy, both functions are usually present, although one or the other can predominate.

Writers on the role of government in the development process have usually stressed the initiating function. Advocates of a limitation of government to a few narrowly circumscribed tasks have justified their position by the argument that concentration on these tasks is necessary to ensure their successful discharge, which in turn is sufficient to produce a powerful igniting effect on economic progress. This expectation is apparent in the following sentence of Adam Smith: "Little else is requisite to carry a state to the highest degree of opulence from the lowest barbarism, but peace, easy taxes, and a tolerable administration of justice." [1] Partisans of a far wider range of activities for the government are similarly given to underlining the initiating character of whatever they want the government to undertake. We have, on the other hand, made the point that, with respect to social overhead capital for instance, the role of the government must frequently be viewed as induced rather than as inducing; and that while it is no doubt of great importance in the former role, it may fail in the latter.

Thus far the initiating function does not resemble too closely the throwing of a stone into a window. Neither maintenance of law and order nor highway construction set up imbalances that *cry out* to be corrected. They are rather conceived as the laying down of what have often been called the "prerequisites" for further development. As such they permit and invite, rather than compel, other activities to follow suit. We have argued that in underdeveloped countries purely permissive sequences may be ineffective in inducing growth; and that in some cases the government may well have to take the first step in the more compulsive sequences that may be indicated, for example through active leadership in industrialization.

We come next to the pressure-relieving function of government. In actual practice, this function is predominant in the many countries where development through market forces has made rapid strides and has in the process led to or revealed serious shortages and shortcomings in education, health, public utilities, and even in the fundamentals of law and order. Nevertheless, the importance of this "catching up" and "filling in" function of government is not often acknowledged by the public authorities themselves, presumably because it is felt that it is undignified for the government to be playing an "induced" role instead of proudly leading the way.

In Chapter 8 we have indicated some reasons for believing that the performance of certain governmental and administrative activities is intrinsically more difficult than the production of physical com-

1. Quoted in Baster, "Recent Literature on the Economic Development of Backward Areas," *Quarterly Journal of Economics, 68* (Nov. 1954), 590.

modities. It is therefore not surprising, and is not really a reflection on the government, that shortages in the supply of governmental services occur in the course of development. Governments that feel restless and slighted when they are forced into this induced role might reflect that indirectly they are still exercising a most important inducing function: for the knowledge on the part of private operators that bottlenecks and shortages will be efficiently taken care of if and when they appear acts as a considerable spur to further development. Frequently, moreover, the induced and inducing functions will coincide. This is the case of any public investment that while curing a shortage creates at the same time excess capacity.

A more interesting type of interaction between the two functions occurs when the government acts first as initiator and when the operations which it undertakes or which it causes to be undertaken in area A cause or reveal deficiencies, which must then be remedied, in some of its own operations in areas B, C, and D. For example, the government promotes industrialization by setting up an iron and steel industry; in the wake of the economic activity that follows, power and transportation shortages appear and inadequacies in education become far more apparent than before, so the government is impelled to improve its performance in these fields. This type of sequence throws some doubt on the validity of the frequently voiced opinion that the government should not get itself involved in making steel ingots when it is not even capable of keeping the roads in passable condition or of teaching the people how to read and write. In some situations, the building of the steel plant may be a necessary detour. For the government may have to *learn* how to maintain a highway system by building a steel plant, for reasons pointed out at length in Chapter 8. Secondly, the construction and operation of the plant and its contribution to industrialization may build up the kind of pressures that will help the government correctly to discharge its "proper" functions—thanks to having first undertaken an "improper" one.

Thus our division of governmental activities into these two "inducing" and "induced" or "unbalancing" and "balancing" functions seems to be useful in a variety of ways. It is not suggested that governments should appoint a Minister for Initiating Growth and a Minister for Restoring Balance; but to think in terms of these two tasks may perhaps serve to give ministers and governments a clearer conception of their role within the development process. The frequently prevailing lack of clarity in this matter is a distinct handicap not only for the peaceful coexistence and collaboration of the public and private sectors but also for the effectiveness of governmental action.

In this respect, the contemporary fashion of drawing up comprehensive development plans or programs is often quite unhelpful. For the very comprehensiveness of these plans can drown out the sense of direction so important for purposeful policy-making. A plan can be most useful if, through its elaboration, a government works out a strategy for development. While the choice of priority areas must of course proceed from an examination of the economy as a whole, it may be best, once the choice is made, to concentrate on detailed concrete programs for these areas, as in the first Monnet Plan for France's postwar reconstruction. The attempt at comprehensive programming usually exacts a high price in terms of articulateness and persuasiveness, qualities that are essential for the plan's ability to come to grips with reality.

The Role of Foreign Capital and Aid

Foreign capital and aid could also be studied from the point of view of the two "pressure-inducing" and "pressure-relieving" functions. But we shall attempt a more unitary definition of their tasks by stating that *it is the role of foreign capital to enable and to embolden a country to set out on the path of unbalanced growth.*[2]

The reasons for which local governments and domestic private investors may be unable or unwilling to undertake the kind of development projects that lead to dynamic growth are several. We have already dealt with the reluctance on the part of the government to concentrate its investment effort in a single region or sector when all regions and sectors are clamoring for help and are in fact badly in need of improvements. As has also been shown, foreign capital serves as a counterforce to this reluctance in a variety of ways. It is less inhibited in picking priorities and in giving one region or one

2. This formulation should be compared with the frequent dictum that foreign aid should be given only upon the presentation of "well-balanced" development programs. Of course, if well-balanced means merely well-conceived, the statement is unexceptionable—and meaningless.

sector a temporary advantage over another. Its availability helps the local government to think in terms of development, rather than in terms of the "pork barrel" type of distribution of public funds. If necessary, it can be given the blame for departures from whatever standards of distributive justice are considered binding upon governments using their own funds.

In the private sphere, foreign capital also helps concentration to take the place of scatter, innovation-type the place of routine-type investment. While the local capitalists are not likely to be subject to the same scruples as the government, they are often unable to come to terms with one another because of what was termed in our first chapter the ego-focused image of change. Therefore, even though savings are generated, they are not combined as is frequently required for the larger projects that will set in motion further growth. Also, local capitalists often prefer the safe investments in trade, real estate, or satellite industries, and shy away from breaking new ground, for they know only too well about all the interlocking vicious circles and are usually unable to realize that their own action will induce actions by others which will mean a change in a seemingly fixed environment. The foreign capitalist does not ordinarily perceive this kind of sequence either; but he is endowed, on the one hand, with greater ability to see and exploit certain profitable opportunities; perhaps more important, he is blessed with ignorance of the actual extent of backwardness—by the time he realizes it he is already committed, and then, fighting to save his investment, he does effect, directly or indirectly, those changes in the environment which eventually ensure success.[3]

In all these instances foreign capital, acting on its own or jointly with local capital, seems to be better equipped than domestic capital alone to take the first "unbalancing" steps in growth sequences. An even more important role is played by foreign capital in connection with the subsequent stages of the process. This subject has been dis-

3. In "Entrepreneurial Error and Economic Growth," *Explorations in Entrepreneurial History*, 4 (May 1952), 199–204, J. E. Sawyer has shown that underestimation of the *cost* of investment projects has often been helpful in getting important ventures underway. If this cost is understood to comprise all difficulties encountered, including those of a nonpecuniary character, Sawyer's point could probably be shown to be particularly pertinent to ventures undertaken by foreign capital.

cussed at length in Chapter 9. As was shown there, foreign capital or aid can have the important function of permitting the country to avoid relative price rises when fundamental reforms and improvements rather than such rises are needed to eliminate the bottlenecks in certain lagging sectors. We also showed that foreign capital is likely to be needed to enable the sectors of an underdeveloped economy that have the highest potential for rapid growth to utilize this potential fully. In other words, the process of unbalanced growth will frequently lead to certain difficulties and pressures that cannot be relieved immediately; in the meantime, foreign capital is needed as a stopgap.

If foreign capital is not forthcoming, the unresolved pressures might do more harm than good by causing inflation and possibly by bringing the original "unbalancing" ventures to grief. Once the economic operators perceive this possibility or if they learn about it through bitter experience, discouragement or extreme caution will ensue. The availability of foreign capital has then the function of restoring or strengthening the spirit of enterprise through the assurance that the pressures and tensions which may arise will not be allowed to boomerrang, but will be temporarily relieved pending a more fundamental solution of the supply difficulties that have been revealed.

In this role, foreign capital is not just a stopgap which in some way detracts from the inducement mechanism that would have been set in motion without it. As we know, the additional imports it makes possible are themselves important and active links in the growth sequence.[4] One example will help to show this clearly. Often an underdeveloped economy faces the vicious circle that an industry cannot be established because a needed raw material input is not being produced domestically; and the raw material is not produced on a commercial scale and at the desired uniform quality because there is no assured market as yet. When, in such cases, the material can be imported temporarily from abroad the problem can be solved in stages: first the manufacturing activity is established with the help of the imported material, and, once the existence of an assured and profitable market is thus demonstrated to the local producers, domestic production is likely to take over in short order.

4. See Ch. 7.

A margin of maneuver for the developing country's balance of payments emerges as the necessary condition for enabling it to take full advantage of the potentialities of our unbalanced growth sequences. A revision of the deeply ingrained idea that aid to underdeveloped countries should always be for specific projects seems therefore desirable. The points made in the first part of this section lead us to think that project lending and direct investments serve a most useful purpose. But, in addition, there is a need for general balance of payments assistance on a stand-by basis as it is impossible to foresee how fast the pressures which a country's economy will experience in the course of its development will result in the appropriate domestic resource shifts. In fact every specific project, *especially* if it has been well conceived, will set up pressures some of which ought to be temporarily amortized through additional importing. Perhaps project loans or grants should therefore be accompanied as a matter of routine by a "repercussions fund" in freely disposable and convertible foreign exchange.

The Argument in Perspective

Looking back upon the main thesis of this book, I cannot help feeling a little uneasy about the importance and creative virtue that I have bestowed on pressures, tensions, and disequilibrium. Actually the argument is no more than an extension of the familiar view which makes economic growth dependent on a continuing outcropping of profitable opportunities. These are, after all, also disequilibria which induce constructive action. But our extension of the concept of disequilibrium to include situations replete not only with opportunities to be grasped but with hindrances, difficulties, and other types of tension, raises the question whether the response to such situations is not at times going to be destructive and whether the process that has been sketched is not therefore a rather risky affair.

We certainly would not want to disregard these dangers. It has just been shown that the pressures generated by unbalanced growth may react adversely on development in the absence of some cushion in the form of foreign capital. Other tensions that have been discussed could lead to the adoption of wholly irrational, rather than of corrective, policies.

208

Nevertheless, for a number of reasons, we do not think it feasible or even desirable to suppress these tensions. In the first place, underdeveloped countries already operate under the *grand tension* that stems from the universal desire for economic improvement oddly combined with many resistances to change. Much is to be said for breaking down this grand tension, a highly explosive mixture of hopes and fears, into a series of smaller and more manageable tensions.

These smaller tensions arise in the course of development. They still harbor many dangers and risks. Indeed, it is a commonplace that development carries with it many strains and stresses. But what has been less well understood is that development also draws new strength from the tensions it creates. By running up against difficulties, development makes it possible to tackle them. In any intellectual inquiry, at least half the job consists in asking the right question; similarly, in the process of social and economic change, an obstacle clearly visualized is an obstacle half overcome.[5]

An attempt to make the most of this positive relation between development and the tensions it creates would lead to a new emphasis and to greater effectiveness in extending technical assistance and policy advice to underdeveloped countries. Economic advisers would be far less given to determining priorities from the outside, after an expert look at the country and its resources; they would instead be intent on discovering under what pressures people are operating and toward what forward steps they are already being impelled. Instead of laying down "first things first" rules, they would try to understand how progress can at times meander strangely through many peripheral areas before it is able to dislodge backwardness from the central positions where it may be strongly entrenched.

Ineffectiveness, which is too often the expert's lot, is also frequently the earmark of official economic policies. It manifests itself in the unsuccessful legislating of progress, in the promulgation of develop-

---

5. It is perhaps the pervasive influence of psychoanalysis that has kept us from seeing this point. For Freud, difficulties, conflict, and anxiety were mainly pathogenic agents; their constructive and educational functions in individual development have been rediscovered only recently by psychologists. Cf. O. H. Mowrer, *Learning Theory and Personality Dynamics* (New York, 1950), ch. 19. Similarly, an anthropologist has recently stressed the value of conflict for societal cohesion; cf. M. Gluckman, *Custom and Conflict in Africa*, Oxford, 1955.

ment plans that nobody takes seriously, in the establishment of abortive reforms and stillborn institutions. But economic policy may be worse than ineffectual: futility can be abruptly replaced by brutality, by utter disregard for human suffering, for acquired rights, for lawful procedures, for traditional values, in short, for the "thin and precarious crust of civilization." Such a course is in fact the natural reaction to a series of *unsuccessful* attempts at promoting development and at introducing improvements and reforms. Thus, after having long been a mirage, the quest for development is apt to turn suddenly into a nightmare.

Both futility and brutality are manifestations of "the inability of the neurotic to have a full encounter with reality." [6] For they stem from a basic disbelief in, and distaste for, the *process* of economic development and from the attempt to jump over it and its difficulties. At first, incantation is used for this purpose. Subsequently, it is decided that all prospective difficulties must be solved at once and the elusive goal be seized through one convulsive investment effort, one large-scale expropriation, or one "short" term of dictatorial rule.

Many developing countries are showing today that their policies need not be confined between these sterile alternatives. They are becoming acquainted with the nature of the development process and are finding out that the pressures and tensions it creates do not necessarily frustrate it, but can be made to help it along. To sharpen the realistic perception of this third way has been the aim of this book.

6. Paul Tillich, *The Courage to Be* (New Haven, Yale Univ. Press, 1952), p. 76.

Author Index

Abruzzi, A., 145
Adler, J. H., 161
Ahumada, J., 77
Allen, R. G. D., 7
Alter, G. M., 169
Arensberg, C. M., 5
Aubrey, H. G., 3, 44, 121, 130

Bain, J. S., 101
Baldwin, R. E., 37
Barlow, E. R., 174
Barnard, C. I., 147
Barnett, H. G., 68
Baster, J., 3, 203
Bator, F. M., 60
Bauer, P. T., 3, 9, 65
Baumol, W. J., 54, 60
Beals, R., 138
Belshaw, C. S., 9
Bergson, H., 201
Bhatt, V. V., 152
Boeke, J. H., 126
Bohr, K. A., 101
Boudeville, J. R., 184
Boulding, K. E., 12
Buchanan, N. S., 20, 67, 109

Cairncross, A. K., 3, 84
Campos, R., viii
Carroll, L., 176
Chaplin, C., 202
Chenery, H. B., 77, 105, 107, 110
Clark, P. G., viii

Dahmén, E., 43
Diamond, W., 3
Dietzel, K., 123
Domar, E. D., 7, 30–1, 33, 54, 73
Duesenberry, J. S., 175–7
Dupréel, E., 178
Dupriez, L. H., 3

Eckaus, R. S., 127
Eckstein, O., 74
Ellis, H. S., 67, 109
Erasmus, C. J., 148

Fahmy, M., 134
Feldman, G. A., 73
Fellner, W., 31, 67, 70, 74–5
Firth, R., 94, 149
Freud, S., 209
Friedmann, G., 148
Fromm, E., 12

Galenson, W., 73–4
Gerschenkron, A., 8–9, 13, 43, 48, 124
Gillin, J., 14–5
Glass, D. V., 179
Gluckman, M., 209
Gold, B., 145
Goodrich, C., 84
Gordon, R. A., 17
Granick, D., 152
Green, F., 143

Haavelmo, T., 8
Haberler, G., 125
Hagen, E. E., 2
Haig, R. M., 183
Hammond, J. L. & B., 130
Harbison, F. H., 136, 146
Harrod, R., 7, 30–1, 33
Hayek, F. A., 111
Heckscher, E. F., 58
Hegel, G. F. W., 59
Hicks, J. R., 33, 40
Higgins, B., 9, 126
Hirschman, A. O., 78, 123, 125, 149, 187
Hitch, C., 79
Holmberg, A. R., 12

Hoselitz, B. F., 8
Hunt, S. P., 139

Ibrahim, I. A., 136

Johnson, H. G., 189

Kafka, A., viii, 116
Kahn, A. E., 77
Kaldor, N., 60
Kapp, K. W., 56
Katona, G., 27, 43
Keynes, J. M., 6, 30, 40, 54
Keyser, V., 113
Kindleberger, C. P., 172
Kluckhohn, C., 4
Kozlovskii, V., 64
Kroeber, A. L., 4
Kuznets, S., 45

Lakdawala, D. T., 172
Lampard, E. A., 183
Landes, D. S., 134
Leibenstein, H., 46, 73–4, 77, 182
Leontief, W., 152
Levasseur, E., 58
Levitt, T., 17
Levy, M. J., 137
Lewis, W. A., 3, 38, 50–1, 126, 153, 159
Linton, R., 4

MacLaurin, R. W., 17
Malinowski, B., 148–9
Malthus, T. R., 46, 177, 178–9
Manne, A. S., 148
Marshall, A., 183
McClelland, D. C., 2, 137
Meade, J. E., 60, 197
Mehta, S. D., 136
Meier, G. M., 37
Mendershausen, H., 174
Mikesell, R. F., 174
Miller, W., 134
Millikan, M. F., viii, 37, 78
Modigliani, F., 175

Montaigne, M., 52
Mowrer, O. H., 209
Murdock, G. P., 4
Myrdal, G., 187, 201

Nelson, R. R., 46
Nurkse, R., 50–1, 84, 156

Orwell, G., 11

Parsons, J. J., 186
Parsons, T., 137
Peacock, A. T., 178
Pearson, H. W., 5
Perroux, F., 74, 183
Phelps-Brown, E. H., 31
Polanyi, K., 5
Prebisch, R., 159

Rao, K. N., 130
Rasmussen, P. N., 108
Reynolds, L. G., viii
Rivlin, H. A. B., 134
Rosenstein-Rodan, P. N., 50–1, 55
Rostow, W. W., 37, 45–6, 115
Ruggles, R., 164

Salveson, M. E., 147
Sargent, S. S., 12
Sawyer, J. E., 206
Say, J. B., 52
Sayres, W. C., 14
Schatz, S. P., 161
Schelling, T. C., viii, 200
Schultz, T. W., 1
Schumpeter, J., 16, 43, 57, 119, 178
Scitovsky, T., 42, 51, 55, 60, 65–7, 69
Sharma, T. R., 146
Simmons, E. J., 8
Simon, H. A., 47–8, 82
Singer, H. W., 5, 53, 159, 176
Sirkin, G., 149
Smith, A., 59, 147, 203
Smith, M. W., 12
Spengler, J. J., 53, 131–2, 171
Spicer, E. H., 12

Stolper, W. F., 174
Sufrin, S. C., 3
Svennilson, I., 74

Tax, S., 14
Taylor, P. S., 12
Tillich, P., 210
Tinbergen, J., 76
Toynbee, A., 145

Udy, S. H., Jr., 141

Van der Kroef, J. M., 126

Veblen, T., 68, 145–6
Viner, J., 53, 56, 109, 197

Wallich, H. C., 138, 156
Watanabe, T., 105, 107, 110
Weber, M., 2, 31, 137
Wender, I. T., 174
Whitehead, A. N., vii
Whyte, W., 17
Wolf, C., Jr., viii, 3
Wolf, E., 15, 138
Wood, R., 113

Yamey, B. S., 3, 9, 65

Subject Index

Ability to invest, 35–40, 42, 49, 177

Abortive development, 44–9, 133–4

Absorptive capacity, 37, 192

Achievement motivation, 2, 137

Adaptation of technology, 130–1, 138

Administrative tasks, 141, 153–5, 203–4

Agriculture, 112, 162–3, 189; and linkage effects, 109–10

Ambivalent attitude toward change, 138–9

Anthropologists, anthropology, 2, 4, 15, 138, 209

Antioquia, 186

Backward vs. developing regions, 94–5, 183–98

Balance of payments: pressures, 62, 156, 166–76, 190, 198; adjustment mechanism, 172–3; assistance, 208. See also Foreign capital and aid

Balanced growth, 50–5, 66, 93, 135; in demand, 50–4, 164–6; in supply, 62–4; of SOC and DPA, 87–90, 92

Barcelona, 186

Basic industries, 118, 168, 184, 191

Birth control, 180–1

Brazil, 20, 112, 181, 189, 195

Capital formation, 1–2, 6, 22, 30, 44; through backward linkage, 113–6

Capital market, 21

Capital-intensive technology: as aid to coordination, 146–53; as spur to savings, 149–50

Capital-output ratio, 30–2, 84

Capitalism, 58, 61, 64

Cargo cult, 94

Central planning, centralization of investment decisions, 56, 59, 61, 69

Challenge and response, 144–5

Change: ego-focused image, 14–20, 23–4, 127, 206; group-focused image, 11–4, 23–4, 48, 191

Classical economics, 63

Cliquishness, 185–7

Cobweb model, 20, 66, 89

Colombia, viii, 112, 143, 186, 189, 195

Commercial policy, 120. See also Protection

Communism, 13, 64

Community development, 12

Comparative advantage, 122–3, 152, 196, 199

Comparative statics, 62

Compensation test, 60

Competition, 135, 148, 160, 196–7

Complementarity, 7, 69–70, 72–5, 103, 135, 160, 197; in production, technical, 58, 67; in use, 68, 100, 159

Complementarity effect of investment, 40–4, 70

Consumption-oriented development, 156

Creative destruction, 57, 59

Customs union, 197

Decision-making ability, 23, 25–6, 44, 80. See also Induced . . . decisions

Defensive ignorance, 138

Demonstration effect, 16, 192

Depression economics, 6, 26, 54

Derived demand, 68

Derived development, 137–8

Development decisions, 26–7. See also Induced . . . decisions

Development plans and programs, 18, 85, 157, 205, 209–10

Dictatorship, 18, 210

Direct investments, 208

Directly productive activities (DPA), 83–99
Disequilibrium. See Unbalanced growth
Disguised unemployment, 5, 151, 188
Disorderliness model, 80–1
Domestic production threshold. See Minimum economic size
Domophobia, 125
Dual level: of wages, 127–30; of capital costs, 127–8
Dualistic development, 52, 125–32, 184
Dynamic equilibrium, 93

Efficient sequences, 76–84
Egypt, 134
Electric power. See Social overhead capital
Enclave-type development, 110–1, 119
Entrained wants, 68, 100, 159
Entrepreneurs, entrepreneurial and managerial abilities, 1, 3, 6, 7, 36, 39, 53, 55, 65, 141, 158, 160, 173, 180, 186, 195, 206
Entrepreneurship, creative and cooperative components, 16–9, 23–4, 137
Equilibrium. See Balanced growth
Exaggerated expectations, 20–3
Exchange rates, 167–8; preferential, 200
Export promotion, 124, 172
Exportability, 169–72
Extended family, 9
External economies and diseconomies, 66–7, 100, 103, 183–5, 194; their internalization, 55–61; and induced investment, 70–2

Factor mobility, 188, 196, 200
Fast- vs. slow-growing sectors, 169–72
Feedback effect, 7
Final touches. See Last-stage industries
Fiscal policy, 26. See also Taxation
Fluctuations in foreign exchange income, 173–5, 179
Ford, Henry, 184
Foreign capital and aid, 38–9, 95, 167, 191–2, 205–8

Foreign exchange illusion, 167–9
Foreign exchange reserves, 167, 208
Foreign experts. See Technical assistance
France, 176, 205

Giannini, A. P., 184
Government's role in development, 54, 65, 85, 165–6, 202–5
Growing points. See Backward vs. developing regions
Growth mentality, 136–7, 140
Growth models, 29–33
Growth poles, 74, 183
Guayaquil, 186
Guild system, 57–9

Hansel and Gretel model, 121–2
Hoarding, 3, 53

Imbalances. See Unbalanced growth
Imports and industrialization, 98–9, 113–6, 120–5, 207
Incentives. See Pressures and incentives, Price signals
Income, 30–2; distribution, 10, 116–7
Indian and mestizo communities, 14–5
Individual firm, conditions for development, 133–9
Indivisibility, 75, 79, 84
Induced and autonomous investment, 26–7, 30–3, 42, 70–2
Induced development and investment decisions, 42–3, 63–4, 89–93, 116–7
Inducement mechanisms, 6, 24–8, 133, 158, 179, 195
Industrial Revolution, 8, 16, 129, 137
Industrialization, vii, 8, 53, 98–132, 134, 159–60, 172, 176, 196, 203–4
Infant industries, 89, 101; prenatal care, 124
Inflation, 21, 96–7, 156–67
Innovation, 60–1
Input-output: analysis, 66, 98, 104, 108, 113–4; statistics, 100, 106–7, 109–10, 117–8
Interdependence, structural, 98–119, 170, 198

International Bank for Reconstruction and Development, 83, 192

International Basic Economy Corporation, 113

International Cooperation Administration, 101

International division of labor, 123, 196

International trade theory, 122

International transmission of growth, 183–4, 195–201

Interregional transmission of growth, 183–201

Investment, 21, 30–6, 65, 157; in showpieces, 144, 190

Investment criteria, 76–83, 140, 153

Investment opportunities, 19, 34–7, 40

Iron and steel industry, 108. *See also* Basic industries

Italy, 185, 189

Japan, 94, 172

Jigsaw puzzle model, 81–2, 117

Labor productivity, 146, 152

Last-stage industries, 111–3, 117–9, 158, 168–9

Latecomers, 7–10, 137–8, 159, 172

Latin America, 4, 14, 16, 113, 185

Latitude for poor performance, 144–6, 154

Learning, 47, 177, 182, 204; Berlitz model, 47–8; of maintenance, 142

Limited wants, 16, 121

Linkage effects: backward, 100–17, 134–5, 158, 168; forward, 100–9, 116–7, 134–5

Liquidity preference, personalized, 20–3

Local capitalists, 206

Machine-paced vs. operator-paced operations, 145–6, 151–2

Maintenance, 46, 139–43, 145, 152; penalties for nonmaintenance, 142–3; signals for maintenance, 145

Management contracts, 39

Manufacturing. *See* Industry

Market and nonmarket forces, 143, 167, 190, 203; in adjustment mechanisms, 63–5

Materials handling, 151–2

Medellín, 186

Mexico, 181

Middle East, 4

Minimum economic size, 101–3, 113–6, 173, 180

Minorities, 2, 4, 186

Modern vs. preindustrial sector, 36–8, 41–2, 125–32. *See also* Dualistic development

Monetary policy, 26, 160–1, 164

Monnet Plan, 205

Muhammad Ali, 134

Multiplier, 43, 71, 119

Natural resources, 1–2

New Guinea, 94

New products, 58–9, 129–32, 160, 171

Nonconventional inputs, 1

Oblomov, 9

Obstacles and difficulties, 1, 10–1, 25, 44, 136, 209

Open and corporate communities, 15

Overhead capital. *See* Social overhead capital

Pacing devices, 6, 26

Pakistan, 4

Permissive vs. compulsive sequences, 23, 81, 89, 93, 195, 203

Petroleum-producing countries, 172

Plant capacity, 148

Plant vs. office activities, 154

Population pressures: reactions to, 176–82; neo-Malthusian models, 46–7, 178, 180, 182

Prerequisites for development, 1, 4–5, 9, 25, 38, 75, 203

Pressures (and incentives), 6, 9, 27, 47, 88, 93, 158, 184, 204, 207–10; on managers to perform, 134–5, 140; on

public authorities, 70, 88, 143, 163, 167
Price-price spiral, 160–4
Price signals, 63, 158–60, 163, 167, 181
Priorities, vii, 13–4, 205. *See also* Efficient sequences, Investment criteria
Product- vs. process-centered industries, 147, 151–4
Profit rate, 20–2
Project lending, 208
Project planning, 191–2
Protection, 89, 116, 120, 122–5, 196–7, 199
Protestant ethic, 185
Psychoanalysis, 139, 209
Psychology, psychologists, 2, 209
Public administration, 2, 153–5, 204. *See also* Administrative tasks
Public investment, 13, 85–6; regional distribution, 190–5; dispersal vs. concentration, 190–3; induced vs. autonomous, 193, 203
Public utilities. *See* Social overhead capital

Rationality, 137
Regional development corporations, 199
Regional problems. *See* Backward vs. developing regions, Interregional transmission of growth
Regional specialization, 197
Reinvestment of profits, 39, 136, 150
Relative backwardness, 8–9
Ritual ceremonies, 141, 148–9
Russia, 13, 61, 64, 94, 172

São Paulo, 186
Satellite industries, 102–4
Savings, 2, 30–2, 35–40; forced, 37, 161, 174–5, 179; frustrated, 37
Say's Law, 52
Sears, Roebuck & Co., 112
Selling costs, 121

Separatism, economic arguments on, 194–6, 198
Service industries, 129
Shortages and bottlenecks, 32, 62, 70, 158–60, 166, 168, 192, 203–4
Skills, 2, 6, 36, 39, 57
Small industry, 44, 129–31
Social marginal productivity, 77
Social overhead capital (SOC), 44, 83–100, 165, 193–4, 203–4; shortage and excess capacity, 86–97
Sovereignty, economic arguments on, 199–200
Stagnation thesis, 176
Substitution vs. postponement choices, 77–8
Supply elasticity, 161–3, 189, 198
Synthetics, 189, 198

Take-off, 45–6, 115
Taxation, 194, 199
Technical assistance, 12, 18, 139, 209
Technological progress, 35; industries beyond active phase of, 119, 138, 159
Tensions. *See* Pressures and incentives
Terms of trade, 159, 189
Theories of economic development, vii, 1–4, 50
Trade vs. aid, 172
Transportation. *See* Social overhead capital
Trickling-down vs. polarization effects, 187–90, 194–200
Turkey, 94

Unbalanced growth, 62–9, 72, 93, 158, 166–7, 184, 205, 207–8
Uncertainty about market, 121
Universalism, 137
Urbanization, 180

Venezuela, 113
Vicious circles, 5, 11, 36, 52, 206

Welfare economics, 60

ALBERT O. HIRSCHMAN was born in Germany, studied in France, England, and Italy, and came to the United States in 1941. He wrote *The Strategy of Economic Development* at Yale University, after five years as financial adviser and economic consultant in Colombia. Subsequently he taught at Columbia and Harvard and in 1974 joined the Institute for Advanced Study at Princeton as Professor of Social Science. His books, which also include *National Power and the Structure of Foreign Trade* (1945), *Journeys Toward Progress* (1963, Norton Library paperback 1973), *Exit, Voice, and Loyalty* (1971), and *The Passions and the Interests* (1977), have established him as an innovative thinker of the first rank.